? **asked** ?

? *&* ?

ANSWERED!

JESUS

CHRIST

speaks to

YOU!!!

a

HAND

Book

Compiled by C.C. Forche

In these pages
are the words of
Jesus Christ
from
MATTHEW
MARK
LUKE
&
JOHN
from the
Bible
The New Testament
The Gospel
Arranged alphabetically in
categories of interest
Don't be confused and think this is all
Christ said. You will also see some verses
used in many categories. This is simply
a **quick reference.** Inspire to read
The Word /The Bible!

Copyright C.C. Forche
a.k.a Cathleen Conner Forche 2015
All Bible verses are public domain
ISBN - 978-0-578-15632-3

Experience the
ARGUMENTS

... what mankind believes to be true and real vs.
God's Truth. Provocative, Angering or
Exhilarating..
It's up to you.
The **BOOK** with 666 decoded in
Hebrew/Greek. ..English ...French ...German...
Italian...Russian...Spanish...Swahili
9 languages   ....5 alphabets...all the same...
What are the odds?
Is this the right answer?
Or is it just one answer?
Does it matter?
We are all responsible and
accountable for everything we think, say and
do. This is true at any point in time. It is NO
accident, as we are each created and are unique
miracles of God and are meant to be alive here
and now. The purpose of life is to give each
one of us freedom to determine the meaning of
our own life.
How is it going?   Oh yea....   The book?

SOME CHRISTIAN STUFF
FOR YOUR BRIEF STAY
ON PLANET EARTH...
by C.C. Forche

THE BEGINNING

OR

THE END

YOU
CHOOSE

Acknowledgments; to God the Father, Jesus Christ the Son and the Holy Spirit... The Way.. The Truth and the Life and to every Christian in every act of faith and every endeavor to spread the Good News.

A

B

C

D

E

F

G

G

H

H

I

J

K

L

L

M

M

N

O

O

P

P

Q

R

R

S

S

S

S

T

T

U

U

V

W

W

W

Y

Z

A DEFINITION

KEY
( ) something I am telling reader
[ ] a related verse... written, not spoken
{ } a related verse/quote by someone else

VISIT
christiantheoriesandconcepts .wordpress.com

Get this book as an APP!!!
Google Apps & Apple App Store

90%...that is what I went for as far as
typo free book. Transfers are character
recognition and tech assumptions. This is
not easy like email.

A   1

ABOVE   MATTHEW 10;24-25

"A student is not greater than his teacher. A servant is not **above** his master. The student shares his teacher's fate. The servant shares his masters! And since I have been called 'Satan' how much more will you! But, don't be afraid of those who threaten you. For the time is coming when the Truth will be revealed: their secret plots will become public information" said Jesus Christ

ACCEPTING ..RECEIVING
MATTHEW 10;40-42

"Those who welcome you are welcoming me. And when they welcome me they are welcoming God who sent me. If you are welcoming a prophet because he is a man of God, you will be given the same reward as the prophet gets. And if you welcome good and godly men because of their godliness, you will be given a reward like theirs.

"And as my representatives, you give even a cup of cold water to a child, you will be surely rewarded." said Jesus Christ

ADULTERY   MATTHEW 5:27-30

" The law of Moses said, 'You shall not commit **adultery.'** But I say: Anyone who even looks at a woman with lust in his eye has already committed [1]

A

ADULTERY MATTHEW 5-27-30 cont'd
  adultery in his heart. So if your eye- even if it is
your best eye!- causes you to lust, gouge it out and
throw it away. Better for part of you to be destroyed
than for all of you to be cast into hell. And if your
hand causes you to sin, cut it off and throw it away.
Better that than find yourself in hell." said Jesus
Christ

AFRAID

MATTHEW 10;28-31

  " Don't be **afraid** of those who can kill only your
bodies- but can't touch your souls! Fear God who
can destroy both soul and body in hell. Not one
sparrow (What do they cost? Two for a penny?)can
fall to the ground without your Father knowing it.
And the very hairs on your head are numbered. So
don't worry! You are more valuable to Him than,
any sparrows." said Jesus Christ

ANGER   MATTHEW 5; 21-26

  " Under the laws of Moses the rule was. 'If you
kill, you must die.' But I have added to that rule,
and tell you that you are only *angry,* even in your
own home, you are in danger of judgment! If you
call your friend an idiot, you are in danger of being
brought before the court. And if you curse him, you
are in danger of the fires of hell."

  "So if you are standing before the altar in the
Temple, offering a sacrifice to God, and suddenly

ANGER   MATTHEW 5;21-16 cont'd

remember that a friend has something against you, leave your sacrifice there beside the altar and go apologize and be reconciled to him and then come and offer your sacrifice to God.

"Come to terms quickly with your enemy before it is too late and he drags you into court and you are thrown into a debtor's cell, for you will stay there until you have paid the last penny." said Jesus Christ

ARRESTED ...Christ
MATTHEW 26; 50, 52-56

Jesus said, "My friend, go ahead and do what you have come for."

"Put away your sword." Jesus told them. "Those using swords will get killed. Don't you realize that I could ask my Father for thousands of angels to protect us and He would send them instantly? But if I did, how would the Scriptures be fulfilled that describe what is happening now?"

The Jesus spoke to the crowd. "Am I some dangerous criminal," he asked, "that you had to arm yourselves with swords and clubs before you could **arrest** me? I was teaching with you daily in the Temple and you didn't stop me then. But all of this happening to fulfill this the words of the prophets as recorded in the Scriptures." said Jesus Christ

4   A

AS YOUSAY

MATTHEW 26;64

"Yes,"Jesus said, "I am . And in the future you will see me, the Messiah, sitting at the right hand of God and returning to the clouds of heaven" .said Jesus Christ

LUKE 23:3

[When confronted by Pilate if Jesus was the Messiah...]

"Yes,"Jesus replied, "It is **as you say**." said Jesus Christ

ASK

MATTHEW 7;7-12

" **Ask** and you will be given what you ask for. Seek and you will find. Knock and the door will be opened. For everyone who asks, receives. Anyone who seeks, finds. If only you will knock the door will open. If a child asks his father for a loaf of bread, will he be given a stone instead? If he **asks** for fish, will he be given a poisonous snake? Of course not! And if you hardhearted, sinful men know how to give good gifts to your children, won't your Father in heaven even more certainly give To those who ask for them?" said Jesus Christ

A 5

AUTHORITY

"Why are you thinking such evil thoughts? I, the Messiah, have the **authority** on earth to forgive sins. But talk is cheap- anybody can say that. So I'll prove it to you by healing this man." said Jesus Chris   MATTHEW 21;24,27

[to the Jewish leaders] "I'll tell you if you answer one question first," Jesus replied. "Was John the Baptist sent from God or not?"

[they were afraid to answer either way] And Jesus said, "Then I won't answer your question either." said Jesus Christ   MATTHEW 28;18

" I have been given all authority in heaven and earth." said Jesus Christ

LUKE 20; 3,8,

"I'll ask you a question before I answer, "he replied. "was John sent by God or was he merely acting under his own **authority?"**

"Then I won't answer your question either." said Jesus Christ   LUKE 5;24

"I, the Messiah, have the **authority** on earth to forgive sins, but talk is cheap- anybody could say that. So I'll prove it to you by healing this man." said Jesus Christ   JOHN 19;17-18

" The Father loves me because I lay down my life that I may have it back again. No one can kill me

6 A

AUTHORITY   JOHN 19;17-18 cont'd
without my consent- I lay down my life voluntarily.
For I have the right and power to lay it down and
take it again. For the Father has given me this
right." said Jesus Christ

B

BACK ... Looking back
LUKE 9;58,60,62

58 "Remember, I don't even own a place to lay
my head. Foxes have dens to live in, and birds have
nests, but I, the Messiah, have no earthly home at
all.
60 "Let those without eternal life concern
themselves with things like that. Your duty is to
come preach the coming of the Kingdom of God to
all the world."
62 " Anyone who lets himself be distracted from
the work I plan for him is not fit for the Kingdom of
God." said Jesus Christ

BACK TO GOD
LUKE 15;7

"Well, in the same way heaven will be happier
over one lost sinner who returns **back to God** than
over ninety-nine others who haven't strayed away."
said Jesus Christ

BETRAYAL   LUKE 21;16

"Even the closest to you- your parents, brothers, relatives and friends will **betray** you and have you arrested and some of you will be killed. And everyone will hate you because you are mine and are called by my name. But not a hair on your head will perish! For if you stand firm, you will win your souls." said Jesus Christ

MATTHEW 10;21-22

"Brother shall betray brother to death, and fathers shall **betray** their own children. Andchildren shall rise up against their parents and cause their deaths. Everyone shall hate you because you belong to me. But all who endure until the end shall be saved." said Jesus Christ

MARK 14;18,20-21

18 "I solemnly declare that one of you will betray me, one of you who are eating with me."20-21 "It is one of you twelve eating with me now. I must die, as the prophets declared long ago: but, oh, the misery ahead of the man by whom I am **betrayed.** Oh, that he had never been born!" said Jesus Christ

LUKE 22;48

"Judas, how can you do this-**betray** the Messiah with a kiss?" JOHN13;18-21, 26, 27

"I am not saying these things to all of you; I know well each one of you I chose. The Scripture declares

8   B

BETRAYAL

JOHN 13;18-21 26,27 cont'd

' One who eats supper with me will **betray** me.' and this will come true. I tell you this now so when it happens, you will believe in me."

"Truly anyone welcoming my message is welcoming me. And to welcome me is to welcome the Father who sent me."

"Yes, it is true-one of you will betray me" 26 "It is the one I honor by giving the bread dipped in the sauce" 27 "Hurry, do it now." said Jesus Christ   MATTHEW 24; 9-11

"Then you will be tortured and killed and hated all over the world because you are mine, and many of you shall fall back into sin and **betray** and hate each other. And many false prophets will appear and lead many astray. Sin will be rampant everywhere and will cool the love of many. But those enduring to the end shall be saved." said JesusChrist

MATTHEW 26;21

"It is the one I served first. For I must die just as prophesied, but woe to the man by whom I am **betrayed.** Far better for that one if he had never been born." said Jesus Christ

BLESSINGS   MATTHEW 5; 3-12

" Humble men are very fortunate! For the Kingdom of Heaven is given to them. Those who mourn are

BLESSINGS   MATTHEW 5; 3-12 cont'd
fortunate for they shall be comforted. The meek and
the lowly are fortunate! For the whole world
belongs to them.

   "**Blessed** are those who long to be just and good,
for they shall be completely satisfied. **Blessed** are
the kind and merciful, for they shall be shown
mercy. **Blessed** are those whose hearts are pure, for
they shall see God. **Blessed** are those who strive for
peace-they shall be called the sons of God.

   "**Blessed** are those who are persecuted because
they are good, for the Kingdom of Heaven is theirs.

   "When you are reviled and persecuted and lied
about because you are my followers-wonderful! Be
happy about it! Be very glad! For a tremendous
reward awaits you up in heaven. And remember the
ancient prophets were persecuted too." said Jesus
Christ

MATTHEW 11;6

   "Then give them this message, '**Blessed** are those
who don't doubt me.' "said Jesus Christ

LUKE 6;20-23

   "What **blessings** there is for you who are poor,
for the Kingdom of Heaven is yours! What
happiness there is for you who are now hungry, for
you are going to be satisfied! What happiness there
is for those of you who weep, for the time will come

BLESSINGS   LUKE 6;20-23 cont'd
when you shall laugh with joy! What happiness it is
when others hate you and exclude you and smear
your name because you are mine! When that
happens, rejoice! Yes, leap for joy! For you will
have great reward waiting for you in heaven. And
you will be in good company-the ancient prophets
were treated that way too!" said Jesus Christ

JOHN 13;17
"You know these things- now do them! That is
the path of blessing." said Jesus Christ

BLIND   MATTHEW 15;14
"Every plant not planted by my Father shall be
rooted up so ignore them. They are **blind** guides
leading the **blind,** and both will fall into the ditch."
said Jesus Christ   MATTHEW 9;29
(when healing two blind men..) "Because of your
faith it will happen." said Jesus Christ

MATTHEW 23;15-17
"Hypocrites! Yes, woe upon you hypocrites. For
you go to all lengths to make one convert and then
turn him into twice the son of hell you are
yourselves. **Blind** guides! Woe upon you! For your
rule is to swear 'By God's Temple means nothing-
you can break the oath, but to swear 'By the gold in
the Temple' is binding! Blind fools!" said Jesus
Christ

BLIND   MARK 10; 49,51,52

49 "Tell him to come here." 51 "What do you want me to do for you?" 52 "All right, it's done. Your faith has healed you." said Jesus Christ

LUKE 6;39

"What good is it for a **blind** man to lead another? He will fall into the ditch and pull the other down with him." said Jesus Christ

JOHN 12;40

"God has **blinded** their eyes and hardened their hearts so they can neither see nor understand nor turn to me to heal them." said Jesus Christ

LUKE 9;39-41

"I have come into the world to give sight to those who are spiritually **blind** and to show those who think they see that they are **blind.**"(the Pharisees ask, "Are you saying we are blind?)"If you were blind, you wouldn't be guilty," Jesus replied. "But your guilt remains because you claim you know what you are doing." said Jesus Christ

BOARD   MATTHEW 7;3

"And why worry about a speck in the eye of your brother when you have a **board** in your own? Should you say,' Friend, let me help you get that speck out of your eye,' when you can't even see because of the **board** in your own? Hypocrite! First get rid of the **board** . Then you can see to help your brother." said Jesus Christ

BOARD cont'd

LUKE 6;42

" And why quibble about a speck in someone else's eye- his little fault-when a **board** is in your own? How can you think of saying to him, 'Brother, let me help you get rid of that speck in your eye,' when you can't see past the **board** in your own? Hypocrite! First get rid of the **board,** and then perhaps you can see well enough to deal with his speck!" said Jesus Christ

BORN AGAIN

JOHN 3;3, 5-8

"With all earnestness I possess I tell you this: Unless you are **born again,** you can never get into the Kingdom of God."

5-8 "What I am telling you so earnestly is this: Unless one is **born** of water and the Spirit, he cannot enter the Kingdom of God. Men can only reproduce human life, but the Holy Spirit gives new life from heaven; so don't be surprised at my statement that you must be **born again!** Just as you can hear the wind, but can't tell where it comes from or where it will go next, so it is with the Spirit. We don't know on whom he will next bestow this life from heaven." said Jesus Christ

B   13

BREAD   MATTHEW 4;4

"No! For the Scriptures tell us that **bread** won't feed men's souls: obedience to every word of God is what we need." said Jesus Christ

LUKE 4;4

"It is written in the Scriptures, 'Other things in life are much more important than **bread!**" said Jesus Christ   JOHN 6;32,33,35, 47-51

"And now He offers you true **Bread** from heaven. The true Bread is a Person-the one sent by God from heaven and gives life to the world."

35 "I am the **Bread** of Life. No one coming to me will ever be hungry again. Those believing in me will never thirst." said Jesus Christ

47-51 "How earnestly I tell you this- anyone who believes in me already has eternal life. Yes, I am the **Bread** of Life! When your fathers in the wilderness ate bread from the skies, they all died. But the Bread from heaven gives eternal life to everyone who eats it. I am the Living **/bread** that came out of heaven. Anyone eating this **Bread** shall live forever; this Bread is my flesh given to redeem humanity." said Jesus Christ

MATTHEW 14;16

[feeding the 5,000 people miracle] "That isn't necessary- you feed them!" said Jesus Christ [and they did]

B

BREAD   MARK 6;31, 37,

  "Let's get away from the crowds for a while and rest."

37 "You feed them." said Jesus Christ

  [5,000 people...and they did with 5 loaves of **bread** and two fish]   LUKE 9;13,14

  "You feed them!"   14 "Just tell them to sit down on the ground in groups of about fifty each." said Jesus Christ (and they fed the 5,000 people)

                    MARK 8;2-3

"Pity these people," he said. "for they have been here three days and have nothing left to eat. And if I send them home without feeding them, they will faint along the road! For some have come a long distance." [so they fed 4,000 with 7 loaves of **bread** and a few small fish.] said Jesus Christ

                 MATTHEW 15; 32,34

  [this time they had 4,000 to feed]" I pity these people- they've been here with me for three days now and have nothing left to eat. I don't want to send them away hungry or they will faint along the road."

 34" How much food do you have?" said Jesus Christ (and then he gave thanks and fed 4,000 with seven loaves of **bread** and a few small fish)

See also: **COMMUNION**

BROTHER(S) and SISTER(S)
MARK 3:33-35

"Who is my mother? Who are my **brothers?**" Looking at those around him he said, "These are my mothers and brothers! Anyone who does God's will is my brother, and my **sister** and my mother." said Jesus Christ

LUKE 22;31-32

"Simon, Simon, Satan has asked to have you, to sift you like wheat, but I have pleaded in prayer for you that your faith should not completely fail. So when you have repented and turned to me again, strengthen and build up the faith of your **brothers.**" said Jesus Christ

(also see anger, betrayal, forgiveness and many others)

BUILD(ERS)   MATTHEW 21;42

"Didn't you read the Scriptures: ' The Stone rejected by the **builders** has been made the honored cornerstone; how remarkable! What an amazing thing the Lord has done'?" said Jesus Christ

MARK 12;10-11

"Don't you remember reading this verse in the Scriptures? ' The Rock the **builders** threw away became the cornerstone, the most honored stone in the **building!** This is the Lord's doing and it is an amazing thing to see." said Jesus Christ

B

BUILD(ERS) LUKE 20; 17

" Then what does the Scripture mean where it says, 'The Stone rejected by the **builders** was made the cornerstone? Whoever stumbles over that Stone shall be broken; and those on whom it falls will crushed to dust." said Jesus Christ

MATTHEW 16;18

"You are Peter, a stone; and upon this rock I will **build** my church; and all powers of hell shall not prevail against it." said Jesus Christ

MATTHEW 23; 29-30

" Yes, woe to you, Pharisees, and you religious leaders-hypocrites! For you **build** monuments to the prophets killed by your fathers and lay flowers on the graves of the godly men they destroyed and say, ' We never would have acted as our fathers did." Said Jesus Christ

MARK 13;2

[answering to a comment of a magnificent building, a temple]

"Yes look! For not one stone will be left upon another, except as ruins." said Jesus Christ

MATTHEW 7; 24-29

" All who listen to my instructions and follow them are wise, like a man who **builds** his house on solid rock. Though the rain comes in torrents, and the floods rise and the storm winds beat against the

B   17

BUILD(ERS)   MATTHEW 7; 24-29 cont'd
house, it won't collapse, for it is built on rock.

"But those who hear my instructions and ignore them are foolish, like a man who **builds** his house on sand. For when the rains and floods come, and the strong winds beat against his house, it will fall with a mighty crash." said Jesus Christ

LUKE 6;46-49

" So why do you call me 'Lord' when you won't obey me? But all of those who come and listen and obey me are like a man who **builds** his house on a strong foundation laid upon underlying rock. When the floodwaters rise and breaks against the house, it stands firm, for it is strongly **built.**

"But those who listen and don't obey are like a man who **builds** a house without a foundation. When the flood sweeps down against the house, it crumbles into a heap of ruins." said Jesus Christ.

C

CHANGE   =repent-be sorry and say so and change... God's Way

MATTHEW 21;28-31

"But what do you think about this? A man with two sons told the older boy, 'Son, go out and work the farm today.' ' I won't.' he answered, but later he **changed** his mind and went. Then the father told

CHANGE= be sorry, say so, and change..
God's Way

MATTHEW 21; 28-31 cont'd
the youngest , 'You go!' and he said 'Yes, sir, I will.' But he didn't. Which one of the two were obeying the father?" {They replied, "The first, of course."}

   "Surely evil men and prostitutes will get into the Kingdom before you do. For John the Baptist told you to repent , **change** and turn to God, and you wouldn't, while very evil men and prostitutes did. And even when you saw this happening, you refused to repent, so you couldn't believe." said Jesus Christ   LUKE 5; 31-32

   " It is the sick who need a doctor, not those in good health. My purpose is to invite sinners to **change,** not spend my time with those who already think themselves good enough." said Jesus Christ
                LUKE 13;2-5

   "Do you think they were worse sinners than other men from Galilee?" he asked. "Is that why they suffered? No. Not at all! And don't you realize that you will also perish unless you leave your evil ways, **change** and turn to God?

   "And what about the eighteen men who died when the Tower of Siloam fell on then? Were there worst sinners in Jerusalem? Not at all! And you, too will perish unless you repent." said Jesus Christ

C   19

CHANGE=be sorry, and say so and change
God's Way

MATTHEW 11;21
"Woe to you, Chorazin, and woe to you,
Bethsaida! For if the miracles I did in your streets
had been done in wicked Tyre and Sidon their
people would have repented and **changed** long ago
in shame and humility." said Jesus Christ

LUKE 15;7
" Well, in the same way heaven will be happier
over one lost sinner who **changes** and returns to
God than over ninety-nine others who haven't
strayed away!" said Jesus Christ
Repent= be sorry and say so and change God's Way

CHARITY

MATTHEW 6;1-4
" TAKE CARE! Don't do your good deeds
publicly, to be admired, for then you will lose the
reward from your Father in heaven. When you give
a gift to a beggar, don't shout about it as hypocrites
do-blowing trumpets in the synagogues and streets
to call attention to their acts of **charity!** I tell you in
earnestness, they have received all the reward they
to call attention to their acts of **charity!** I tell you in
earnestness, they have received all the reward they
will ever get. But when you do kindness to

C

CHARITY MATTHEW 6;14cont'd
someone, do it secretly-don't tell your left hand
what your right hand is doing. And your Father who
knows your secrets will reward you." said Jesus
Christ

MATTHEW 19;21-22

" If you want to be perfect, go sell everything
you have and give the money to the poor, you will
have treasure in heaven; and come follow me." said
Jesus Christ (but the young man went away sadly,
for he was very rich.)

MARK 10;21

"You lack only one thing," he told him; "go sell
everything you have and give the money to the
poor and you shall have treasure in heaven-and com
follow me." said Jesus Christ (but sadly the man
went away for he was very rich)

MARK 12;43-44

"That poor widow has given more than all those
rich men put together! For they gave a little extra
fat, while she gave up her last penny." said Jesus
Christ

LUKE 21;3-4

" Really," he remarked, "this poor widow has
given more than all the rest combined. For they
have given a little of what they didn't need, but she,
poor as she is, has given everything she has." said
Jesus Christ

C 21

CHEEK MATTHEW 5;38-42

"The law of Moses says, 'If a man gouges out another's eye, he must pay with his own eye. But I say: Don't resist violence! If you are slapped on one **cheek,** turn the other too." said Jesus Christ

LUKE 6;29

"If someone slaps you on one **cheek.** Let him slap the other too!." said Jesus Christ

CHILDREN

MATTHEW 18;3-6

"Unless you turn to God from your sins and become like little **children,** you will never get into the Kingdom of Heaven. Therefore anyone who humbles himself like a little **child** is greatest in the Kingdom of Heaven. And any of you who welcomes a little **child** like this because you are mine , is welcoming and caring for me. But if any of you causes one of these little ones who trusts me to lose his faith, it would be better for you to have a rock tied to your neck and thrown to sea." said Jesus Christ

MATTHEW 19; 14

"Let the little **children** come to me, and don't prevent them. For of such is the Kingdom of Heaven" said Jesus Christ

CHILDREN   MARK 9;37

"Anyone who welcomes a little **child** like this in my name is welcoming me, anyone who welcomes me is welcoming my Father who sent me!" said Jesus Christ

MARK 10; 14-15

"Let the little **children** come to me, for the Kingdom of God belongs to such as they. Don't send them away! I tell you seriously as I know how anyone who refuses to come to God as a little **child** will never be allowed into His Kingdom." said Jesus Christ

LUKE 9;47

"Anyone who takes care of a little **child** like this is caring for me! And whoever cares for me is caring for God who sent me! Your care for others is the measure of your greatness." said Jesus Christ

LUKE 18;16-17

" Let the little children come to me! Never send them away! For the Kingdom of God belongs to men who have hearts as trusting as these little **children's.** And anyone who doesn't have their kind of faith will never get within the Kingdom's gates." said Jesus Christ

C   23

CHOSEN

LUK*E* 10;21-22

"I praise you, O Father, Lord of Heaven and earth, for hiding these things from intellectuals and worldly wise and for revealing them to those who have **chosen** to be trusting as little children. Yes, thank you, Father, for that is the way you wanted it. I am the Agent of my Father in everything; and no one really knows the Son except the Father, and no one really know the Father except the Son and those to whom the Son choose to reveal him." said Jesus Christ

MARK 13;20

(referring to end times)

" And unless the Lord shortens the time of calamity, not a soul on in all the earth will survive. But for the sake of his **chosen** ones, he will limit those days." said Jesus Christ

LUKE 10;41-42

But the Lord said to her, "Martha dear friend, you are so upset over all these details! There is really only one thing worth being concerned about. Mary has **chosen** it- and I won't take it away from her!" said Jesus Christ

CHRIST...family

MATTHEW 8;21

"My mother and brothers are all those that want to hear the message of God and obey it." said Jesus Christt   LUKE ;12 51-53

"Do you think I have come to give peace on earth? No! Rather, strife and division! From now on **families** will be split apart, three in favor of me and two against- or perhaps the other way around. A father will decide one way about me; his son, the other; mother and daughter will disagree; and the decision of an honored mother-in-law will be spurned by her daughter-in-law." said Jesus Christ

CHRIST ...NAME

MATTHEW 6-9

"Hallowed be Your **name**"'prayed Jesus Christ

CHRIST... in his name

MATTHEW 18;20

" For where two or more gathered together in my **name,** I will be right there among them." said Jesus Christ

MATTHEW 28;19

" Therefore go and make disciples in all the nations, baptizing them into the **name** of the Father and of the Son and of the Holy Spirit, and teach these new disciples to obey all the commands I have given you; and be sure of this-I am with you until the end of the world." said Jesus Christ

CHRIST's..name

"If anyone so much as gives you a cup of water in my **name**- I say this solemnly- he will not lose his reward." said Jesus Christ

MARK 11;9

"Blessed is he who comes in the **name** of the Lord!" said Jesus Christ

JOHN 10;1-4 (our name)

"ANYONE REFUSING TO walk through the gate into a sheepfold, who sneaks over the wall, must be a thief! For a shepherd comes through the gate. The gatekeeper opens the gate for him, and the sheep hear his voice and come to him; and he calls his own sheep by **name** and he leads them out." said Jesus Christ   JOHN 14;13

"In solemn truth I tell you, anyone believing in me shall do the same miracles I have done, and even greater ones, because I am going to be with the Father. You can ask for *anything,* using my **name,** and I will do it, for this will bring praise to the Father because of what I, the Son, will do for you. Yes, ask *anything* using my **name** and I will do it." SAID Jesus Christ   JOHN 15;16

" You didn't choose me! I chose you! I appointed you to go and produce lovely fruit always, so no matter what you ask for from the Father, using my **name** , He will give it to you." said Jesus Christ

26   C

CHRIST'S NAME
JOHN 16;23-24

"At that time you won't need to ask me for anything, for you can go directly to the Father and ask Him, and He will give you what you ask for because you use my name. You haven't tried this before, but begin now. Ask using my **name,** and you will receive, and your cup of joy will overflow." said Jesus Christ

CHRIST'S PRAYERS (speaking to God about the disciples and about you, the future believer)
JOHN 17;1-5 (for himself)

"Father, the time has come. Reveal the glory of Your Son so that he can give glory back to You. For You have given him authority over every man and woman on earth. He gives eternal life to each one You have given him. And this is the way to eternal life-by knowing you, the only True God, and Jesus Christ, the one You sent to earth! I brought glory to you here on earth by doing everything you told me to. And now, Father reveal my glory as I stand in Your presence, the glory we shared before the world began." said Jesus Christ

Cont'd in JOHN 17; 6-19 (for the disciples)

"I have told these men all about You. They were in the world, but then You gave them to me; and they have obeyed You. Now they know everything I have is a gift from You, for I have passed on the

C   27

CHRIST'S PRAYERS

commands You gave me; and they accepted them and know of certainty that I came down to earth from You and they believe You sent me."

"My Plea is not for the world but those You have given me because they belong to You. And all of them, since they are mine, belong to You and You have given them back to me with everything else of yours, and *so they are my glory!* Now I am leaving the world and leaving them behind, and coming to You. Holy Father, keep them in your own care- all those You have given me. I guarded them so that not one perished, except the son of hell as Scriptures foretold."

"And I am now coming to You. I have told them many things while I was with them so that they would be filled with my joy. I have given them Your commands. And the world hates them because they don't fit in with it, just as I don't. I'm not asking You to keep them out of the world, but to keep them safe from Satan's power. They are no part of this world any more than I am. Make them pure and holy through teaching them Your words of truth. As You sent me into the world, I am sending them into the world, and I consecrate myself to meet their need for growth in truth and holiness." said Jesus Christ

CHRIST'S PRAYERS cont'd

JOHN 17 20-26 (future believers)

"I am not **praying** for these alone but also for future believers who will come to me because of the testimony of these. My **prayer** for all of them is that they will be of one heart and mind, just as You and I are, Father-as You are in me and I am in You., so they will be in us and the world will believe You sent me."

"I have given them the glory You gave me- the glorious unity of being one-so that the world will be perfected into one- so that the world will know You sent me and will understand that You love them as much as you love me. Father, I want them with me- so that they can see my glory. You gave me the glory because You loved me before the world began."

" O righteous Father, the world doesn't know You, but I do; and these disciples know You sent me. And I have revealed You to them, and will keep on revealing You so the mighty love you have for me may be in them, and I in them" said Jesus Christ

LUKE 22; 42 (before crucifixion)

"Father, if You are willing , please take away this cup of horror from me. But I want Your will, not mine." said Jesus Christ

(also see the Lord's Prayer.)

CHURCH,TEMPLE

MATTHEW 12;6

"And truly, one is here who is greater than the **Temple!** But if you had known the meaning of the Scripture verse, ' I want you to be merciful more than I want your offerings,' you would not have condemned those that are not guilty! For, I,the Messiah, am master even of the Sabbath."said Jesus Christ

MATTHEW 16;18-19

" YOU ARE Peter, a stone; and upon this rock I will build my **church;** and all the powers of hell shall not prevail against it. And I will give you the keys of the Kingdom of Heaven; whatever doors you lock on earth shall be locked in heaven; and whatever doors you open on earth shall be opened in heaven!" said Jesus Christ

MATTHEW 18; 17-20

"If he still refuses to listen, take your case to the **church,** and if the church's verdicts favor you, but he won't accept, excommunicate him. And I tell you this- whatever you bind on earth is bound in heaven, whatever you free on earth is free in heaven."

"I also tell you this- if two of you agree down here on earth concerning anything you ask for, my Father in Heaven will do it for you. For where two or three gather together because they are mine, I will be right there among them." said Jesus Christ

CHURCH, TEMPLE

MARK 11;17

"It is written in the scriptures. 'My **Temple** is a place of prayer for all nations,' but you have turned it into a den of robbers." said Jesus Christ

JOHN 2; 19, 21

" All right," Jesus replied, "this is the miracle I will do for you: Destroy this **sanctuary (temple)** and in three days I will raise it up!" 21. [but by "this sanctuary" he meant his body.] said Jesus Christ

COMFORT (ER)

MATTHEW 5; 4

"Those who mourn are fortunate for they will be **comforted!**" said Jesus Christ

(See also Holy Spirit)

COMMANDMENTS

MATTHEW 19;18-19

"Don't kill, don't commit adultery, don't steal, don't lie, honor your father and mother and love your neighbor as yourself!" said Jesus Christ

MATTHEW 22;37-40

" 'Love the Lord your God with all your heart, soul and mind'. This is the first and greatest commandment. The second most important is similar: ' Love your neighbor as much as yourself.' all other commandments and all demands of the prophets stem from these two laws and are fulfilled if you obey them. Keep only these and you will find

COMMANDMENT
MATTHEW 22; 37-40 cont'd
that you are obeying all others." said Jesus Christ
MARK 12;29--33

"The one that says. 'Hear, O Israel! The Lord our God is the one and only God. You must love Him with all your heart, soul, and mind and strength.' "

"The second is: ' You must love others as much as yourself.' no other **commandment**s are greater than these." said Jesus Christ

COMMANDMENT 11th NEW
JOHN 13;34-35

"And so I am giving a **new commandment** to you now- love each other just as much as I have loved you. Your strong love for each other will prove to the world that you are my disciples." said JesusChrist

COMMUNION
MATTHEW 26; 18,23-29

"Go into the city and see Mr. So-and So, and tell him, 'Our Master says, my time has come, and I will eat the Passover meal with my disciples at your house.'"

23,24 -29 "It is the one I served first. For I mustdie just as was prophesied, but woe to the man by whom I have been betrayed. Far better for that one that he had never been born."

"Take it and eat it for this is my body."

COMMUNION MATTHEW 18; 23-29 cont'd

"Each drink from it, for this is my blood, sealing the new covenant. It is poured out to forgive the sins of multitudes. Mark my words- I will not drink this wine again until the day I drink it new with you in my Father's kingdom." said Jesus Christ

MARK 14;22,24-26

"Eat it- this is my body." 24 " This is my blood, poured out for many, sealing the new agreement between God and man. I solemnly declare that I shall never again taste wine until the day I drink a different kind in the Kingdom of God." said Jesus Christ

LUKE 22;19, 20-22

"This is my body, given for you. Eat it in remembrance of me."

20-22 "This wine is a token of God's new agreement to save you- an agreement sealed with blood I shall pour out to purchase back your souls.. But here at this table, sitting among us as a friend, is the man who will betray me. I must die. It is part of God's plan. But, oh, the horror awaiting that man who betrays me." said Jesus Christ

COMPARE   MATTHEW 11;16-19

" To what can I **compare** this generation? These are like children playing who say to their friends, 'We played wedding and you weren't happy, so we

COMPARE   MATTHEW   11;16-19 cont'd
played funeral and you weren't sad.' For the John
the Baptist doesn't even drink wine and often goes
without food, and you say, 'He's crazy.' and I, the
Messiah, feast and drink and you complain that I am
a glutton and drinking man, and hang around the
worst of sinners! But brilliant men like you can
justify your every inconsistency!"said Jesus Christ
LUKE 7;31-35

"What can I say about such men? With what shall
I **compare** them? They are like a group of children
who complain to their :friends. 'You don't like it if
we play "wedding" and you don't like it if we play
funeral"! For John the Baptists used to go without
food and never took a drop of liquor all his life and
you say, 'He must be crazy!"But I eat my food and
drink my wine, and you say, 'What a glutton Jesus
is! And he drinks! And has the lowest sort of
friends!' But I am sure you can always justify your
inconsistencies!" said Jesus Christ

CONCEIT   JOHN 7;17-19

"I'm not teaching you my own thoughts, but
those of God who sent me. If any of you really
determines to do God's will, then you will certainly
know whether my teaching is from God or is merely

CONCEIT   JOHN 7;17-19 cont'd
 my own. Anyone presenting his own ideas is
looking for praise for himself, but anyone seeking
to honor the One who sent him is a good and true
person." said Jesus Christ

CONFLICT   MATTHEW 10;34-38
   "Don't imagine that I came to bring peace on
earth! No, rather a sword. I have come set man
against father, and daughter against mother, and a
daughter-in-law against mother-in-law- a man's
worst enemies will be right in his own home! If you
love your father and mother more than you love me,
you are not worthy of being mine; or if you love
your son or your daughter more than me, you are not
worthy of being mine. If you refuse to take up your
cross and follow me, you are not worthy of being
mine." said Jesus Christ

CRIPPLED   MARK 9;45-46
   "If your foot carries you toward evil, cut it off!
Better to be **crippled** and live forever than have two
feet carry you to hell!" said Jesus Christ

CROSS   MATTHEW 10;38
   " If you refuse to take up your **cross** and
follow me, you are not worthy of being mine."
said Jesus Christ   MATTHEW 16;24
   "If anyone wants to be a follower of mine, let him

CROSS   MATTHEW 16;24 cont'd
deny himself and take up the **cross** and follow me."
said Jesus Christ

MARK. 8;34

"If any of you want to be my follower, you must
put aside your own pleasures and shoulder your
cross and follow me closely." said Jesus Christ

LUKE 9;24

" Anyone who wants to follow me must put aside
his own desires and conveniences and carry his
cross with him every day and keep close to me!"
said Jesus Christ

CRUCIFIXION,CRUCIFIED

MATTHEW 26;2

"As you know, Passover Celebration begins in
two days, and I shall be betrayed and
crucified." said Jesus Christ

LUKE 22; 40-42

THE GARDEN PRAYER

"Pray to God that you will not be overcome by
temptation."…."Father, if You are willing, please
take this cup of poison away from me. But, Your
will be done, not mine." said Jesus Christ

LUKE 22;48

THE KISS OF BETRAYAL

But Jesus said, "Judas, how can you do this-
betray the Messiah with a kiss?" said Jesus Christ

CRUCIFIXION   LUKE 22;51-53 DON'T RESIST

But Jesus said, " Don't resist anymore. Am I a robber, that you have come with swords to arrest me? Why didn't you arrest me in the Temple? I was there every day. But this is your moment, the time when Satan's power reigns supreme." said Jesus Christ   LUKE 22;69-70

BEFORE THE COUNCIL

"If I tell you , you won't believe me or let me present my case. But the time is soon coming when I, the Messiah, shall be enthroned beside Almighty" said Jesus Christ

JOHN 18; 5,7,8,11,20-23

""Whom are you looking for?"" I am he." 7, "Whom are you searching for? " 8, "I told you I am he." 11 "Put your sword away. Shall I not drink from the cup the Father has given me?" 20 "What I teach is widely known, for I have preached regularly in the Temple; I have been heard by all the Jewish leaders and teach nothing in private that I have not said in public. Why are you asking me this question? Ask those who heard me. You have some of them here. They know what I said." 23 " If I lied, prove it, should you hit a man for telling the truth?" said Jesus Christ

CRUCIFIXION

PILATE   JOHN 18;34,36

"King as *you* use the word or as the Jews use it?" 36 "I am not an earthly king. If l were, my followers would have fought when I was arrested by the Jewish leaders. But my Kingdom is not of this world." 37 "I was born for that purpose. And I came to bring truth to the world. All who love the truth are my followers." said Jesus Christ

THE DENIAL   LUKE 22; 61

"Before the rooster crows tomorrow morning, you will deny me three times." said Jesus Christ

                LUKE 23;28-31, 34

CONSEQUENCES

"Daughters of Jerusalem, don't weep for me, but for yourselves and for your children. For the days are coming when women who have no children will be counted fortunate indeed. Mankind will beg mountains to fall on them and crush them and hills to bury them. For if such things as these are done to me, The Living Tree, what will they do to you?" 34 "Father, forgive these people for they don't know what they are doing." said Jesus Christ

38 C

CRUCIFIXION

CONSEQUENCES

(speaking to Pilate)

JOHN 19;11

"You would have no power at all over me unless it were given to you from above. So those who brought me to you have the greater sin." said Jesus Christ

LAST WORDS

LUKE 23; 43,45,46

"Today you will be with me in Paradise. This is a solemn promise."

46 "Father, I commit my spirit unto you." said Jesus Christ

JOHN 19; 28

"I'm thirsty. It is finished." said Jesus Christ

D

DEATH   MATTHEW 16; 27-28

"For I, the Son of Mankind, shall come with angels in the glory of my Father and judge each person according to his deeds. And some of you standing right here now will certainly live to see me coming in my Kingdom." said Jesus Christ

DEATH   JOHN 5;24-29

"I say emphatically that anyone who listens to my message and believes in God who sent me has eternal life, and will never be damned for their sins, but has already passed out of **death** into life. And I solemnly declare that the time is coming, in fact it is here, when the dead shall hear my voice- the voice of the Son of God- and those who listen to me shall live. The Father has life in Himself, and has granted the Son to have life in himself, and to judge the sins of all mankind because he is the Son of Man. Don't be surprised! Indeed the time is coming when all of the dead in their graves shall hear the voice of God's Son, and shall rise again-those who have done good, to eternal life; and those who have continued in evil, to judgment." said Jesus Christ

JOHN 8;51

" With all the earnestness I have, I tell you this- no one who obeys me shall ever **die!**" said Jesus Christ   JOHN 11;4

"The purpose of his illness is not **death,** but for the glory of God. I, the Son, will receive glory from this situation." said Jesus Christ

DEATH PREDICTION

MATTHEW 16;21-23

[From then on Jesus began to speak plainly to his

40   D

DEATH PREDICTION

MATTHEW 16;21-23 cont'd

[disciples about going to Jerusalem, and what would happen to him there- that he would suffer at the hands of the Jewish leaders, that he would be killed and three days later he would be raised to life again.]

[But Peter took him aside to remonstrate with him. "Heaven forbid, sir," he said, "this is not going to happen to you!"]

Jesus turned to Peter and said, "Get away from me, you Satan! You are a dangerous trap to me. You are thinking merely from a human point of view, and not from God's" said Jesus Christ.

MATTHEW 20;18-19

"I will be betrayed to the chief priests and other Jewish leaders and they will condemn me to **die.** And they will hand me over to the Roman government, I will be mocked and **crucified,** and on the third day I will rise to life again." said Jesus Christ

MATTHEW 26;2

"As you know, the Passover celebration begins in two days, and I shall be betrayed and **crucified."** said Jesus Christ

MARK 9;31

"I, the Messiah, am going to be betrayed and

DEATH PREDICTION

MARK 9;31 cont'd

killed and three days later I will come to life again."
said Jesus Christ   MARK 10;33-34

"When we get there, "he told them' "I, the
Messiah, will be arrested and taken before the chief
priests and the Jewish leaders, who will sentence
me to **die** and hand me over to the Romans to be
killed. They will mock me and spit on me and flog
me with their whips and kill me; but after three
days, I will come back to life again." said Jesus
Christ   LUKE 9;44

"Listen to me and remember what I say. I, The
Messiah, am going to be betrayed." said Jesus
Christ   JOHN 12;23-33, 35- 37

Jesus replied that the time had come for him to
return to his glory in heaven and that , "I must **die**
and fall like a kernel of wheat that falls in the
furrows of the earth. Unless I **die** -I will be alone- a
single seed. But my **death** will produce many new
wheat kernels- a plentiful harvest of new lives. If
you love your life down here- you will loose it. If
you despise your life down here- you will exchange
it for eternal glory."

"If the Greeks want to be my disciples, tell them
come and follow me, for my servants are where I

42   D

DEATH PREDICTION

JOHN 12;23 -33, 35-37 cont'd

am. And if they follow me, the Father will honor them. Now my soul is deeply troubled. Shall I pray, ' Father save me from what lies ahead?' But that is the very reason why I came! Father, bring glory and honor to Your name."

{Then a voice spoke from Heaven saying. "I have already done this and I will do it again."}
[When the crowd heard the voice, some of them thought it was thunder, while others declared an angel had spoken to him.]

Then Jesus told them, "The voice was for your benefit, not mine. The time of judgement for the world has come- and the time with Satan, the prince of this world shall be cast out. And when I am lifted up on the cross, I will draw everyone to me. [He said this to indicate how he was going to die.]

{"Die?" asked the crowd. " We understood that the Messiah would live forever and never die. Why are you saying he will die? What Messiah are you talking about?"}

Jesus replied. "My light will shine out for you just a little while longer. Walk in it while you can and go where you want to go before darkness falls, for then it will be too late to find your way. Make use of the light while there is still time: then you will become light bearers." After saying these

DEATH PREDICTION

JOHN 12; 23-33 35-37 cont'd

things, Jesus went away and was hidden from them.

DEATH REMEMBERED

MATTHEW 26;10-13

Jesus knew what they were thinking and said, "Why are you criticizing her? For she has done a good thing to me. You will always have poor among you, but you won't always have me. She has poured this perfume on me to prepare **my body for burial.** And she will always be **remembered** for this deed. The story of what she has done will be told throughout the whole world, wherever the Good News is preached." said Jesus Christ

DEBT (financial and spiritual)

LUKE 7;40-43

"Simon," he said to the Pharisee, "I have something to say to you...."A man loaned money to two people.- $5,000 to one and $500 to the other. But neither of them could **pay him back,** so he kindly forgave them both, letting them keep the money! Which do you suppose loved him most after that?"

"Correct." Then he turned to the woman and said to Simon, "Look! See this woman kneeling here! When I entered your home, you didn't bother to offer me water to wash the dust from my feet, but she washed them with her tears and wiped them

DEBT   LUKE 7;40-43 cont'd

with her hair, You refused me the customary kiss of greeting, but she has kissed my feet again and again from the time I first came in. You neglected the usual courtesy of olive oil to anoint my head, but she covered my feet in rare perfume. Therefore her sins-and they are many-are forgiven, for she loved me much; but one who is forgiven little, shows little love." said Jesus Christ.

DEMON -DEMONIC POSSESSION
MARK 5;18-19

[So he got back into the boat. The man who had been possessed by the **demon** begged Jesus to go along,] but Jesus said, "No."

"Go home to your friends," he told him, "and tell them all the wonderful things God has done for you; how merciful he has been."said Jesus Christ

MARK 7;29

"Good!" he said. "You have answered well- so well that I have healed your little girl. Go home for the **demon** has left her!" said Jesus Christ

MARK 9;25,29

"0 **demon** of deafness and dumbness. "he said, "I command you to come out of this child and enter him no more!"

"Cases like this require prayer."said Jesus Christ

DEMON- DEMONIC POSSESSION
cont'd

LUKE 9;41, 43

"O you stubborn faithless people," Jesus said to his disciples, "how long should I put up with you? Bring him here." said Jesus Christ
[But Jesus ordered the demon to come out and healed the boy and handed him over to his father. 43 Awe gripped the crowd as they saw the display of the power of God.]

DENIAL - PREDICTION

MATTHEW 26; 21

Jesus told him, (Peter) "The truth is that this very night, before the cock crows at dawn, you will **deny** me three times." said Jesus Christ

MARK 14;30

" Peter," Jesus said, 'before the cock crows a second time tomorrow morning you will **deny** me three times." said Jesus Christ

[MARK 14;72 And immediately the rooster crowed the second time. Suddenly Jesus' words flashed through Peter's mind: "Before the cock crows twice, you will deny me three times." And he beganto cry.]

DIRTY   MATTHEW 15; 16-20

"Don't you understand? "Jesus asked him. "
Don't you see that anything you eat passes through
the digestive tract and out again? But evil words
come from an evil heart, and defiles a man who says
them. For from the heart comes evil thoughts,
murder, adultery, fornication, theft, lying and
slander. These are what defile; but there is no
spiritual defilement from eating without first going
through the ritual of ceremonial hand washing!"
said Jesus Christ

DISCIPLES   MATTHEW 10;5

Jesus set them out with these instructions: "Don't
go to the Gentiles or the Samaritans, but only to the
people of Israel- God's lost sheep. Go and
announce to them the Kingdom of Heaven is near.
Heal the sick, raise the dead, cure the lepers, and
cast out demons."

"Give as freely as you have received!"

" Don't take money with you; don't even carry a
duffle bag with extra clothes or shoes, or even a
walking stick; for those who help you should feed
and care for you. Whenever you enter a city or
village, search for a godly man and stay at his home
until you leave for the next town. When you ask
permission to stay, be friendly, and if it turns out to
be a godly home, give it your blessing; if not, keep
the blessing. Any city or home that does not

DISCIPLES   MATTHEW 10; 5-42 cont'd
welcome you- shake off the dust of that place from
your feet as you leave. Truly the wicked of Sodom
and Gomorrah will be better off on Judgment Day
than they.

" I am sending you out as sheep among wolves.
Be as wary as serpents and harmless as doves. But
beware! For you will be arrested and tried, and
whipped in the synagogues. Yes, you must stand
trial before governors and kings for my sake. This
will give you the opportunity to tell the world about
me, yes, to witness to the world.

"When you are arrested, don't worry about what
to say at your trial, for you will be given the right
words at the right time. For it won't be you doing
the talking-it will be the Spirit of your heavenly
Father speaking through you!

"Brother shall betray brother to death, and fathers
shall betray their own children. And children shall
rise against their parents and cause their deaths.
Everyone shall hate you because you belong to me.
But all of you who endure until the end shall be
saved.

" When you are persecuted in one city flee to the
next! I will return before you've reached them all! A
student is not greater than his teacher. A servant is
not above his master. The student shares his
teacher's fate. The servant shares his master's! And

48   D

DISCIPLES MATTHEW 10; 5-42 cont'd
since I, the master of the household, have been
called Satan, how much more will you! But don't be
afraid of those who threaten you. For the time is
coming when the truth will be revealed: their secret
plot will become public information.

"What I tell you now in the gloom. Shout abroad
when daybreak comes. What I whisper in your ears,
proclaim it from the housetops!

"Don't be afraid of those who can kill only your
bodies- but can't touch your souls! Fear only God
who can destroy both soul and body in hell. Not one
sparrow (What do they cost? Two for a penny?)
can fall to the ground without your Father knowing
it. And the very hairs of your head are all numbered.
So don't worry! You are more valuable to Him than
many sparrows.

"If anyone publically acknowledges me as as
his friend, I will openly acknowledge him as a
friend before my Father in heaven.

" Don't imagine that I came to bring peace to the
earth! No, rather a sword. I have come to set man
against his father, a daughter against her mother
and a daughter-in-law against her mother-in-law- a
man's worst enemies will be right in his own home!
If you love your father and mother more than you
love me, you are not worthy to be mine; or if you
love your son or daughter more than me, you are not

DISCIPLES   MATTHEW 10;5-42 cont'd
worthy to be mine. If you refuse to take up your
cross and follow me, you are not worthy of being
mine.

"If you cling to your life, you will lose it; but if
you give it up for me, you will save it.

" Those who welcome you are welcoming me.
And when they welcome me they are welcoming
God who sent me. If you welcome a prophet
because he is a man of God, you will be given the
same reward a prophet gets. And if you welcome
good and godly men because of their godliness, you
will be given a reward like theirs.

"And if, as my representatives, you give even a
cup of cold water to a little child, you will be
rewarded." said Jesus Christ

MARK. 1;17

Jesus called out to them, " Come follow me! And
I will make you fishermen for the souls of men!"
said Jesus Christ

MARK 16;15-18

And he told them, "You are to go into all the
world and preach the Good News to everyone,
everywhere. Those who believed and are baptized
will be saved. But those who refuse to believe will
be condemned.

"And those who believe shall use my authority to

DISCIPLES   MARK 16;15-18 cont'd
cast out demons, and they shall speak new languages. They will be able to even handle poisonous snakes with safety and if they drink anything poisonous, it won't hurt them; and they will be able to place their hands on the sick and heal them." said Jesus Christ

JOHN 6;61-65,67,70

Jesus knew within himself that his disciples were complaining and said to them, "Does this offend you? Then what will you think if you see me, the Messiah, return to heaven again? Only the Holy Spirit gives eternal life. Those born only once, with physical birth, will never receive the gift. But now I have told you how to get this true spiritual life. But some of you don't believe me." {For Jesus knew from the beginning who didn't believe and knew the one who would betray him,}

And he remarked, "That is what I meant when I said that no one can come to me unless the Father attracts him to me."
67 "Are you going too?" 70 "I choose twelve of you and one is the devil." said Jesus Christ

JOHN 8;31

"You are truly my **disciples** if you live as I tell you to live." said Jesus Christ

D 51

JOHN 13;34

"And so I am giving a new commandment to you now-love one another just as much as I love you. Your strong love for one another will prove to the world that you are my **disciples."** said Jesus Christ

JOHN 15;5-15

" Yes, I am the Vine; you are the branches. Whoever lives in me and I in him shall produce a large crop of fruit. For apart from me you can't do a thing. If anyone separates from me, he is thrown away like a useless branch, withers, and is gathered into a pile with all the others burned. But if you stay in me and obey my commands, you may ask any request you like and it will be granted! My true **disciples** will produce bountiful harvests. This brings great glory to my Father.

"I have loved you even as the Father has loved me. Live within my love. When you obey me you are living in my love, just as I obey my Father and live in His love. I have told you this so that you can be filled with my joy. Yes, your cup will overflow! I demand that you love one another as I love you. And here is how to measure it- the greatest love is shown when a person lays down his life for his friends; and you are my friends if you obey me. I no longer call you slaves, for a master doesn't confide in his slaves; now you are my friends, proved by the

DISCIPLES   JOHN 15;5-15 cont'd

fact that I have told you everything the Father told me." said Jesus Christ

MATTHEW 28;18-20

He told the disciples, "I have been given all authority in heaven and earth. Therefore go and make **disciples** in all nations, baptizing into the name of the Father and of the Son and of the Holy Spirit, and teach these new **disciples** to obey all the commands I have given you; and be sure of this- that I am with you always, even to the end of the world." said Jesus Christ

DIVIDED

MATTHEW 12;25-30

Jesus knew their thoughts and replied, " A **divided** kingdom ends in ruin. A city or home **divided** against itself cannot stand. And if Satan is casting out Satan, he is fighting himself, and destroying his own kingdom. And if you claim I am casting out demons by invoking powers of Satan, then what power do your own people use when they cast them out? Let them answer your question! But if I am casting out demons by the Spirit of God, then the Kingdom of God has arrived among you. One cannot rob Satan's kingdom without frrst binding Satan. Only then can his demons be cast out! Anyone who isn't helping me is harming me." said Jesus Christ

DIVIDE

PLEASE READ   MARK 3; 23-27
                     LUKE 11;17-28
                     LUKE 12; 51-53

"Do you think I have come to give peace on earth? No! Rather, strife and **division!** From now on families will be split apart, three in favor of me and two against- or perhaps the other way around. A father will decide one way about me and the son, the other; mother and daughter will disagree; and the decision of an honored mother-in-law will be spurned by her daughter-in-law." said Jesus Christ

DIVORCE / MARRIAGE

MATTHEW 19; 6-12

"And no man may **divorce** what God has joined together."

{" Then why," they asked, " did Moses say a man may divorce his wife by merely writing her a letter of dismissal?'}

Jesus replied, "Moses did that in recognition of your hard and evil hearts, but it is not what God originally intended. And I tell you this, anyone who **divorces** his wife, except for fornication, and marries another commits adultery."

{"If that is how it is, it is better not to marry!"} "Not everyone can accept this statement," Jesus said. "Only those whom God helps. Some are born without the ability to **marry,** and some are disabled

54 D

DIVORCE *I*MARRIAGE

MATTHEW 19;6-12 cont'd

by men, and some refuse to **marry** for the sake of the Kingdom of Heaven. Let anyone who can accept my statement." said Jesus Christ

MARK 10;3,5-9

"What did Moses say about **divorce?**" asked Jesus.

5 "And why did he say that?" Jesus asked. "**I'**ll tell you why-it was a concession to your hard hearted wickedness. But certainly it isn't God's Way. For from the very first He made man and woman to be joined together permanently in **marriage** therefore a man is to leave his father and mother, and he and his wife are united as one. And no man may separate what God has joined together." said Jesus Christ

DOCTOR   MATTHEW 9;12

{ The Pharisees were indignant. "Why does your teacher associate with men like that?"}

" Because people who are well don't need a **doctor!** It's the sick people who do!"was Jesus' reply. "Now go away and learn the meaning of this verse of Scripture,

'It isn't your sacrifices and your gifts I want- I want you to be merciful.'

"For I have come to urge sinners to , not the self-righteous, back to God."said Jesus Christ

DOCTOR   LUKE 4;23-24

Then he said," Probably you will quote me that proverb, **'Physician** heal yourself -meaning. 'Why don't you do miracles here in your hometown like those you did in Capernaum? But I solemnly declare to you that no prophet is accepted in his own home town!" said Jesus Christ

DON'T BELIEVE
JOHN10;25-31 34-38

"I have already told you, and you **don't believe** me, "Jesus replied. " The proof is in the miracles I do in the name of my Father. But you **don't believe** me because you are not part of my flock. My sheep recognize my voice, and I know them and they follow me. I give them eternal life and they shall never perish. No one shall snatch them away from me, for my Father has given them to me, and He is more powerful than anyone else, so no one can kidnap them from me. I and the Father are one."

[Then the Jewish leaders picked up stones to kill him.]

Jesus said, "At God's direction, I have done many a miracle to help the people. For which one are you killing me?

{They replied, "Not for any good work but, for blasphemy; you a mere man, have declared yourself to be God."}

DON'T BELIEVE

JOHN 10; 25-31 34-38 cont'd

"In your law it says men are gods!" he replied. "
So if the Scriptures, which cannot be untrue, speaks
of those as gods to whom the message of God came,
do you call it blasphemy when the one sanctified
and sent into the world by the Father says, 'I am the
Son of God'? **Don't believe** me unless I do miracles
of God. But if you do, believe them even if you
don't believe me. Then you will become convinced
that the Father is in me, and I in the Father." said
Jesus Christ

[Once again they started to arrest him. But he
walked away and left them, and went beyond the
Jordon River to stay near the place where John was
first baptizing. And many followed him.]

{ "John didn't do miracles," they remarked to one
another, "but all his predictions concerning this
man have come true."} [And many came to the
decision that he was the Messiah.]

DOOR   MATTHEW 6;6

"But when you pray, go away by yourself , all
alone and shut the **door** behind you and pray to your
Father secretly, and your Father knows your secrets,
will reward you." said Jesus Christ

D 57

DOOR   MATTHEW 7;7

"Ask, and you will be given what you ask for.
Seek and you will find. Knock and the **door** will be
opened. For anyone who asks receives. Anyone who
seeks, finds. If you only knock the **door** will be
opened." said Jesus Christ

LUKE 13;24

And he replied, "The **door** to heaven is narrow.
Work hard to get in, for the truth is that many will
try to enter, but when the head of the house has
locked the door, it will be too late. Then if you stand
outside knocking, and pleading, 'Lord, open the
door for us,' He will reply, 'I do not know you.'"
said Jesus Christ

E

ELIJAH and MOSES VISIT
MATTHEW 17;1-13

[Six days after he took Peter and James and his
brother John to the top of the high and lonely hill,
and as they watched, his appearance changed so that
his face shone like the sun and his clothing became
dazzling white.]

[Suddenly Moses and **Elijah** appeared and were
talking to him.] { Peter blurted out, " Sir, it is
wonderful that we can be here! If you want me to,
I'll make three shelters, one for you and one for

58   E

ELIJAH and MOSES VISIT
MATTHEW 17; 1-13 cont'd

Moses and one for **Elijah."]**

[But even as he said it, a bright cloud came over them and a voice from the cloud said.] { "This is my beloved Son, and I am wonderfully pleased with him. Obey him.}

[At this, the disciples fell face downward to the ground, terribly frightened. Jesus came over and touched them.] " Get up, "he said, "don't be afraid."

[And when they looked, only Jesus was with them.]

[As they were going down the mountain. Jesus commanded them not to tell anyone what they had seen until he was risen from the dead.]

{His disciples asked. "Why do the Jewish leaders insist **Elijah** must return before the Messiah comes?'}

Jesus replied, "They are right. **Elijah** must come and set everything in order. In fact, he has already come, but wasn't recognized, and was badly mistreated by many. And I the Messiah shall also suffer at their hands." said Jesus Christ

[Then the disciples realized that he was speaking of John the Baptist]

END TIMES SIGNS
MATTHEW 24;2-34

But he told them, "all of these buildings will be knocked down and not one stone left on top of the other."

{"When will this happen?"} [the disciples asked him later, as he sat on the slopes of the Mount of Olives.] {"What events will signal your return, and the end of the world?}

Jesus told them, " Don't let anyone fool you. For many will come in my name For many will come claiming to be the Messiah, and will lead many astray. When you hear of wars beginning, this does not signal my return; these must come, but **the end** is not yet. The nations and kingdoms of the earth will up against each other and there will be famines and earthquakes in many places. But this will all be only the beginning of the horrors to come.

"Then you will be tortured and killed and hated all over the world because you are mine, and many of you shall fall back into sin and betray and hate each other. And many false prophets will appear and lead many astray. Sin will be rampant everywhere and cool the love of many. But those enduring until **the end** will be saved.

"And the Good News about the Kingdom will be preached throughout the whole world, so that all nations will hear it.

E

END TIMES SIGNS

MATTHEW 24;2-34 cont'd

" So, when you see a horrible thing (told about by Daniel the prophet) standing in a Holy place {Note to reader: You know what is meant! }, then those in Judea must flee to the Judean hills. Those on their porches must not even go back inside to pack before they flee. Those in fields should not return to their homes for their clothes.

" And woe to pregnant women and to those with babies in those days. And pray your flight will not be in winter, or on the Sabbath. For there will be persecution like the world has never seen in all its history and never will see again.

" In fact, unless those days are shortened, all mankind will perish. But they will be shortened for the sake of God's chosen people.

" Then if anyone tells you, ' The Messiah has arrived at such and such a place or has appeared here or there', don't believe it. For false christs shall arise and false prophets will do wonderful miracles, so that even if it were possible, God's chosen ones would be deceived. See, I have warned you.

"So if someone tells you the Messiah has returned and is out in the desert, don't believe it! For as lightning flashes across the sky from east to west

E 61

END TIMES SIGNS

MATTHEW 24;2-34, cont'd

so shall my coming be, when I , the Messiah return. And wherever the carcass is, the vultures will gather.

"Immediately after the persecution of those days, the sun will be darkened and the moon will not give light, and stars will seem to fall from the heavens and the powers overshadowing the earth will be convulsed.

" And when at last the **signal** of my coming will appear in the heavens and there will be deep mourning all around the earth. All nations of the world will see me arrive in the clouds of heaven, with power and great glory. I'll shall send forth my angels with a sound of a mighty trumpet blast and they shall gather my chosen from the farthest ends of the earth and heaven.

"Now learn a lesson from the fig tree. When her branch is tender and the leaves begin to sprout, you know that summer is almost here. Just so, when you see all of things happen, you can know that my return is near, even at the doors." said Jesus Christ

END TIMES PARABEL OF VIRGINS

MATTHEW 25;1-13

" THE Kingdom of Heaven can be illustrated by the story of the ten bridesmaid **virgins** who took lamps and went to meet the bridegroom. But only

62   E

END TIMES PARABEL OF VIRGINS
MATTHEW 25;1-13 cont'd

five of them were wise enough to fill their lamps with oil, while the other five were foolish and forgot.

" So when the bridegroom was delayed, they lay down and rest until midnight, they were roused by the shout, 'The bridegroom is coming! Come out and welcome him!'

" All the girls jumped up and trimmed their lamps. The five who hadn't any oil begged the others to share with them, for their lamps were going out.

"But the others replied, 'We haven't enough. Go instead to the shops and buy some for yourselves.'

"But while they were gone, the bridegroom came and those who were ready went in with him to the marriage feast, and the door was locked.

"Later, the other five returned, they stood outside calling, 'Sir, open the door for us.'

"But he called back, ' Go away! It is too late.'

"So stay awake and be prepared for you do not know the date or moment of my return." said Jesus Christ

READ   MARK 13; 5-37

END TIMES   MARK 13; 32-37

"However, no one, not even the angels in heaven, nor I myself, knows the day or hour when these things will happen: only the Father knows. And since you don't know when it will happen, stay alert. Be on watch for my return.

"My coming can be compared with a man who went on a trip to another country. He laid out his employees' work for them to do while he was gone, and told the gatekeeper to watch for his return.

"Keep a sharp lookout! For you do not know when I will come, at evening, at midnight, early dawn or late daybreak. Don't let me find you sleeping. Watch for my return! This is my message to you and everyone else." said Jesus Christ

ENEMIES   MATTHEW 5;43-48

"There is a saying, ' Love your friends and hate your **enemies.**' But I say: Love your **enemies!** Pray for those who persecute you! In that way you will be acting as true sons of your Father in heaven. For He gives His sunlight to both evil and good, and sends rain on the just and unjust too. If you love only those that love you, what good is that? Even scoundrels do that much. If you are friendly only to your friends, how are you different from anyone else? Even heathen do that. But you are to be perfect, even as your Father in Heaven is perfect." said Jesus Christ

64   E

ENEMIES CHEEK

LUKE 6;27-31

"Listen, all of you. Love your **enemies.** Do good to those who hate you. Pray for the happiness of those who curse you; implore God's blessing on those who hurt you.

" If someone slaps you on one cheek , let him slap you on the other too! If someone demands your coat, give him your shirt besides. Give what you have to anyone who asks for it; and when things are taken away from you, don't worry about getting
them back. TREAT OTHERS AS YOU WOULD HAVE THEM TREAT YOU." said Jesus
Christ (above is what we call "The Golden Rule")

ETERNAL LIFE ETERNITY

MATTHEW 19;17-22

"When you call me good, you are calling me God, "Jesus replied, "for God alone is truly good. But to answer your question, you can get to Heaven by keeping the commandments."

{"Which ones?" the man asked}

And Jesus replied, "Don't kill, don't commit adultery, don't steal, don't lie, honor your father and mother, and love your neighbor as yourself."

{"I've always obeyed every one of them." the youth replied. "What else must I do?"}

Jesus told him, "If you want to be perfect, go and

ETERNAL LIFE ETERNITY

MATTHEW 19;29cont'd
sell everything you have and give the money to the
poor, and you will have treasure in heaven; and
come follow me." {But when the young man heard
this, he went away sadly, for he was very rich.}
Again in   **MARK 10;17 & LUKE 10;25**

MATTHEW **19;29**
" And anyone who gives up his home, brother,
sisters, father, mother, wife children or property to
follow me shall have **eternal life.** But many who
are first now will be last then; and some who are
last now will be first then." said Jesus Christ

LUKE 16; 8-12
" The rich man had to admire the rascal for being
so shrewd. And it is true that the citizens of this
world are more clever {in dishonesty} than the
godly are. But shall I tell *you* to act that way, to but
friendship through cheating? Will this ensure your
entry into an **everlasting** home in heaven? *No!* For
unless you are honest in small matters, you won't be
in large ones. I f you cheat even a little, you won't
be honest with greater responsibilities. And if you
are untrustworthy about worldly wealth, who will
trust you with true riches of heaven? And if you are
not faithful with other people's money, why should
you be entrusted with money of your own?" said
Jesus Christ

66 E

ETERNAL LIFE ETERNITY

JOHN 3;16

"For God loved the world so much that He gave His only Son so that anyone who believes in him shall not perish but have **eternal life**. God did not send His Son into the world to condemn it, but to save it." said Jesus Christ

JOHN 12;44-50

Jesus shouted to the crowds, " If you trust me, you are really trusting God. For when you see me, you are seeing the one who sent me. I have come as aLight to shine upon this dark world, so that all who put their trust in me will no longer wander in the darkness. If anyone hears me and doesn't obey me, I am not his judge- for I have come to save the world and not judge it. But all who reject me and my message will be judged on the Day of Judgment by the truths I have spoken. For these are not my ideas, but I have told you what the Father said to tell you. And I know His instructions lead to **eternal life**." said Jesus Christ

JOHN 17; 1-3

When Jesus had finished saying all these things, he looked up to Heaven and said, "Father, the time has come. Reveal the glory of your Son so that he can give the glory back to you. For you have given him authority over every man and woman in all the earth. He gives **eternal life**-by knowing you, the

ETERNAL LIFE ETERNITY
JOHN 17;1-3 cont'd

only true God, and Jesus Christ, the one You sent to earth!" said Jesus Christ

EVIDENCE   JOHN 14;11

"Just believe it- that I am in the Father and the Father in me. Or else believe it because of the miracles you have seen me do." said Jesus Christ.
(See **MIRACLES, FOOLISH , FOLLOW**)

EXPERTS   LUKE 11;52

"Woe to you **experts** in religion! For you hide the truth from people. You won't accept it for yourselves and you prevent others from believing it!" said Jesus Christ

F

(Everything about Christ is faith. Examples)

FAITH   MATTHEW 17;20

"Because of your little **faith,** "Jesus told them. "For if you had **faith** as tiny as a mustard seed you could say to this mountain, 'Move!' and it would go far away. Nothing would be impossible." said Jesus Christ   MATTHEW 21;21

Then Jesus told them, "Truly, if you can have **faith,** and don't doubt, you can do things like that and much more. You can say to this mount of olives, 'Move over to the ocean' and it will. You

68   F

FAITH   MATTHEW 21;21 cont'd
can get anything-anything you ask for in prayer- if
you believe." said Jesus Christ

MARK 11;24

"Listen to me! You can pray for anything and if
you believe, you have; it's yours !But when you are
praying, first forgive anyone you have a grudge
against, so your Father in heaven will forgive your
sins too." said Jesus Christ

LUKE 7;50

And Jesus said to the woman, "Your **faith** has
saved you; go in peace." said Jesus Christ.

LUKE 12;28-31

"And if God provides clothing for the flowers that
are here today and gone tomorrow, don't you
suppose that He will provide clothing for you, you
doubters? And don't worry about food- what to eat
and what to drink; don't worry at all God will
provide it for you. All of mankind scratches for
daily bread, but your Heavenly Father knows your
needs. He will always give you all you need from
day to day if you make the Kingdom of God your
primary concern." said Jesus Christ

LUKE 18;6-9

Then the Lord said, ' If even an evil judge can be
worn down like that, don't you think that God will
surely give justice to His people who plead with
Him day and night? Yes! He will answer them

FAITH   LUKE 18;6-9 cont'd

quickly! But the question is: When I, the Messiah, return, how many will I find who have **faith**?" said Jesus Christ

JOHN 14;12-13

I shall do the same miracles I have done, and even greater ones, because I am going to be with the Father. You can ask Him *anything,* using my name and I will do it, for this will bring praise to the

"Father because of what I, the Son, will do for you. Yes, ask *anything* in my name and I will do it." said Jesus Christ

FALSE PROPHETS, TEACHERS

MATTHEW 7;15-21

"Beware of **false teachers** who come disguised as harmless as sheep, but are wolves and will tear you apart. You can detect them by the way they act, just as you can identify a tree by its fruit. You need never confuse grapevines with thorn bushes or figs with thistles. Different kinds of fruit trees can be quickly identified by examining their fruit. A variety that produces delicious fruit never produces an inedible kind. And a tree producing an inedible kind can't produce what is good. So trees having inedible kind are chopped down and thrown into the fire. Yes, the way to identify a tree or a person is the

FALSE PROPHETS and TEACHERS

MATTHEW 7;15-21 cont'd

kind of fruit produced.

"Not all who sound religious are really godly people. They may refer to me as 'Lord,' but still won't get to Heaven." said Jesus Christ

LUKE 20;46-47

"Beware of these experts in religion, for they love to parade in dignified robes and be bowed to by people as they walk along the street. And how they love seats of honor in the synagogues and religious festivals!"

"But even while they are praying long prayers with great outward piety, they are planning schemes to cheat widows out of their property. Therefore God's heaviest sentence awaits these men." said Jesus Christ

FAMILY   MATTHEW 12;46-50

As Jesus was speaking in a crowded house, his mother and brothers were outside, wanting to talk with him. When someone told him they were there, he remarked, "Who is my mother? Who are my brothers?" He pointed to his disciples. "Look", he said, "these are my mothers and brothers." Then he added, "Anyone who obeys my Father in heaven is my brother and sister." said Jesus Christ

FASTING   MATTHEW 6;16-18

"And now about **fasting**. When you fast,

F   71

FASTING   MATTHEW 6;16-18 cont'd
declining your food for spiritual purpose, don't do it publicly like hypocrites do, who try to look wan and disheveled so people will feel sorry for them. Truly, that is the only reward they will ever get. But when you **fast,** put on festive clothing, so no one will suspect you are hungry, except your Father who knows every secret. And He will reward you." said Jesus Christ

FEAR   LUKE 12;4-5
"Dear friends, don't be afraid of those that want to kill the body; they have no power over your souls. They can only kill the body; they have no power over your souls. But I tell you whom to **fear- fear** God who has the power to kill and cast into hell." said Jesus Christ

FEEDING (also see **BREAD**)
LUKE 14; 12-14
Then he turned to his host. "When you put on a dinner," he said, " don't invite friends, brothers, relatives and rich neighbors! For they will return the invitation. Instead, invite the poor, the crippled, the lame and the blind. Then at resurrection of the godly, God will reward you for inviting those who can't repay you." said Jesus Christ
LUKE 14;16-24
Jesus replied with this illustration: "A man prepared a great feast and sent out many invitations.

FEEDING   LUKE 14;16-24 cont'd

When all was ready, he sent his servant around to notify the guests that it was time for them to arrive. But they began making excuses. One said he had just bought a field and wanted to inspect it, and asked to be excused. Another said he bought 5 pair of oxen and wanted to try them out. Another had just been married and for that reason he couldn't **come."**

"The servant returned and reported to his master what they had said. His master was angry and told him to go quickly into the streets and alleys of the city and invite the beggars, crippled, lame and blind. But even then there was still room."

"'Well then,' said his master, ' go out into the country lanes and behind the hedges and urge anyone you find to come, so the house will be full. For none of those that I invited first will get even the smallest taste of what I prepared for them." said Jesus Christ

FEET   JOHN 13;7-17

Jesus replied, "You don't understand now why I am doing it; someday you will,"

{"No,"Peter protested, "you shall never wash my **feet."}**

"But if I don't, you can't be my partner."Jesus replied.

{ Simon Peter exclaimed, "Then wash my hands and

FEET   JOHN 13;7-17cont'd

Head as well- not just my feet!}

Jesus replied, "One who has bathed all over only needs to have his **feet** washed to be entirely clean. Now you are clean-- but that isn't true of everyone here." for Jesus knew who would betray him. That is what he meant when he said, "Not all of you are clean."

After washing their **feet** he put on his robe again and sat down and asked , "Do you understand what I was doing? You call me 'Master' and 'Lord' and you do well to say it, for it is true. And since I, the Lord and Teacher, have washed your feet, you ought to wash each other's **feet** I have given you an example to follow; do as I have done to you. How true is it that a servant is not greater than his master Nor the messenger more important than the one who send him. You know these things -now do them! That is the path of blessing." said Jesus Christ

FEW   MATTHEW 7; 13-14

" Heaven can be entered only through a narrow gate! The highway to hell is broad and the gate is wide enough for all the multitudes that choose its easy way. But the Gateway to Life is small, and the road narrow, only a **few** will ever find it." said Jesus Christ

FISH FISHING (*also* see MIRACLES)
MATTHEW 4;19

And Jesus called out, "Come along with me and I'll show how to **fish** for the souls of men!"(And they left their nets at once and went with him.)said Jesus Christ   MATTHEW 12;40-41

But then Jesus replied, "Only and evil, faithless nation would ask for further proof: and no one will be given except what happened to Jonah the prophet! For as Jonah was Ina great **fish** for three days and three nights, so I, the Messiah, shall be in the heart of the earth three days and three nights. The men of Ninevah shall arise against this nation at the judgment and condemn you. For when Jonah preached to them, they repented and turned to God from their evil ways. And now a greater than Jonah is here -and you refuse to believe him!" said Jesus Christ

FOLLOW also see **CROSS**
MATTHEW 8; 22

But Jesus told him, **"Follow me *now!*** Let those who are spiritually dead care for their own dead." said Jesus Christ   JOHN 10;25-30

"I have already told you, and you don't believe me, "Jesus replied. "the proof is in the miracles I

FOLLOW   JOHN 10;25-30 cont'd

do in the name of my Father. But you don't believe me because you are not part of my flock. My sheep recognize my voice, and I know them and they follow me. I give them eternal life and they shall never perish. No one shall ever snatch them away from me, for my Father has given them to me, and He is more powerful than anyone else, so no one can kidnap them from me. I and the Father are one" said Jesus Christ

FOOD   MATTHEW 6;25-27

" So my counsel: Don't worry about things-food, drink, clothes. For you already have life and a body-and they are far more important than what you eat and wear. Look at the birds! They don't worry about what to eat-they don't need to sow or reap or store up food-for your heavenly Father **feeds** them. And you are far more valuable to Him than they are. Will all your worries add one single moment to your life?" said Jesus Christ   LUKE 12; 22-25

Then turning to his disciples he said, "Don't worry about whether you have enough **food** to eat or clothes to wear. For life consists of far more than food and clothes. Look at the ravens- they don't plant or harvest or have barns or store away their **food** and they get along all right-for God **feeds** them And you are far more valuable than any birds!" said Jesus Christ

F

FOOD   JOHN 4;32-34

Meanwhile the disciples were urging Jesus to eat. "No", he said, "I have some **food** you don't know about."

{Who brought it to him? The disciples asked each other?}

Then Jesus explained, "My nourishment comes from doing the will of God who sent me, and from finishing His work." said Jesus Christ

JOHN 6;27

" But you shouldn't be so concerned about perishable things like **food.** No, spend your energy seeking eternal life that, I, the Messiah can give you." said Jesus Christ

FOOL, FOOLISH   MATTHEW 7;26-29

"But those who hear my instructions and ignore them are **foolish,** like a man who builds his house on sand. For when the rains and floods come, and the storm winds beat against his house, it will fall with a mighty crash." { the crowds were amazed at Jesus' sermons, for he taught as one who had great authority, and not as their Jewish leaders.} said Jesus Christ   LUKE 11;40

"Fools! Didn't god make the inside as well as the outside? Purity is best demonstrated by generosity." said Jesus Christ   LUKE 12;20-21

. "But God said to **him, 'Fool!** Tonight you will die! Then who will get it all?'

FOOL...FOOLISH LUKE 12; 20-21 cont'd

"Yes, every man is a **fool** who gets rich on earth and not in heaven!" said Jesus Christ

LUKE 24;25-26

Then Jesus said to them, " You are such **foolish, foolish** people! You find it so hard to believe all that the prophets wrote in the Scriptures! Wasn't it clearly predicted that the Messiah would have to suffer all of these things before entering his time of Glory?" said Jesus Christ

FORGIVE, (NESS), FORGIVING

MATTHEW 6;14-15

" Your heavenly Father will **forgive** you if you **forgive** those who sin against you; but if *you* refuse to **forgive** *them, He* will not **forgive** *you.* " said Jesus Christ MATTHEW 18;21-22
}[Then Peter came to him and asked, " Sir, how often should I **forgive** a brother who sins against me? Seven times?]

"No, seventy times seven!" said Jesus Christ (the number 7 represents complete, whole, perfect Also see MATTHEW 9;6)

MARK.2;8-10

Jesus could read their minds and said to them at once, " Why does this bother you ? I, the Messiah, have the authority on earth to **forgive** sins. But talk is cheap- anybody could say that. So I'll prove it to you by healing this man." said Jesus Christ.

FORGIVE (NESS) cont'd

MARK. 3;29

"I solemnly declare that any sin of man can be **forgiven,** even blasphemy against me, but blasphemy against the Holy Spirit can never be **forgiven.** It is the eternal sin." said Jesus Christ

MARK 11;25

"But when you are praying, first **forgive** anyone you are holding a grudge against so that your Father in Heaven will **forgive** your sins too." said Jesus Christ   MATTHEW 26;27-28

And he took a cup of wine and gave thanks for it and gave it to them and said, "Each drink from it, for this is my blood sealing a New Covenant. It is poured out to **forgive** the sins of multitudes." said Jesus Christ

LUKE 7;47

"Therefore her sins- and they are many- are **forgiven,** for she loved me much; but one who is **forgiven** little, shows little love." And he said to her, "Your sins are **forgiven".** said Jesus Christ

LUKE 23;34

"Father **forgive** these people," Jesus said, "for they don't know what they are doing" said Jesus Christ

LUKE 24;45-48

Then he opened their mind to understand many Scriptures! And he said, "Yes, it was written long

FORGIVE (NESS) cont'd

LUKE 24;25-28 cont'd

ago that the Messiah must suffer and die and rise from the dead on the third day; and that this message of salvation should be taken to Jerusalem and all the nations: *There is **forgiveness** of sins for all those who turn to me.* You have seen these prophecies come true." said Jesus Christ

Also see LUKE 5;21 5;24 6;37 11;4 17;3-4

JOHN 20;21-23

He spoke to them again and said, "As the Father has sent me, even so I am sending you." Then he breathed on them and told them, " Receive the Holy Spirit. If you **forgive** anyone's sins, they are **forgiven.** If you refuse to **forgive** them, they are unforgiving. " said Jesus Christ (to the disciples)

FORSAKEN   MATTHEW 27;46

About three o'clock, Jesus shouted, "Eli, Eli, lama sabachthani," which means, "My God, My God why have you **forsaken** me?" said Jesus Christ

(this showed beyond a doubt that he was experiencing everything in a human way, like us)

FOUNDATION   Spirit of

MATTHEW 7; 24-27

" All those who listen to my instructions and follow them are wise, like a man who **builds his house on solid rock.** Though the rain comes in torrents, floods rise and winds beat against his

FOUNDATION •Spirit of

MATTHEW 7;24-27 cont'd
house, it won't collapse, for it is built on rock." said
Jesus Christ

FREE   JOHN 8; 32

Jesus said to them, " You are truly my disciples if
you live as I tell you to, and you will know the truth
and the truth will set you **free."** said Jesus Christ

JOHN 8;36

" So if the Son sets you **free,** you'll indeed
be **free-"** said Jesus Christ

G

GAMBLING   MATTHEW 21;12-16

[Jesus went to the Temple, drove out the
merchants, and knocked over the money
changers' tables and the stalls of those selling
doves.]

" The Scriptures say my Temple is a house of
prayer," he declared, "but you have turned it into a
den of thieves."

[And now the blind and crippled came to him and
he healed them there in the Temple. But then the
chief priests and other Jewish leaders saw these
wonderful miracles and heard even the little
children in the Temple shouting,] {"God bless the
Son of David," they were disturbed and indignant
and asked him," Do you hear what the children are

GAMBLING   MATTHEW 21;12-16
saying?"}

"Yes," Jesus replied. "Didn't you ever read the Scriptures? For they say even the babies shall praise him!" said Jesus Christ

MARK 11;15-17

[When they arrived back to Jerusalem he went to the Temple and began to drive out the merchants and their customers, and knocked over tables of moneychangers and the stalls of those selling doves, and he stopped everyone from bringing in loads of merchandise.]

He told them, " It is written in the Scriptures, 'My Temple is to be a place of prayer for all nations', but you have turned it into a **den of robbers."**

GARDEN   MATTHEW 26; 36-42

[Then Jesus brought them to a **garden** grove, Gethsemane, and told them to sit down and wait while he went on ahead to pray. He took Peter with him and Zebedee's two sons James and John, and began to be filled with anguish and despair.]

Then he told them, "My soul is crushed with horror and sadness to the point of death...stay here...stay awake with me."

He went forward a little, and fell face downward on the ground, and prayed, "My father! If it is possible, let this cup be taken away from me. But I want Your Will be done not mine."

GARDEN   MATTHEW 26; 36-42 cont'd

Then he turned to the three disciples and found them asleep. "Peter," he called, " couldn't you even stay awake with me one hour? Keep alert and pray. Otherwise, temptation will overpower you. For the spirit indeed is willing, but how weak the body is!"

Again he left them and prayed, "My Father! If this cup cannot go away until I drink it all, your will be done." said Jesus Christ

MARK 14;32-38

And now they came to an olive grove called the **Garden of Gethsemane,** and he instructed his disciples, "Sit here, while I go and pray."

He took Peter, James and John with him and began to be filled with horror and deep distress. And he said to them, "My soul is crushed with sorrow to the point of death; stay here and watch with me."

He went a little further and fell to the ground and prayed that if it were possible the awful hour awaiting him might never come.

"Father, Father," he said, "everything is possible for you. Take away this cup from me. Yet, I want your will not mine." [Then he returned to the three disciples and found them asleep.]

"Simon", he said, "Asleep? Couldn't you watch

GARDEN , GIVE IT UP, ADMIT TO,
REPENT   MARK 14;32-38cont'd

with me even one hour? Watch with me and pray lest the Tempter overpower you. For though the spirit is willing, the body is weak." said Jesus Christ

LUKE 13;2-9

"Do you think they were worse sinners than other men from Galilee?" he asked. "Is that why they suffered? Not at all !And don't you realize that you will also perish unless you leave your evil ways and turn to God?"

"And what about the eighteen men who died when the Tower of Siloam fell them? Were they the worst sinners in Jerusalem? Not at all! And you too will perish unless you **repent."**

Then he used this illustration: " A man planted a fig tree in his **garden** and came again and again to see if there was any fruit on it., but he was always disappointed. Finally he told his gardener to cut it down. 'I've waited three years and there hasn't been a single fig!' he said. 'Why bother with it any longer? It is taking up space we can use for something else'

" ' Give it one more chance,' the gardener answered. 'Leave it another year, and I'll give it special attention and plenty of fertilizer. I f we get figs next year, fine, if not, I'll cut it down.'" said Jesus Christ

84 G

GOD FROM   JOHN 7;16-18

So Jesus told them, "I am not teaching my own thoughts, **but those of God who sent me.** If any of you really determine to do God's will then you will certainly know whether my teaching is from God or merely my own. Anyone presenting his own ideas is looking for praise for himself, but anyone seeking to honor the one who sent him is a good and true person." said Jesus Christ

GOD SENT   JOHN 7;28-29

So Jesus said, " When you have killed the Messiah, then you will realize that I am he and that I have not been telling you my own ideas, but spoken what the Father taught me. **And He who sent me is** with me-He has not deserted me- for I always do things pleasing to Him." said Jesus Christ

JOHN 8;34-42

Jesus replied, "You are slaves of sin, every one of you. And slaves don't have rights, but the Son has every right there is! So if the Son sets you free, you will indeed be free-Yes, I realize you are descendants of Abraham! And yet, some of you are trying to kill me because my message does not find a home within your hearts. I am telling you what I saw when I was with my Father. But you are following the advice of your father."

GOD SENT   JOHN 8;38-42 cont'd

["Our father is Abraham!" they declared]

"No," Jesus replied, " for if he were, you would follow his good example. But instead you are trying to kill me-all because I told you the truth I heard **from God.** Abraham wouldn't do a thing like that! No, you are obeying your real father when you act that way."

{They replied, "We were not born out of wedlock- our true father is God himself."}

Jesus told them, "If that were so, then you would love me, **for I have come to you from God. I am not here on my own, but He sent me.** Why can't you understand that?" said Jesus Christ

GOD   THE FATHER

LUKE 18;19

"Do you realize what you are saying when you call me 'good'? Jesus asked him. **"Only God** is truly good." said Jesus Christ

See also UNDERSTAND *I* JOHN 16; 29-33

GOLDEN RULE   LUKE 6;31

"Treat others as you want them to treat you." said Jesus Christ

GOOD NEWS APPOINTED TO SET FREE   MATTHEW 11;4-6

Jesus told them, " Go back to John and tell him about the miracles you've seen me do- the blind people I've healed, and the lame people now

86   G

GOOD NEWS   MATTHEW 11;4-6

walking without help, and the cured lepers, and the deaf who hear, and the dead raised to life; and tell him about my preaching the **Good News** to the poor. Then give him this message, 'Blessed are those who don't doubt me.'" said Jesus Christ

MARK 16;15

And he told them, "You are to go into all the world and preach the **Good News** to everyone, everywhere. Those who believe and are baptized will be saved. But those who refuse to believe will be condemned." said Jesus Christ

LUKE 4; 18-19

" The Spirit of the Lord is upon me; He has appointed me to preach the **Good News** to the poor; He has sent me to heal the brokenhearted and to announce that captives shall be released and the blind shall see, that the downtrodden shall be freed from their oppressors, and that God is ready to give blessings to all who come to Him. "said Jesus Christ

LUKE 4;43

But he replied, "I must preach the **Good News** of the Kingdom of God in other places too, for that is why I was sent." said Jesus Christ

LUKE 7;20-23

The two disciples found Jesus while he was curing many sick people of their various diseases-healing the lame and the blind and casting out evil spirits.

GOOD NEWS LUKE 7;20-23 cont'd

When they asked him John's question, this was his reply: " Go back to John and tell him all that you have seen and heard here today: how those who were blind can see. The lame are walking without a limp. The lepers are completely healed. The deaf can hear again. The dead come back to life. And the poor are hearing the **Good News**. And tell Him .'Blessed is the one who does not lose his faith in me." said Jesus Christ

GOOD SAMARITAN
LUKE 10; 30-37

Jesus replied with an illustration: " A Jew going on a trip from Jerusalem to Jericho was attacked by bandits. They stripped him of his clothes and money and beat him up and left him lying half dead beside the road.

"By chance a Jewish priest came along; and when he saw the man lying there, he crossed to the other side of the road and passed him by. A Jewish Temple-assistant walked over and looked at him lying there but went on.

"But a despised Samaritan came along, and when he saw him, he felt deep pity. Kneeling beside him the Samaritan soothed his wounds with medicine and bandaged them. Then he put the man on his donkey and walked along beside him until they came to an inn, where he nursed him through the

GOOD SAMARITAN

LUKE 10;30-37 cont'd

night. The next day he handed the innkeeper two twenty-dollar bills and told him to take care of the man. 'If this bill runs higher than that', he said, ' I'll pay the difference next time I am here.'

"Now which one of these three would you say was a neighbor to the bandit's victim?"

{The man replied, " The one who showed him some pity."}

Then Jesus said, "Now go and do the same." said Jesus Christ

GREED ...POWER

LUKE 12;14-15

But Jesus replied, "Man, who made me a judge over you to decide such things as that? Beware! Don't always be **wishing for what you don't have.** For real life and real living are not related to how rich we are." said Jesus Christ

LUKE 12; 16-21

The he gave this illustration: "A rich man had a fertile farm that produced fine crops. In fact, his barns were full to overflowing-he couldn't get everything in. He thought about this problem, and finally exclaimed, 'I know, I'll tear down my barns and build bigger ones! Then I'll have room enough. And I'll sit back and say to myself, 'Friend, you have enough stored away for years to come. Now take it easy! Wine, women and song for you!"

"But God said to him," Fool! Tonight you die.

GREED POWER   LUKE 12; 16-21 cont'd

Then who will get it all?'

"Yes, every a **man** is a **fool who** gets **rich** on earth, but not in heaven." said Jesus Christ.

"A nobleman living in a certain province was called away to a distant capital of the empire to be crowned king of his province. Before he left he called together ten assistants and gave them each $2000 to invest while he was gone. But some of his people hated him and sent him their declaration of independence, stating that they had rebelled and "would not acknowledge him as their king.

"Upon his return he called in the men to whom he had given the money, to find out what they had done with it, and what their profits were.

The first man reported a tremendous gain-ten times as much as the original amount!.

"'Fine!,' the king exclaimed. 'You are a good man. You have been faithful with the little I entrusted you, and as your reward , you will governor of ten cities.'

"The next man also reported a splendid gain - five times the original amount.

"'All right!' his master said. 'You can governor over five cities.

"But the third man brought back only the money he had started with. 'I've kept it safe,' he said

G

GREED ..POWER   LUKE19;12-27 cont'd
'because I was afraid you would demand my profits,
for you are a hard man to deal with, taking what
isn't your and confiscating the crops that others
plant.' 'You vile and wicked slave,' the king roared.
'Hard am I? That's exactly how I will be toward
you! If you know so much about me and how
toughI am, then why didn't you deposit the money
in thebank so that I could at least get some interest
on it?'

   "Then turning to the others standing by he
ordered. 'Take the money away from him and give
it to the man who earned the most.'

   " 'But, sir,' they said, 'he has enough already!'

   " ' Yes,' the king replied, 'but it is always true
that those who have, get more, and those who have
little, soon lose even that. And now about these
enemies of mine who revolted- bring them in and
execute them before me.'" a story told by Jesus
Christ

GRIEF   JOHN 16;17-28
   { "Whatever is he saying? "some of his disciples
asked. "What is this about going to the 'Father'?
We don't know what he means.'}

   Jesus realized that they wanted to ask him so he
said, "Are you asking yourselves what I mean? The
world will greatly rejoice over what is going to
happen to me, and you will weep. But your weeping

GRIEF JOHN16; 17-28 cont'd

shall suddenly be turned into joy (when you see me again!) It will be the same joy as a woman in labor when her child is born- her anguish gives place to rapturous joy and pain is forgotten. You have sorrow now, but I will see you again and then you will rejoice and no one can rob you of that joy. At that time you won't need to ask me for anything, for you can go straight to the Father and ask Him and He will give you what you ask for because you use my name. You haven't tried this before, but begin now. Ask using my name, and you will receive and your cup of joy will overflow.

" I have spoken of these matters very guardedly, but the time will come when this will not be necessary and I will tell you plainly about the Father. Then you will present your petitions over my signature! And I won't need to ask the Father to grant you these requests, for the Father Himself loves you dearly because you love me and believe that I came from the Father. Yes, I came from the Father into the world and will leave the world and return to the Father." said Jesus Christ.

H

HARD HEARTED

MARK 10;5,

" And why did he say that?" Jesus asked. **"I**'ll tell

HARD HEARTED MARK 10;5 cont'd
you why- it was a concession to your **hard hearted**
wickedness. But it certainly isn't God's way." said
Jesus Christ
(see also MARRIAGE)

HARVEST   MATTHEW 9;35-38

[Jesus traveled through all the cities and villages
of that area, teaching in Jewish synagogues
announcing the Good News and about the
Kingdom. And wherever he went he healed people
of every sort of illness. And what pity he felt for the
crowds that came, because their problems were so
great and they didn't know what to do or where they
would go for help. They were like sheep without a
shepherd.]

"The **harvest** is so great, and the workers are so
few, "he told his disciples. "So pray to the One in
charge of **harvesting**, and ask Him to recruit more
workers for His harvest fields." said Jesus Christ

HATE..•HATES•..HATED DESPISE
MATTHEW 10;22

"Everyone shall **hate** you because you belong to
me. But all of you who endure until the end shall be
saved." said Jesus Christ

LUKE 6;22,27

" What happiness it is when others **hate** you and
exclude you and insult and smear your name
because you are mine! When that happens, rejoice!,

HATE,HATE,HATED,DESPISE

LUKE 6;22,27 cont'd

leap for joy! For you will have a great reward awaiting you in heaven! And you will be in good company-the ancient prophets were treated like that too!"

27 "Listen, all of you. Love your enemies. Do good to those who **hate** you. Pray for the happiness of those who curse you; implore God's blessings on those who hurt you." said Jesus Christ

LUKE 16;13

" For neither you nor anyone else can serve two masters. You will **hate** one and love the other or the other way around-you'll be enthusiastic about one and **despise** the other. You cannot serve both God and money" said Jesus Christ

JOHN 3;20

"They **hated** the heavenly Light because they wanted to sin in the darkness. They stayed away from that Light for fear their sins would be expose and they would be punished. But those doing right come gladly to the Light to let everyone see that they are doing what God wants them to." said Jesus Christ   JOHN 12;25

"If you love your life down here- you will lose it. If you **hate** your life down here- you will exchange it for eternal glory." said Jesus Christ

H

HATE..HATES.•·HATED··DESPISE
JOHN 15; 16-19

" You didn't choose me! I chose you! I appointed you to go out and produce lovely fruit always, so that no matter what you ask from the Father, using my name, He will give it to you. I demand that you love each other, for you get enough bate from the world. But then it hated me before it hated you. The world would love you if you belonged to it; but you don't- for I chose you to come out of the world, and so it bates you. Do you remember what I told you? A slave isn't greater than his master! So since they persecuted me, naturally they will persecute you." said Jesus Christ

HEALING

There are numerous accounts of Jesus healing throughout the New Testament. These are some examples that attempt to give an overview of many of the things he said. Please see other Bibles passages to look up at the end of these Scriptures.

MATTHEW 8; 2-4

{Look! A leper is approaching! He kneels before him worshiping. "Sir", the leper pleads, "if you want to, you can heal me.'}

HEALING MATTHEW 8; 2-4 cont'd

Jesus touches the man, "I want to."he says. "Be **healed."** and instantly the leprosy disappears.

The Jesus says to him. "Don't stop to talk to anyone; go right over to the priest to be examined; take with you an offering required by Moses' law for lepers who are **healed-a** public testimony of your cure." said Jesus Christ

MATTHEW 9;19-22

[As Jesus and the disciples were going into a rabbi's home, a woman who had been sick for twelve years with internal bleeding came up behind him and touched a tassel on his robe., for she thought, if I only touch him, I will be healed.]

Jesus turned around and spoke to her. " Daughter," he said, "all is well! Your faith has **healed** you." And the woman was well from that moment. said Jesus Christ

MATTHEW 9; 25-26

When Jesus arrived at the Rabbi's home and saw the noisy crowds and heard the funeral music, he said, "Get them out, for the little girl is not dead; she is only sleeping!" Then how they all scoffed and sneered at him! Said Jesus Christ

[When the crowd was finally outside. Jesus went in where the little girl was lying and took her by the hand, and she jumped up all right! The report of this wonderful miracle swept the countryside]

96   H

HEALING

[And so they reached Jericho. Later, as they left town, a great crowd was following. Now it happened that a blind beggar named Bartimaeus < the son of Timaeus, was sitting beside the road as Jesus was going by.]

{ When Bartimaeus heard that Jesus from Nazareth was near , he began to shout out, "Jesus , Son of David, have mercy on me!"}

{ "Shut up!"some of the people yelled at him. But he only shouted louder, again and again. " 0, Son of David, have mercy on me!"}

When Jesus heard him, he stopped there in the road and said, "Tell him to come here."
{[So they called to the blind man "You lucky fellow, "they said, "come on, he's calling you." Bartimaeus yanked off his coat and flung it aside, jumped up and came to Jesus.}

"What do you want me to do for you?" Jesus asked

["O Teacher," the blind man said, "I want to see!"]

And Jesus said, "All right, it's done. Your faith has **healed** you."

{And instantly, the blind man could see, and followed Jesus down the road.} said Jesus Christ

HEALING   LUKE 7; 12-23

[A funeral procession was coming out as he approached the village gate. The boy who had died was the only son of his widowed mother, and many mourners from the village were with her.]

When the Lord saw her, his heart overflowed with sympathy. "Don't cry!." he said. Then he walked over to the coffin and touched it, and the bearers stopped. "Laddie", he said "come back to life again."

[Then the boy sat up and began to talk to those around him! And Jesus gave him to his mother.]

{ A great fear swept the crowd and they exclaimed praises to God. "A mighty prophet has risen among us," and " We have seen the hand of God at work today."}

[The report of what he did that day raced from end to end of Judea and even out across the borders.]

{The disciples of John the Baptist soon heard all that Jesus was doing. When they told John about it, he sent two of his disciples to Jesus to ask him, " Are you really the Messiah?" Or shall we keep looking for him?"}

[The two disciples found Jesus while he was curing many sick people of various diseases-healing the lame and blind and casting out evil spirits.] When they asked him John's question, this was his

H

HEALING   LUKE 7; 12-23 cont'd

reply, "Go back to John and tell him all that you've seen and heard today: how those who were blind can see. The lame are walking without a limp. The lepers are completely **healed.** The deaf can hear again. The dead come back to life. And the poor are hearing the "Good News". And tell him 'Blessed is the one who does not lose his faith in me.'" said Jesus Christ   JOHN 9;1-17

   As he was walking along, he saw a man blind from birth.

   {"Master," his disciples asked him, "why was this man born blind?" Was it a result of his own sins or those of his parents? "}

   "Neither," Jesus answered. " But to demonstrate the power of God. All of us must quickly carry out our tasks assigned us by the One who sent me, for there is little time left before the night falls and all work comes to an end. But while I am still here in the world, I give it my light."

   Then he spat on the ground and made a mud from the spittle and smoothed the mud over the blind man's eyes, and told him, " Go and wash in the pool of Siloam." (the word 'Siloam' means Sent") so the man went where he was sent and washed and came back up seeing!

   { His neighbors and others who knew him as a blind beggar asked each other, "Is this the same

HEALING   JOHN 9; l-17 cont'd
fellow-that beggar?"}

{Some said yes and some said no. "It can't be the same man," they thought, "but it sure looks like him!"}

{And the beggar said, "I am the same man!"}
{ They asked him how in the world he could see. What had happened?}

{And he told them, " A man they call Jesus made mud and smoothed it over my eyes and told me to go to the Pool of Siloam and wash off the mud and I did and now I can see!"}

{"Where is he now?" they asked}

{"I don't know ."he replied}

[Then they took the man to the Pharisees. Now as it happened, this all occurred on the Sabbath. Then the Pharisees asked him about it. So he told them how Jesus smoothed mud over his eyes and now he can see!]

{ Some of them said. "Then this fellow Jesus is not from God because he is working on the Sabbath.}

{Others said, "But how could an ordinary sinner do such miracles?" So there was deep division of opinion among them}

{Then the Pharisees turned to the man who had been blind and demanded, "This man who opened your eyes- who do you say he is?"}

100   H

{"I think he must be a prophet sent by God." the man replied }

HEALING A FEW OTHER PASSAGES

MATTHEW 12;15,22...14;14...15;29,30...l7;18
             19;2, 21;14
MARK   5;23,29,34...6;13,56
LUKE   4;40...5;15...6;18,19...7;7...
             8;47,48, 50   ... 9;6,11,42...
             13;14...14;4...17;15...18;42...22;51
JOHN   5;10,13...7;23

HEAR..HEARING ...HEARD ...LISTEN
MATTHEW 11;15

"If ever you were willing to **listen, listen now!**" said Jesus Christ   MATTHEW 13;14

"...they **hear** but they don't understand." said Jesus Christ   MARK 4;12

He replied, "You are permitted to know some truths about the Kingdom of God that are hidden from those outside the Kingdom:

        'Though they **hear,** they will not understand or turn to God or be forgiven of their sins."
        said Jesus Christ
        LUKE 12;3

"Whatever they have said in the dark shall be heard in the light, and what you have whispered in inner rooms shall be broadcast from the housetops for all to **hear!**" said Jesus Christ

HEAR..HEARING,,HEARD..LISTEN

LUKE16;31

"But Abraham said,' If they won't **listen** to Moses and the prophets, they won't **listen** even though someone rises from the dead." said Jesus Christ

JOHN 5; 24-25

" I say emphatically that anyone who **listens** to my message and believes in God who sent me has eternal life, and will never be damned for his sins, but already has passed out of death into life. And I solemnly declare that a time is corning, in fact it is here, when the dead shall **hear** my voice-the voice of the son of God- and those who **listen** shall live." said Jesus Christ

JOHN 6;45

"As it is written in the Scriptures, 'They shall be taught of God. Those that the Father speaks to, who **listen,** learn the truth from Him, will be attracted to me. Not that anyone actually sees the Father; for only I have seen Him." said Jesus Christ

JOHN 8;46-47

"Which one of you can truthfully accuse me of one single sin? No one! And since I am telling you the truth, why don't you believe me? Anyone whose Father is God **listens ,hears** gladly to the words of God. Since you don't, it proves you aren't His children." said Jesus Christ

HEART

MATTHEW 5;8

" Happy are those whose **hearts** are pure, for they shall see God." said Jesus Christ

MATTHEW 5;27-28

" The laws of Moses said, 'You shall not commit adultery.' But I say :Anyone who even looks at a woman with lust in his eyes has already committed adultery with her in his **heart.**" said Jesus Christ

MATTHEW 6;21

" Don't store up treasures here on earth where they can erode away or may be stolen. Store them in heaven where they will never lose their value, and are safe from thieves. If your profits are in heaven your **heart** will be there too." said Jesus Christ

MATTHEW 15;18-19

"But evil words come from an evil **heart,** and defile the man who says them. For from the **heart** come evil thoughts, murder, adultery, fornication, theft, lying and slander." said Jesus Christ

MARK 12;30

Jesus replied, "The one that says, 'Hear, 0 Israel! The Lord our God is the one and only God. And you must love with all your **heart** and soul and mind and strength,'" said Jesus Christ

LUKE 6;43-45

"A good man produces good deeds from a good

H   103

HEART   LUKE 6;43-45 cont'd

heart. An evil man produces evil deeds from his hidden wickedness. Whatever is in the **heart** overflows into speech." said Jesus Christ

LUKE 16;15

Then he said to them, "You wear a noble, pious expression in public, but God knows your evil **hearts.** Your pretense brings you honor from the people, but it is an abomination in the sight of God." said Jesus Christ

JOHN 12;40-41

"God had blinded their eyes and hardened their **hearts** so that they could neither see or understand nor turn to me to heal them." said Jesus Christ

HEART HOME   JOHN 14; 1-4

"LET NOT YOUR **heart** be troubled. You are trusting God, now trust in me. There are many **homes** up there where my Father lives and I am going to prepare them for your coming. When everything is ready, I will come and get you, so that you can always be with me where I am. If this weren't so, I would tell you plainly. And you know where I am going and how to get there." said Jesus Christ

HEAVEN

(Obviously there are many, many things that Christ told us about Heaven. The following represent a small sampling of some main ideas

HEAVEN

and points of discussion we often choose. All the Gospels are full of brilliance and everything that Christ said on all subjects, every word was about heaven.) see also CHILDREN, DOOR,

MATTHEW 5; 19

" And so if anyone breaks the least commandment, and teaches others to, he shall be the least in the Kingdom of **Heaven**, But those who teach God's laws and obey them shall be great inthe Kingdom of **Heaven**." said Jesus Christ

MATTHEW 7;21-23

"Not all who sound religious are really godly people. They may refer to me as 'Lord' but still won't get into **Heaven**. At the Judgment many will tell me, ' Lord, Lord we told others about you and used your name to cast out demons and do many other great miracles. But I will reply, 'You have never been mine. Go away your deeds are evil." said Jesus Christ   MATTHEW 19;21-24

Jesus told him, "If you want to be perfect, go and sell everything you have and give the money to the poor, and you will have treasure in **Heaven;** and come follow me." But when the young man heard this, he went away sadly, for he was very rich.

Then Jesus said to the disciples, "It is almost impossible for a rich man to get into the Kingdom

HEAVEN MATTHEW 19;21-24

of **Heaven**. I say it again-it is easier for a camel to go through the eye of a needle than for a rich man to enter the Kingdom of God!." said Jesus Christ

MATTHEW 24;35-36

"**Heaven** and earth will disappear, but my words remain forever. But no one knows the date and hour when the end will be-not even the angels. No, nor even God's Son. Only the Father knows." said Jesus Christ MATTHEW 26;64

"Yes," Jesus said, "I am.And in the future you will see me, the Messiah, sitting at the right hand of God returning on the clouds of **Heaven**." said Jesus Christ MATTHEW 28;18

He told the disciples, "I have been given all authority over **Heaven** and earth." said Jesus Christ

MARK 1;10

(note to reader; Christ did not say this...just read and you'll see why I put it in this book. His Father...Our Father did the talking.)

[Then one day Jesus came from Nazareth to Galilee, and was baptized by John there in the Jordan River. The moment Jesus came up out of the water, he saw the **heavens** open and the Holy Spirit in the form of a dove descending on him, and a voice from heaven said, "You are my beloved Son, You are my Delight."]

H

HEAVEN   MARK 13;25

"After the tribulation ends, then the sun will grow dim and the moon will not shine, and the stars will fall- the **heavens** will convulse." said Jesus Christ

LUKE IO; I8-20

"Yes," he told them, "I saw Satan falling from **Heaven** as a flash of lightening! And I have given you authority over all the power of the Enemy, and to walk among serpents and scorpions and crush them. Nothing shall injure you! However the important thing is not that demons obey you, but your names are registered as citizens of **Heaven.**" said Jesus Christ

LUKE 12;32-34

" So don't be afraid, little flock. For it gives your Father great happiness to give you the Kingdom. Sell what you have and give to those in need. This will fatten your purses in **Heaven!** And the purses of **Heaven** have no rips or holes in them. Your treasures will never disappear; no thief can steal; no moth can destroy them. Wherever your treasure is, there your heart and thoughts will also be." said Jesus Christ

JOHN 3; 10-17

Jesus replied, "You, a respected Jewish teacher, and yet you don't understand these things? I am telling you what I know and have seen- and yet you

HEAVEN   JOHN 3; 10-17 cont'd

won't believe me. But even if you won't believe me when I tell you about such things as these that happen among men, how can you possibly believe what is going on in **heaven?** For only I, the Messiah, have come to earth and will return to **heaven.** And as Moses in the wilderness lifted up the bronze image of a serpent on a pole, even so I must be lifted up on a pole, so that anyone who believes in me shall have eternal life. For God loved the world so much that He gave His only Son so that anyone who believes in him shall not perish but have eternal life. God did not send His Son into the world to condemn it but to save it." said Jesus Christ

(This underlined verse is spoken frequently.)

JOHN 6;32-33

Jesus said, "Moses didn't give it to them. My Father did. And now He offers you true Bread from **Heaven.** The true Bread is a Person- the one sent by God from **Heaven** and he gives life to the world." said Jesus Christ

JOHN 6;38

"For I have come here from **Heaven** to do the will of God who sent me, not to have my own way. And this is the will of God that I should not lose even one of all those that He has given me, but I should raise them to eternal life on the Last Day.

HEAVEN   JOHN 6;38 cont'd

For it is my Father's will that everyone who sees His Son and believes in him should have eternal life- that I should raise him on that Last Day." said Jesus Christ

HIDDEN TRUTHS

MATTHEW 11;25-29

And Jesus prayed this prayer: "O Father, Lord of Heaven and earth, thank you for **hiding the truth** from those who think of themselves as wise, for revealing it to the little children. Yes, Father, for it is pleased you do it this way!" said Jesus Christ

LUKE 10; 21-24

Then he was filled with joy of the Holy Spirit and said, "I praise you, O Father, Lord of Heaven and earth, for **hiding** these things from the intellectuals and worldly wise and for revealing them to those who are as trusting as little children. Yes, thank you Father, for that is the Way you wanted it. I am the Agent of my Father in everything and no one really knows the Son except the Father and no one really knows the Father except the Son and those to whom the Son chooses to reveal him." said Jesus Christ

HOLD ON   MARK 11;25

"But when you are praying, first forgive anyone you are **holding** a grudge against, so that your Father in Heaven will forgive your sins too." said Jesus Christ

JOHN 16;1-4

"I HAVE TOLD you these things so that you won't be staggered by all that lies ahead. For you will be excommunicated from the synagogues, and indeed the time is coming when those who kill you think that they are doing God a service. This is because they have never known the Father or me. Yes, I am telling you these things now so that when they happen you will remember I warned you. I didn't tell you earlier because I was going to be with you a while longer." said Jesus Christ

HOLY SPIRIT

There are numerous references to the Holy Spirit throughout the entire New Testament including what Christ said. These are just a sampling. Please read the Gospels of MATTHEW, MARK, LUKE and JOHN.

MATTHEW 12;31-32

"Even blasphemy or any other sin can be forgiven- all except one: speaking against the **Holy Spirit** shall never be forgiven, either in this world or the in the world to come." said Jesus Christ

110   H

HOLY SPIRIT MARK 3:28-29

"I solemnly declare that any sin of man can be forgiven, even blasphemy against me; but blasphemy against the **Holy Spirit** can never be forgiven. It is an eternal sin" said Jesus Christ

LUKE 11;13

"And even sinful persons like yourselves give children what they need, don't you realize your heavenly Father will do at least as much, and give the **Holy Spirit** to those who ask for him?" said Jesus Christ   LUKE 12;11-12

"And when you are brought to trial before the Jewish rulers and authorities in the synagogues, don't be concerned about what you say in your own defense, for the **Holy Spirit** will give you the right words even as you are standing there." said Jesus Christ

JOHN 14;26

"But when the Father sends the Comforter instead of me- and by the Comforter I mean the **Holy Spirit-he** will teach you much, as well as remind you of everything I, myself have told you." said Jesus Christ   JOHN 20;22

Then he breathed on them and told them, " Receive the **Holy Spirit.** If you forgive anyone's sins, they are forgiven. If you refuse to forgive anyone's sins, they are unforgiven." said Jesus Christ

HOMETOWN HONOR

MATTHEW 13;57

"A prophet is **honored** everywhere except his own country, among his own people!" said Jesus Christ {And so he only did a few great miracles there, because of their unbelief.}

MARK. 6; 4-6

Then Jesus told them, "A prophet is **honored** everywhere except in his **hometown** and among relatives and by his own family. And because of their unbelief he couldn't do any mighty miracles among them except place his hands on a few sick people and heal them. And he couldn't hardly accept the fact that they wouldn't believe him." Said Jesus Christ

LUKE 4;24

"But I solemnly declare to you that no prophet is accepted is his own **hometown!**" said Jesus Christ

JOHN 4;44

"A prophet is **honored** everywhere except his own country!" said Jesus Christ

JOHN 5; 22-23

"And the Father leaves all judgment of sin to His Son , so that everyone will honor the Son as much as they honor the Father. But if you refuse to **honor** God's Son, whom He sent to you, then you are certainly not **honoring** the Father." said Jesus Christ

HOMETOWN...HONOR

JOHN 7;18

" Anyone presenting his own ideas is looking for praise for himself, but anyone seeking to **honor** the One who sent him is a good and true person." said Jesus Christ

JOHN 12; 26

" If these Greeks want to be my disciples, tell them to come and follow me, for my servants must be where I am. And if they follow me, the Father will **honor** them. Now my soul is deeply troubled. Shall I pray' Father, save me from lies ahead'? But that is the very reason why I came! Father, bring glory and **honor** to your name." said Jesus Christ (also see COMMANDMENTS)

HOUSES HOMES

MATTHEW 10;26

Jesus knew what their thoughts and replied, " A kingdom divided ends in ruin. A city or **home** divided against itself cannot stand." said Jesus Christ

MATTHEW 19;29

"And anyone who gives up his **home,** brothers sisters, father mother, wife, children or property to follow me shall receive a hundred times as much in return, and shall have eternal life." said Jesus Christ

HOUSES,HOME

MARK 12; 39-40

"They love to sit in the best seats in the synagogues, and places of honor at banquets- but shamelessly cheat widows out of their homes and then to cover up what kind of men they really are, they pretend to be pious praying in public. Because of this their punishment will be greater." said Jesus Christ JOHN 4;53

Jesus told them, " Your son is healed." said Jesus Christ {And the officer and the entire household believed that Jesus was the Messiah.}

HUMAN   LIFE VERSUS SPIRITUAL

MATTHEW 18; 7-9

"Woe upon the world for all of its evils.. Temptation to do wrong is inevitable, but woe to the man who does the tempting. So if your hand or foot causes you to sin, cut it off and throw it away. Better to enter heaven crippled than to be in hell with both of your hands and feet. And if your eye causes you to sin, gouge it out and throw it away. Better to enter heaven with one eye than be in hell with two.

" Beware that you don't look down upon a single one of these little children. For I tell you that in Heaven their angels have constant access to my Father. And I the Messiah, have come to save the lost." said Jesus Christ

HUMAN LIFE...VERSUS SPIRITUAL
MARK 9;43-49

" If your hand does wrong, cut it off.. Better live forever with one hand than be thrown into the unquenchable fires of hell with two. If your foot carries you toward evil, cut iit off! Better be lame and live forever than have two feet carry you into hell!

"And if your eye is sinful gouge it out. Better to enter the Kingdom of God half blind than have two eyes to see the fires of hell, where the worm never dies, and the fire never goes out- where all are salted with fire." said Jesus Christ

HUMAN WITNESS VERSUS GODLY
JOHN 5; 31-40

" When I make claims about myself they aren't believed, but someone else, yes, John the Baptist, is making these claims for me too. You have gone out to listen to his preaching, and I can assure you all he says about me is true! But the truest witness I have is not from a human, Though, I have reminded you about John's witness so that you will believe in me and be saved. John shone brightly for a while, and you benefited and rejoiced, but I have a greater witness than John. I refer to the miracles that I do; these have been assigned me by the Father, they prove the Father has sent me. And the Father himself has also testified about me, though not

H   115

HUMAN WITNESS VERSUS GODLY
appearing to you personally, or speaking to you directly. But you are not listening to Him, for you refuse to believe me- the One sent to you with God's message." said Jesus Christ
JOHN 8;14-17
" These claims are true even though I make them concerning myself. For I know where I came from and where I am going, but you don't know this about me. You pass judgment on me without knowing the facts. I am not judging you now; but if I were, it would be an absolutely correct judgment in every respect, for I have with me the Father who sent me. Your laws say if two men agree on something that has happened their witness is accepted as fact. Well, I am one witness and my Father who sent me is the other." said Jesus Christ

HUMBLE   MATTHEW 11;29-30
" Wear my yoke- for if it fits perfectly- let me teach you; for I am gentle and **humble,** and you shall find rest for your souls; for I give you only light burdens." said Jesus Christ
MATTHEW 18;4
"Therefore anyone who **humbles** himself as this little child, is the greatest in the Kingdom of Heaven. And anyone of you who welcomes a little child like this because you are mine, is welcoming

HUMBLE   MATTHEW 18;4 cont'd
and caring for me." said Jesus Christ

MATTHEW 23;11-12

"The more lowly your service is to others, the greater you are. To be the greatest, be a servant. But those who think themselves great shall be disappointed and **humbled;** and those who **humble** themselves shall be exalted." said Jesus Christ

LUKE 14;11

"For everyone who tries to honor himself shall be **humbled** ; and he who **humbles** himself shall be exalted." said Jesus Christ

HYPOCRITES

MATTHEW 6; 1-6

" TAKE CARE! DON'T do your good deeds publicly, to be admired, for then you will lose your reward from your Father in Heaven. When you give a gift to a beggar, don't shout about it as the **hypocrites** do-blowing trumpets at synagogues and streets to call attention to their acts of charity! I tell you in all earnestness, they have received all the reward they will ever get. But when you do a kindness to someone, do it secretly-don't tell your left hand what your right hand is doing. And you Father who knows all secrets will reward you."

"And now about prayer; When you pray, don't be like the **hypocrites** who pretend piety by praying publicly on street comers and in synagogues where

HYPOCRITES

MATTIIEW 6;1-6

everyone can see them. Truly that is all the reward they will ever get. But when you pray, go away by yourself, all alone, and shut the door behind you and pray to your Father, who knows your secrets and will reward you." said Jesus Christ

MATTHEW 7;1-5

"DON'T CRITICIZE, and then you won't be criticized. For others will treat you as you treat them. And why worry about a speck in the eye of your brother when you have a board in your own? Should you say, 'Friend let me help you get that speck out of your eye, when you can't even see because of the board in your own? **Hypocrite!** First get rid of the board . Then you can see to help your brother." said Jesus Christ

MATTHEW 23; 13-30

"Woe to you, Pharisees, and you other religious leaders. **Hypocrites!** For you won't let others enter the Kingdom of Heaven, and won't go in yourselves. And you pretend to be holy, with all your long public prayers in the streets, while you are evicting widows from their homes. **Hypocrites!** Yes, woe upon you **hypocrites!** For you go all the length to make one convert, and then turn him into twice the son of hell you are yourselves. Blind guides! Woe upon you! For your rule is that to swear 'By God's Temple' means nothing -you can

HYPOCRITES MATTHEW 23;13-30 cont'd break an oath, but to swear 'By the gold in the Temple' is binding! Blind fools! Which is greater, the gold or the Temple that sanctifies the gold? And you say you take an oath. "By the altar' can be broken, but to swear 'By the gifts of the altar' is binding! Blind for which is greater, the gift at the altar, or the altar itself that sanctifies the gift? When you swear 'By the altar' you are swearing by it and everything on it, and when you swear 'By the Temple' you are swearing by it, and by God who lives in it. And when you swear 'By heavens' you are swearing by the throne of God and by God Himself.

"Yes, woe upon you, Pharisees and you other religious leaders-**hypocrites**! For you tithe down to the last mint leaf in your garden, but ignore the important things like justice and mercy and faith. Yes, you should tithe, but you shouldn't leave the more important things undone. Blind guides! You strain out a gnat to swallow a camel.

"Woe to you, Pharisees, and you religious leaders-**hypocrites**! You are so careful to polish the outside of the cup, but the inside is foul with extortion and greed. Blind Pharisees! First cleanse the inside of the cup and then the whole cup will be clean.

"Woe to you, Pharisees and you religious leaders!

H   119

HYPOCRITES MATTHEW 23; 13-30 cont'd
You are like beautiful mausoleums-full of dead men's bones, and of foulness and corruption. You try to look like saintly men, but underneath those pious robes of yours are hearts besmirched with every sort of **hypocrisy** and sin.

"Yes, woe to you, Pharisees and you religious leaders-hypocrites! For you build monuments to the prophets killed by your fathers and lay flowers on the graves of godly men they destroyed and say, 'We certainly never would have acted as our fathers did.'"said Jesus Christ

MARK 7; 6-9
Jesus replied, " You bunch of hypocrites! Isaiah the prophet described you very well when he said, 'These people speak very prettily about the Lord but they have no love for Him at all. Their worship is a farce, for they claim that God commands the people to obey their petty rules. How right Isaiah was! For you ignore God's specific orders and substitute your own traditions. You are simply rejecting God's laws and trampling them under your feet for the sake of tradition." said Jesus Christ

LUKE 6;42
" And why quibble about the speck in someone else's eye- his little fault-when a board is in your own? How can you think of saying to him, 'Brother, let me help you get rid of that speck in your eye,'

H

HYPOCRITES LUKE 6;42contd
when you can't see past the board in yours?
Hypocrite! First get rid of the board, and then
perhaps you can see well enough to deal with his
speck!" said Jesus Christ

LUKE 12;1-3

[MEANWHILE THE CROWDS grew until
thousands upon thousands were milling about
crushing each other.] He turned now to the disciples
and warned them, "More than anything else,
beware of the Pharisees and the way they pretend to
be good when they aren't. But such **hypocrites**
cannot be hidden forever. It will become as evident
as yeast in dough. Whatever they have said in the
dark shall be heard in the light, and what you have
whispered in the inner rooms shall be broadcast
from the housetops for all to hear!" said Jesus
Christ

LUKE 12;55-57

" When the south wind blows you say, 'Today
will be a scorcher.' And it is. **Hypocrites!** You
interpret the sky well enough, but you refuse to
notice the warnings all around you about the crisis
ahead. Why do you refuse to see for yourselves
what is right?" said Jesus Christ

IDIOT   MATTHEW 5;21-23

"Under the law of Moses the rule was, 'If you kill, you must die.' but I have added to that rule, and tell you that if you are only *angry,* even in your own home, you are in danger of judgment! If you call your friend an **idiot,** you are in danger of being brought before the court. And if you curse him, you are in danger of the fires of hell."said Jesus Christ

IDLE WORDS   MATTHEW 12; 33-37

" You brood of snakes! How could evil men like you speak what is good and right? For a man's heart determines his speech. A good man's speech reveals his the rich treasures within him. And evil-hearted man reveals his venom, and his speech reveals it. And I tell you this, that **you must give account on Judgment Day for every idle word you speak.** Your words now reflect your fate then: either you will be justified by them or you will be condemned." said Jesus Christ

IMPORTANT   MATTHEW 6;25-27

" So my counsel is: don't worry about *things*-food, drink and clothes. For you already have a life and a body- they are far more **important** than what you eat and wear! Look at the birds! They don't worry about what to eat- they don't sow and reap and store up food-for your heavenly Father feeds them. And you are far more valuable to Him than

122 I

IMPORTANT MATTHEW 6; 25-27 cont'd
they are. Will all your worries add one single
moment to your life?" said Jesus Christ
                    MATTHEW 23;23
    "Yes, woe upon you, Pharisees, and you other
religious leaders-hypocrites! For you tithe down to
the last mint leaf in your garden, but ignore the
important things like justice and mercy and
faith." said Jesus Christ   MARK 9;35
    "All these will be his here on earth and in the
world to come he shall have eternal life. But many
people who seem to be **important** now will be the
least **important** then; and many who are considered
the least here shall be the greatest there." said Jesus

INSIDE (WITHIN)   MARK 7;23
    "And he added, "It is the thought life that
pollutes. For from **within,** out of men's hearts
comes evil thoughts of lust, theft, murder and
adultery, wanting what belongs to others,
wickedness deceit ,lewdness, envy, slander, pride
and all other folly. All these things come from
within: they are what pollute you and make you
unfit for God." said Jesus Christ
                    LUKE 11;39-41
    Then Jesus said to him, " You Pharisees wash the
outside, but **inside** you are still dirty-full of greed
and wickedness! Fools! Didn't God make the **inside**
as well as the outside? Purity is best demonstrated

by generosity." said Jesus Christ

INVEST   MARK 4; 18-25

"The thorny ground represents the hearts of people who listen to the Good News and receive it, but all too quickly the attractions of this world and the delights of wealth, and the search for success and the lure of nice things come in and crowd out God's message from their hearts, so that no crop is produced."

"But the good soil represents the hearts of those who truly accept God's message and produce plentiful; harvest for God- thirty, sixty even a hundred times as much as planted in their hearts. " Said Jesus Christ

J

JERUSALEM   LUKE 13;34-35

" 0 **Jerusalem, Jerusalem!** The city that murders the prophets. The city that stones those sent to help her. How often have I wanted to gather your children together even as a hen protects her brood under wings, but you won't let me. And now your house is left desolate. And you will never again see me until you say, 'Welcome to him who comes in the name of the Lord.'" said Jesus Christ

(Jerusalem is mentioned over and over again by Christ as a place and an attitude. Read the Gospels.

124   J

JESUS ABOUT HIMSELF
JOHN 8;12

Later on in one of his talks, Jesus said to the people, "I am the light of the world. So if you follow me, you won't be stumbling through the darkness, for the living light will flood your path." said Jesus Christ   JOHN 8; 23-27

Then he said to them, "You are from below, I am from above. You are of this world; I am not. That is why I said you will die in your sins; for unless you believe I am the Messiah, the Son of God, you will die in your sins.

{"Tell us who you are." they demanded.}

He replied, "I am the one I have always claimed to be. I could condemn you for much and teach you much, but I won't, for I say only what I am told to by the One who sent me and He is the Truth." [But they still didn't understand he was talking about God] said Jesus Christ   JOHN 8;51

"No," Jesus said, "I have no demons in me. For I honor the Father- and you dishonor me. And though I have no wish to make myself great, God wants this for me and judges those who reject me. With all earnestness I have to tell you this- no one who obeys me shall ever die!" said Jesus Christ

JESUS...ABOUT HIMSELF
JOHN 12;44-50

Jesus shouted to the crowds. "If you trust **me,** you are really trusting God. For when you see **me,** you are seeing the one who sent **me. I have** come as a Light to shine in this dark world, so that all who put their trust in **me** shall no longer wander in the darkness. If anyone hears **me** and doesn't obey me, I **am** not his judge-for I have come to save the world and not judge it. But all who reject **me** and my message will be judged on the Day of Judgment by the Truths I **have** spoken. For they are not my own ideas, but I have told you what the Father said to tell you. And I **know** His instructions lead to eternal
life; so whatever He tells **me** to say, I say!" said Jesus Christ

JOHN THE BAPTIST
MATTHEW 11;7-15

When **John's** disciples had gone, Jesus began talking about him to the crowds. " When you went into the barren wilderness to see **John;** what did you expect him to be like? Grass blowing in the wind? Or were you expecting to see a man dressed as a prince in a palace? Or a prophet of God? Yes, he is more than just a prophet. For **John** is the man mentioned in the Scriptures-a messenger to precede me, to announce my coming, and prepare people to receive me.

126   J

JOHN THE BAPTIST
MATTHEW 11; 7-15 cont'd

"Truly of all men ever born, none shines more brightly than **John the Baptist.** And yet even the lesser lights in the Kingdom of Heaven will be greater than he is! And from the time John the Baptist began preaching and baptizing until now, ardent multitudes have been crowding toward the Kingdom of Heaven, for all laws and prophets looked forward to the Messiah. Then **John** appeared, and if you are willing to understand what I mean, he is Elijah, the one the prophets said would come at the time the Kingdom begins. If ever you were willing to listen, listen now!" said Jesus Christ (see also Luke 7; 24-35

JONAH
MATTHEW 12;39-41

But Jesus replied, "Only a faithless nation would ask for further proof; and none will be given except what happened to **Jonah** the prophet! For as **Jonah** was in the great fish for three days and three nights, so I the Messiah, shall be in the heart of the earth for three days and three nights. The men of Ninevah shall arise against this nation in judgment and condemn you. For when **Jonah** preached to them, they repented and turned to God from all their evil ways. And now greater than **Jonah** is here- and you refuse to believe him." said Jesus Christ

JONAH

LUKE 11; 29-30

As the crowd pressed in upon him, he preached them this sermon: "These are evil times, with evil people. They keep asking for some strange happening in the skies to prove I am the Messiah, but the only proof! will give them is a miracle like that of **Jonah,** whose experienced proved to the people of Ninevah that God had sent him. My similar experience will prove God has sent me to these people." said Jesus Christ

JOY HAPPINESS

MATTHEW 13;20-21

"The shallow, rocky soil represents the heart of man who hears the message and receives it with real **joy,** but he doesn't have much depth in life, and the seeds don't root very deeply, and after a while trouble comes, or persecution begins because of his beliefs his enthusiasm fades and he drops out." said Jesus Christ

MARK. 4;16

" The rocky soil the hearts of those who hear the message with **joy,** but like young plants their roots don't go very deep, and though at first they got along fine, as soon as persecution begins, they wilt." Said Jesus Christ

LUKE 6;20-23

Then he turned to his disciples and said, " What

JOY.HAPPINESS LUKE 6;20-23

happiness there is for you who are poor, for the kingdom of God is yours. What **happiness** there is for you who are now hungry, for you are going to be satisfied. What **happiness** there is for you who weep, for the time will come when you laugh with joy! What happiness it is when others hate you and exclude you and insult you and smear your name because you are mine! When that happens, **rejoice**! Yes, leap for **joy**! For you will have a great reward waiting for you in heaven. And you will be in good company-the ancient prophets were treated that way too." said Jesus Christ

JOHN 15;9-11

"I have loved you even as the Father has loved me. live within my love. When you obey me you are living within my love, just as I obey my Father and live within His love. I have told you this so you will be filled with my **joy.** Yes, your cup of **joy** will overflow! I demand that you love each other as much as I love you!" said Jesus Christ

JOHN 16; 20-22

" The world will greatly rejoice over what is going to happen to me, and you will weep. But your weeping shall suddenly be turned into wonderful **joy** when you see me again. It will be the same **joy** as a woman in labor when her child is born-her anguish gives way to rapturous **joy** and the pain is forgotten.

JOY...HAPPINESS   JOHN 16;20-22 cont'd
You have pain now, but I will see you again and then you will **rejoice** and no one can rob you of that **joy."** said Jesus Christ

JUDGE   JUDGING   JUDGMENT JUSTICE   MATTHEW 7;1-2

" Don't **criticize,** and then you won't be **criticized.** For others will treat you as you treat them." said Jesus Christ

MATTHEW 5;21-22

"Under the law of Moses the rule was, 'If you kill, you must die.' But I have added to that rule, and tell you that if you are angry in your own home, you are in danger of **judgment!** If you call your friend an idiot, you are in danger of being brought before the court. And if you curse him, you are in danger of the fires of hell." said Jesus Christ

MATTHEW 12;36

"And I tell you this, that you must give account on **Judgment** Day for every idle word you speak. Your words now reflect your fate then: either you will be justified by them or condemned." said Jesus Christ

MATTHEW 12;41
(speaking to Jewish leaders)

"The men of Ninevah shall arise against this nation at the **judgment** and condemn you. For when Jonah preached to them, they repented and turned to

130   J

JUDGE JUDGING JUDGMENT
JUSTICE   MATTHEW 12;41 cont'd

God from all of their evil ways. And now greater than Jonah is here and you refuse to believe him." said Jesus Christ

LUKE 18; 1-8

[One day Jesus told his disciples a story to illustrate their need for constant prayer and show them they must keep praying until the answer comes.]

"There was a city **judge**," he said, "a very godless man who had great contempt for everyone. A widow of that city came to him frequently to appeal for **justice** against a man who had harmed her. The **judge** ignored her for a while, but eventually she got on his nerves."

" ' I fear neither God nor man,' he said to himself, 'but this woman bothers me. I am going to see that she gets **justice** for she is wearing me out with her constant complaining.'"

Then the Lord said, "If even an evil **judge** can be worn down like that, don't you think God will surely give **justice** to his people who plead with him day and night? Yes, He will answer them quickly! But the question is: When I, the Messiah, return, how many will I find who have faith and are praying?" said Jesus Christ

JUDGE JUDGING JUDGMENT
JUSTICE   JOHN; 5;22

" And the Father leaves all **judgment** of sin to His Son, so that everyone will honor the Son just as they honor the Father. But if you reuse to honor God's Son, whom He sent to you, then you are certainly

not honoring the Father. "said Jesus Christ

JOHN 5;30

" But I pass no **judgment** without consulting the Father. I **judge** as I am told. And my **judgment** is absolutely fair and just, for it is according to the Will of God who sent me and is not merely my own." said Jesus Christ

JOHN 16;8-11

" And when he, the Holy Spirit, has come he will convince the world of its sin, and the availability of God's goodness, and of the deliverance of **judgment.** The world's sin is unbelief in me; there is righteousness available because I go to the Father and you shall see me no more; there is deliverance from **judgment** because the prince of this world has already been **judged."** said Jesus Christ

K

KINGDOM   OF GOD.....OF HEAVEN

(There are so many Scriptures that tell us what Christ said, that I chose different ones to provide a variety of answers. Look at the end of this section

132   K

KINGDOM OF GOD.. HEAVEN
Cont'd- for more verses to look up.
Also see HEAVEN)

MATTHEW 13;18-23

"Now here is the explanation of the story I told you about the farmer planting grain: the hard path where some of the seeds fell represents the heart of the person who hears the Good News about the **Kingdom** and doesn't understand it: then Satan comes along and snatches away the seeds from his heart. The shallow, rocky soil represents the heart of a man who hears the message and receives it with real joy , but he doesn't have much depth in his life, and the seeds don't root very deeply, and after a while trouble comes, or persecution begins because of his beliefs, his enthusiasm fades and he drops out. The ground covered with thistles represents a man who hears the message, but the cares of his life and his longing for money chokes out God's Word, and he does less and less for God. The good ground represents the heart of a man who listens to the message and understands it and goes out and brings thirty, sixty or even a hundred others into the **Kingdom.**" said Jesus Christ

KINGDOM..OF GOD. HEAVEN
MATTHEW 20;1-16

Here is another illustration of the **Kingdom of Heaven.** " The owner of an estate went out early one morning to hire workers to harvest his field. He agreed to pay them $20 a day. And sent them out to work.

"A couple of hours later he was passing a hiring Hall and saw some men standing around waiting for jobs, so he sent them also into his fields, telling them he would pay them whatever was right at the end of the day. At noon and around three o'clock he did the same thing.

" At five o'clock that evening he was in town again and saw some more men standing around and asked them, 'Why haven't you been working today?'

" ' Because no one hired us,' they replied.

" 'Then go out and join the others in my fields,' he told them.

" That evening he told the paymaster to call the men in and pay them, beginning with the last men first. When the men hired at five o'clock were paid, each received $20. So when the men hired earlier came to get theirs, they assumed they would receive much more. But they too, were paid $20.

" 'They protested, 'These fellows worked only one hour, and yet you've paid them as much as those

KINGDOM..OF GOD...HEAVEN

MATTHEW 20; 1-16 cont'd
who worked all day in the scorching heat!'

"'Friend,' he answered. 'I did you no wrong! Didn't you agree to work all day for $20? Take it and go. It is my desire to pay all the same; is it against the law to give away my money if I want to? Should you be angry because I am kind? And so it is, the last shall be the first and the first shall be the last." said Jesus Christ

MATTHEW 25; 34-46

"Then I, the King, shall say to those at my right, 'Come, blessed of my Father into the **Kingdom** prepared for you from the founding of the world. For I was hungry and you fed me; I was thirsty and you gave me water; I was a stranger and you invited me into your homes; naked and you clothed me; sick and in prison and you visited me.'

"Then these righteous ones will reply, 'Sir, when did we ever see you hungry and feed you? Or thirsty and give you anything to drink? Or a stranger, and help you? Or naked and clothe you? When did we ever see you sick and in prison and visit you?'

"And I, the King, will tell them, 'When you did it to these my brothers, you were doing it to me!' Then I will turn to those on my left and say, 'Away with you, you cursed ones, into the eternal

KINGDOM OF GOD HEAVEN
MATTHEW 25;34-46 cont'd

fire prepared for the devil and his demons. For I was hungry and you wouldn't feed me, thirsty and you give me anything to drink; a stranger, and you refused me hospitality; naked and you wouldn't clothe me; sick and in prison and you wouldn't visit me.'

"Then they will reply, 'Lord, when did we ever see you hungry or thirsty or a stranger or naked or sick or in prison and not help you?'

" And I will answer, 'When you refused to help the least of these, my brothers, you were refusing to help me.'

"And they shall go away into eternal punishment; but the righteous into everlasting life." said Jesus Christ

MARK 4;11-12

" You are permitted to know some of the truths about the **Kingdom of God** that are hidden to those outside the **Kingdom:**

Though they see and hear, they will not understand or turn to God, or be forgiven for their sins. But if you can't understand this simple illustration, what will you do about all the others I am going to tell?" Said Jesus Christ

KINGDOM...OF GOD
HEAVEN   MARK 13;24-27

"After the Tribulation ends, then the sun will grow dim and the moon will not shine, and the stars will fall -the heavens will convulse.

"Then all of mankind will see me, the Messiah, coming in the clouds with great power and glory. And I will send out the angels to gather together my chosen ones from all over the world- from the farthest bounds of earth and **Heaven.**" said Jesus Christ   LUKE 10;18-20

"Yes,"he told them. "I saw Satan falling from **Heaven** as a flash of lightning! And I have given you authority over all the power of the Enemy, and to walk among serpents and scorpions and to crush them. Nothing shall injure you! However, the important thing is not that demons obey you, but your names are registered as citizens of **Heaven.**" said Jesus Christ   LUKE 12;32-34

"So don't be afraid little flock. For it gives your Father great happiness to give you the **Kingdom.** Sell what you have and give to those in need. This will fatten your purses in **Heaven!** And the purses in **Heaven** have no rips or holes in them. Your treasures will never disappear; no thief can steal them; no moth can destroy them. Wherever your treasure is, there your thoughts and heart will be also." said Jesus Christ

K   137

KINGDOM ...OF GOD
HEAVEN   LUKE 13;18-21

Now he began teaching them again about the **Kingdom of God.** "What is the **Kingdom** like?" he asked. "How can I illustrate it? It is like a tiny mustard seed planted in a garden ; soon it grows into a tall bush, and birds live among its branches. It is like yeast kneaded into dough, which work is unseen until it is risen high and light." said Jesus Christ

LUKE 17; 20-21

{ One day the Pharisees asked Jesus, " When will the **Kingdom of Heaven** begin?" } Jesus replied. " the **Kingdom of God** isn't ushered in by visible signs. You won't be able to say, ' It has begun here in this place or there in that part of the country. For the **Kingdom of God** is within you." said Jesus Christ

JOHN 3;10-17

Jesus replied, " You, a respected Jewish teacher, and yet, you don't understand these things. I am telling you what I know and have seen- and yet you won't believe me. But if you don't even believe me when I tell you about such things that happen here among men, how can you possibly believe if I tell you what is going on in **Heaven?** For only I, the Messiah, have come to earth and will return to **Heaven** again. And as Moses in the wilderness

138   K

KINGDOM...OF GOD...HEAVEN
JOHN 3;10-17

lifted up the bronze image of the serpent on a pole, even so, I must be lifted up upon a pole, so that anyone who believes in me will have eternal life. <u>For God loved the world so much that He gave His only Son so that anyone who believes in him shall not perish but have eternal life.</u> God did not send His Son into the world to condemn it, but to save it." said Jesus Christ

JOHN 6;32-33

Jesus said, "Moses didn't give it to them. My Father did. And now He offers you true bread from Heaven. The true Bread is a Person- the one sent by God from **Heaven,** and he gives life to the world. " said Jesus Christ

JOHN 6;38

"For I have come here from **Heaven** to do the Will of God who sent me, not to have my own way. " said Jesus Christ

KNOCK

MATTHEW 7;7-12

"Ask and you will be given what you ask for. Seek and you will find. **Knock** and the door will be opened. For everyone who asks, receives. Anyone who seeks finds. If only you will **knock,** the door will open. If a child asks his father for a loaf of bread, will he be given a stone instead? If he asks

K   139

KNOCK   MATTHEW 7;7-12 cont'd
...for fish, will he be given a poisonous snake? Of course not! And if you hardhearted sinful men know how to give gifts to your children, won't your Father in Heaven even more certainly give good gifts to those who ask for them?

"Do for others what you want them to do for you. This is the teaching of the laws of Moses in a nutshell." said Jesus Christ**(THE GOLDEN RULE)
LUKE 11; 8-10
"But I tell you this- though he won't do it as a friend, if you keep **knocking** long enough, he will get up and give you everything you want just because of your persistence. And so it is with prayer-keep on asking and you will keep on getting; keep on looking and you will keep on finding; **knock** and the door will be opened. Everyone who asks receives, all who seek, find; and the door is opened to everyone who **knocks.**" said Jesus Christ

L

LAMP...LIGHT MATTHEW 5;14-16
"You are the world's **light**- a city on a hill, glowing in the night for all to see. Don't hide your **light!** Let it shine for all; let your good deeds glow for all to see so that they will praise your Heavenly Father." said Jesus Christ

140   L

LAMP,LIGHT,EYES

MATTHEW 6;22

" If your eye is pure, there will be **sunlight** in your soul. But if your eye is clouded with evil thoughts and desires, you are in deep spiritual darkness. Oh how deep that darkness can be." said Jesus Christ   **MARK 4;21-25**

"Then he asked them, "When someone **lights** a **lamp,** does he put a box over it to shut out the **light?** Of course not! The light couldn't be seen or used. A **lamp** is placed on a stand to be seen and useful.

"All that is now hidden will someday come to **light."** said Jesus Christ

LUKE 8;16-18

[Another time he asked,] " Whoever heard of someone **lighting a lamp** and then covering it up to keep it from shining? No, lamps are mounted in the open where they can be seen. This illustrates the fact that someday everything in men's hearts shall be brought to **light** and plain to all. So be careful how you listen; for whoever has, to him shall be given more; and whoever does not have, even what he thinks he has shall be taken away."said Jesus Christ

LUKE 11; 33-36

"No one **lights a lamp** and hides it! Instead he puts it on a stand to give **light** for all who enter the

LAMP...LIGHT,EYES

LUKE 11;33-36 cont'd

room. Your eyes **light** up your inward being. A pure eye lets sunshine into your soul. A lustful eye shuts out **light** and plunges you onto darkness. So watch that the sunshine is not blotted out. If you are filled with **light** within, no dark comers, then your face will be radiant too, as though a floodlight isbeamed upon you." said Jesus Christ

JOHN 3; 18-21

"Their sentence is based on this fact: that the **Light** from Heaven came into the world, but they loved the darkness more than the Light, for their deeds were evil. They hated the heavenly **Light** for fear their sins would be exposed and they would be punished. But those doing right gladly came to the **Light** to let everyone see that they are doing what God wants them to." said Jesus Christ

JOHN 8;12

"I am the **Light** of the world. So if you follow me, you won't be stumbling through the darkness, for living **light** will flood your path" said Jesus Christ

JOHN 9;5

"But while I am still here in this world, I give it my **light.**" said Jesus Christ

142   L

LAMP..LIGHT.EYES

JOHN 12;35-36

Jesus replied, "My **Light** will shine out for you just a little while longer. Walk in it while you can, and go where you want before darkness falls, for then it will be too late for you to find your way. Make use of the **Light** while there is still time; then you will become **Light** bearers." {After saying this, Jesus went away and was hidden from them.} said Jesus Christ   JOHN 12;44-50

Jesus shouted to the crowds, "If you trust me, you are really trusting God. For when you see me, you are seeing the One who sent me. I have come as a **Light** to shine in this dark world, so that all who put their trust in me will no longer wander in the darkness. If anyone hears me and doesn't obey me, I am not his judge- for I have come to save the world and not to judge it. But all who reject me and my message will be judged at the Day of Judgment by the truths I have spoken. For these are not my own ideas, but I have told you what the Father said to tell you. And I know His instructions lead to eternal life; so whatever He tells me to say, I say." said Jesus Christ

LAST   MATTHEW 19;30

"But many who are first now will be **last** then; and some who are **last** now, will be first then." said Jesus Christ

LAST   JOHN 6; 39-40

" And this is the will of God that I should not even lose even one of those He has given me, but I should raise them to Eternal Life on the **Last** Day. For it is my Father's Will that everyone who sees His Son and believes him shall have eternal life- that I should raise them on the **Last** Day." said Jesus Christ

LAWS   MATTHEW 5;17-19

" Don't misunderstand why I have come- it isn't to cancel the Jaws of Moses and the warnings of the prophets. No, I came to fulfill them and make them all come true. With all the earnestness I have I say: every law in the book will continue until its purpose is achieved. And so if anyone breaks the least commandment, and teaches others to, he shall be the least in the Kingdom of Heaven. But those who teach God's laws and obeys them shall be great inthe Kingdom of Heaven. " said Jesus Christ

MATTHEW 7;12

"Do for others what you want them to do for you. This is the teaching of the **Law** of Moses in a nutshell." said Jesus Christ

MATTHEW 22;37-40

Jesus replied, "Love the Lord with all of your heart, soul and mind. This is the greatest commandment. The second most important is similar. 'Love your neighbor as much as you love

LAWS   MATTHEW 22; 37-40 cont'd

yourself. All other commandments and all the demands of the prophets stem from these two **laws** and are fulfilled if you obey them. Keep only these and you will find that you are obeying all the others." said Jesus Christ

LUKE 16;15-17

Then he said to them, "You wear a noble, pious expression in public, but God knows your evil hearts. Your pretense brings you honor from the people, but it is an abomination in the sight of God. Until John the Baptist began to preach, the **laws** of Moses and the messages of the prophets were your guides. But John introduced the Good News that the Kingdom of God would come soon. And now eager multitudes are pressing in. But that doesn't mean the **Law** has lost its force in even the smallest point. It is as strong and unshakeable as Heaven and Earth." said Jesus Christ

LAZARUS   JOHN 11;11, 14,15,23, 25,26

Then he said, "Our friend Lazarus has gone to sleep, but now I will waken him!"

14-15 "**Lazarus** is dead. And for your sake I am glad I wasn't there, this will give me another opportunity to believe in me. Come, let's go to him." 23 "Your brother will come back to life again."

25-26 "I am the one who raises the dead and gives

LAZARUS   JOHN 11; 35-36 cont'd
them life again. Anyone who believes in me, even
though he dies like everyone else, shall live again.
He is given eternal life for believing in me and shall
never perish. Do you believe this, Martha?" said
Jesus Christ

LEADS   JOHN 10;1-5
"Anyone refusing to walk through the gate and
into the sheepfold, who sneaks over the wall, must
surely be a thief! For a shepherd comes through the
gate. The gatekeeper opens the gate for him, and the
sheep hears his voice and come to him: and he calls
his own sheep by name and **leads** them out. He
walks ahead of them; and they follow him for they
recognize his voice. They won't follow a stranger,
but run from him, for they don't recognize his
voice." said Jesus Christ

LEAST   MATTHEW 25;45
"And I will answer, 'When you refused to help the
least of these my brother, you refused to help me. "
said Jesus Christ   LUKE 7;28
" In all humanity there is no one greater than John.
And yet the **least** citizen in the Kingdom of God is
greater than he is." said Jesus Christ
(see IMPORTANT >MARK 9;35)

L

LIAR(S), LIE(S) LIED, LYING

MATTHEW 5;11

"When you are reviled and persecuted and **lied** about because you are my followers-wonderful! Be *happy* about it! Be *very glad!* For a *tremendous award* awaits you up in Heaven. And remember the ancient prophets were persecuted too." said Jesus Christ

JOHN 8;42-45

Jesus told them, "If that were so then you would love me, for I have come to you from God. I am not here on my own, but He sent me. Why can't you understand what I am saying? It is because you are prevented from doing so! For you are the children of the devil and you love the evil things he does. He was a murderer from the beginning and a hater of truth-there is not one iota of truth in him. When he **lies** it is perfectly normal; for he is the father of **liars.** And so when I tell you the truth, you naturally don't believe it." said Jesus Christ

JOHN 8; 54-55

"If l am merely boasting about myself, it doesn't count. But it is my Father-and you claim Him as your God- who is saying these glorious things about me. But you do not even know Him. I do. If I said otherwise I would be as great a **liar** as you. But it is true- I know Him and fully obey Him." said Jesus Christ

LIFE   MATTHEW 6;25

" So my counsel is: Don't worry about *things-*food drink and clothes. For you already have **life** and a body- they are far more important than what to eat and wear. " said Jesus Christ

MATTHEW 10;39

" If you cling to your **life,** you will lose it; but if you give it up for me, you will save it." said Jesus Christ   MATTHEW 16;25

"For anyone who wants to keep his **life** for himself shall lose it; and anyone who loses his **life** for me shall find it again. What profit is there if you gain the whole world- and lose eternal life? What can be compared to eternal **life?** " said Jesus Christ

MATTHEW 19;29

"And anyone who gives up his home, brothers, sisters, father, mother, wife, children or property to follow me, shall receive a hundred times as much in return and have eternal **life."** said Jesus Christ

MATTHEW 20;28

" Your attitude must be like my own, for I, the Messiah, did not come to be served, but to serve, and give my **life** as ransom for many," said Jesus Christ

MATTHEW 25;46

"And they shall go away into eternal punishment; but the righteous into everlasting **life."** said Jesus Christ

LIFE   MARK 8;35

"If you insist on saving your **life**, you will lose it. Only those who throw away their **lives** for my sake or the sake of the Good News will ever know what it is like to truly **live**. " said Jesus Christ

MARK 10;44-45

"As you know, the kings and the great men of this earth lord it over people; but among you it is different. Whoever wants to be great among you must be your servant. And whoever wants to be greatest of all must be a slave to all. For even I, the Messiah, am not here to be served, but to help others, and give my **life** as a ransom for many. " said Jesus Christ

LUKE 9;24

"Whoever loses his **life** for my sake will save it, but whoever insists on keeping his will lose it; and what profit is there to gaining the whole world when it means forfeiting one's self?" said Jesus Christ

LUKE 12;15

" Beware! Don't always be wishing for what you don't have. For real **life** and real living are not related to how rich we are." said Jesus Christ

LUKE 12;22-26

"Don't worry about whether you have enough food to eat or clothes to wear. For **life** consists of far more than food and clothes. Look at the ravens-they don't plant or harvest or have barns or store

LIFE   LUKE 12;22-26 cont'd

away their food and yet they get along all right- for God feeds them. And you are far more valuable to Him than any birds!

"And besides, what is the use of worrying? What good does it do? Does it add one single day to your **life?** Of course not! And if worry can't even do such little things as that, what's the use of worrying over bigger things?" said Jesus Christ

LUKE 14;26

"Anyone who wants to be my follower must love me more than he does his own father, mother, wife, children, brothers, or sisters- yes, more than his own life-otherwise he cannot be my disciple." said Jesus Christ   LUKE 17;33

"Whoever clings to his **life** shall lose it, and whoever loses his **life** shall save it." said Jesus Christ

JOHN 3;16

" For God loved the world so much that He gave His only Son so that anyone who believes in him shall not perish but have eternal **life."** said Jesus Christ   JOHN 3;39

"All who trust him-God's Son- to save them have eternal **life;** those who don't believe and don't obey him shall never see Heaven, but the wrath of God remains on them," said Jesus Christ

L

LIFE   JOHN 5;24-29

"I say emphatically that anyone who listens to my
message and believes in God who sent me has
eternal **life,** and will never be damned for his sins,
but has already passed out of death into **life.** And I
solemnly declare that the time is coming, in fact, it
is here, when the dead shall hear my voice-the Son
of God- and those who listen shall live. The Father
has life in Himself, and has granted His Son to have
life in himself, and to judge the sins of all mankind
because he is the Son of Man. Don't be so
surprised! Indeed the time is coming when all the
dead in their graves shall hear the voice of God's
Son, and shall rise again-those who have done good,
to eternal **life;** and those who have continued in evil
to judgment. "said Jesus Christ

JOHN 6;40

"For it is my Father's will that everyone who sees
His Son and believes shall have eternal **life**- that I
should raise them on the Last Day." said Jesus Christ

JOHN 6; 47-51,53-54

"How earnestly I tell you this- anyone who
believes in me already has eternal **life!** Yes, I am the
Bread of **Life!** When your fathers in the wilderness
ate bread from the skies, they all died. But the Bread
from Heaven gives eternal **life** to everyone who eats
it. I am that **Living** Bread that came down from
Heaven. Anyone eating this Bread shall **live** forever,

LIFE JOHN 6;47-51,53-54 cont'd

this Bread is my flesh given to redeem humanity.
53 So Jesus said it again, " With all the earnestness
I possess I tell you this: unless you eat the flesh of
the Messiah and drink his blood, you cannot have
eternal **life** within you. But anyone who does eat my
flesh and drink my blood has eternal **life,** and I will
raise them on the Last Day." said Jesus Christ

JOHN 6; 61-64

"Does this offend you? Then what will you
think when you see me, the Messiah, return to
Heaven again? Only the Holy Spirit gives eternal
life. Those born only once, with physical birth will
never receive this gift. But now I have told you how
to get this true spiritual **life.** But some of you don't
believe me." said Jesus Christ

JOHN 10;17-18

"The Father loves me because I lay down my **life**
that I may have it back again. No one can kill me
without my consent- I lay down my **life** voluntarily.
For I have the right and the power to lay it down
when I want to and also the right and the power to
take it again. For the Father has given me this
right." said Jesus Christ

JOHN 10;28-30

"I give them eternal **life** and they shall never
perish. No one shall snatch them away from me, for
my Father has given them to me, and He is more

LIFE   JOHN 10; 28-30 cont'd
powerful than anyone else, so no one can kidnap
them from me. I and the Father are one." said Jesus
Christ   JOHN 11; 25-26

  "I am the one who raises the dead and gives
them **life** again. Anyone who believes in me, even
though he dies like everyone else, shall **live** again.
He is given eternal **life** for believing in me and shall
never perish. Do you believe this, Martha?" said
Jesus Christ   JOHN 12;25

  "If you love your **life** down here-you will lose it. If
you despise your **life** down here- you will exchange
it for eternal glory." said Jesus Christ
             JOHN 12;50

  " And I know His instructions lead to eternal
life; so whatever He tells me to say, I say." said
Jesus Christ   JOHN 14;6

  "I am the Way-yes, the Truth and the **Life.** No
one can get to the Father except by means of me."
said Jesus Christ   JOHN 15; 12-15

  " I demand that you love each other as much as I
love you. And here is how you measure it- the
greatest love is shown when a person lays down his
life for his friends; and you are my friends if you
obey me. I no longer call you slaves, for a master
does not confide in slaves; now you are my friends,
proved by the fact that I told you everything the
Father has told me."said Jesus Christ

LIFE   JOHN 17;2-3

"Father, the time has come. Reveal the glory of your Son so that he can give glory back to You. For You have given him authority over every man and woman in all the earth. He gives eternal **life** to each one You have given him. And this is the way to eternal **life**- by knowing you, the only true God and Jesus Christ, the one You sent to earth! I brought glory to you here on earth by doing everything you told me to. And now Father, reveal my glory as I stand in your presence, the glory we shared before the world began." said Jesus Christ

LIP SERVICE   MATTHEW 15;8-10

"These people say they honor me, but their hearts are far away. Their worship is worthless, for they teach their man-made laws instead of those from God." said Jesus Christ

LORD'S PRAYER MATTHEW 6; 9-15

"Pray along these lines: Our Father who art in Heaven, we honor your Holy name. May Your Kingdom come, May Your Will be done on Earth as it is in Heaven. Give us this day our daily bread and forgive our sins as we forgive those that have sinned against us. Don't lead us into temptation, but deliver us from evil. A-men ....Your Heavenly Father will forgive you if you forgive those who have sinned against you; but if you refuse to forgive them, He will not forgive you" said Jesus Christ

154   L

LORD'S PRAYER (also as Christ's prayers)
LUKE 11;2-4

LOST,LOSE   MATTHEW 18;10-14

"Beware you don't look down on any one of these little children. For I tell you that in Heaven their angels have constant access to my Father. And I the Messiah came to save the **lost.**

"If a man has a hundred sheep, and one wanders away and is **lost,** what will he do? Won't he leave the ninety-nine others and go into the hills and search for the **lost** one? And if he finds it, he will rejoice over it more than the ninety-nine others safe at home! Just so, it is not my Father's Will that even one of these little ones should perish." said Jesus Christ   LUKE 15;7

"Well, in the same way Heaven will be happier over one **lost** sinner who returns to God than over ninety-nine others who haven't strayed away." said Jesus Christ   (read the Prodigal Son.LUKE15;11-32
JOHN 6;38-40

"For I have come here from Heaven to do the Will of God who sent me, not to have my own way. And this is the Will of God that I should not **lose** even one of all those He has given me, but I should raise them to eternal life on the Last Day. For it is my Father's Will that everyone who sees His Son and believes in him shall have eternal life- that I should raise them on the Last Day." said Jesus Christ

LOST...LOSE   JOHN 12;25

"If you love your life down here, you will **lose** it. If you despise your life down here-you will exchange it for eternal glory." said Jesus Christ

JOHN 18;9

"I told you, I am he," Jesus said; "and since I am the one you are after, let the others go. He did this to carry out the prophecy he just made, "I have not **lost** a single one you gave me." said Jesus Christ

LOVE (is written about throughout the entire Bible, especially in all the Gospels. These verses represent just some, of the ultimate commands Christ said of how and who we are to love.)

MATTHEW 5;43

" There is a saying, '**Love** your *friends* and hate your enemies, But I say: **Love** your *enemies!* Pray for those who persecute you! In that way you will be acting as true sons of the Father in heaven. For He gives sunlight to both the evil and the good, and sends rain on the just and unjust too. If you **love** only those who **love** you, what good is that? Even scoundrels do that much. If you are friendly only to your friends, how are you different from anyone else? Even heathen do that. But you are to be perfect, even as you Father in Heaven is perfect." said Jesus Christ

156   L

LOVE   MATTHEW 19;19

And Jesus replied," Don't kill, don't commit adultery, don't steal, don't lie, honor your father and mother and **love** your neighbor as yourself.." said Jesus Christ   MATTHEW 22;37-40

Jesus replied, " **Love** the Lord your God with all of your heart, soul and mind. This is the first and greatest commandment. The second most important is similar, 'Love your neighbor as much as you love yourself.' all other commandments and demands of the prophets stem from these two laws and are fulfilled if you obey them. Keep only these and you will find you are obeying all others." said Jesus Christ   MATTHEW 24;11-13

"And many false prophets will appear and lead many astray. Sin will be rampant everywhere and will cool the **love** of many. But those enduring until the end shall be saved." said Jesus Christ

JOHN 3:16-17

"For God **loved** the world so much that He gave His only Son so that anyone who believes in him shall not perish, but have eternal life. God did not send His Son into the world to condemn it, but to save it, " said Jesus Christ

JOHN 5;42

"Your approval or disapproval means nothing to me, for as i know so well, you don't have God's

LOVE   JOHN 5;42 cont'd
love within you." said Jesus Christ
                    JOHN 13;34

"And so I am giving a new commandment to you now- **love** one another as much as I **love** you. Your strong **love** for each other will prove to the world you are my disciples." said Jesus Christ

JOHN 14;15

"If you **love** me obey me; and I will send you another Comforter, and he will never leave you. He is the Holy Spirit who leads into all truth." said Jesus Christ   JOHN 14;21,23-25

"The one who obeys me is the one who **loves** me and because he **loves** me, my Father will **love** him; and I will too, and I will reveal myself to him." 23 Jesus replied, "Because I will only reveal myself to those who **love** me and obey me. The Father will **love** them too, and we will come to them and live with them. Anyone who doesn't obey me doesn't **love** me. And remember, I am not making up this answer to your question! It is the answer given by the Father who sent me. I am telling you these things now while I am still with you. But when the Father sends the Comforter instead of me-and by the Comforter I mean the Holy Spirit- he will teach you much, as well as remind you of everything I myself have told you." said Jesus Christ

LOVE   JOHN 14;30-31

"I don't have much more time to talk to you, for the evil prince of this world approaches. He has no power over me, but I will freely do whatever the Father requires of me so the world will know that I **love** the Father. Come, let's be going." said Jesus Christ   JOHN 15;9-14

"I have **loved** you even as the Father has **loved** me. Live within my **love.** When you obey me, you are living within my **love,** just as I obey my Father and live in His **love.** Yes, I have told you this so that you will be filled with my joy. Yes, your cup will overflow! I demand that you **love** each other as much as I **love** you. And here is how to measure it- the greatest **love** is shown when a person lays down his life for his friends; and you are my friends if you obey me." said Jesus Christ

JOHN 15;17

"I demand that you **love** each other, for you get enough hate from the world! But then, it hated me before it hated you. The world would **love** you if you belonged to it, but you don't- for I chose you to come out of the world, and so it hates you." said Jesus Christ   JOHN 17;25-26

"O, righteous Father, the world doesn't know You, but I do; and these disciples know You sent me. And I have revealed You to them, and will keep on revealing You so the mighty **love** you have for

L   159

LOVE   JOHN 17;25-26 cont'd
me may be in them and I in them." said Jesus Christ
JOHN 21;15,-18

After breakfast Jesus said to Simon Peter,
"Simon, son of John, do you **love** me more than
these others?"

{"Yes." Peter replied. "You know I am your
friend."}

"Then feed my lambs." Jesus told him.

Jesus repeated the question: "Simon, son of John,
do you *really* **love** me?"

{"Yes. Lord," Peter replied, "You know I am your
friend." }

"Then take care of my sheep." Jesus said.

Once more Jesus asked him, "Simon, son of
John, are you even my friend?"

[Peter was grieved at the way Jesus asked the
question the third time.]

Jesus said, "Then feed my little sheep. When you
were young you were able to do as you liked and go
wherever you wanted to; but when you are old you
will stretch out your hands and others will direct
you and take you where you don't want to go." said
Jesus Christ

LOVE/LOYALTY   MATTHEW 19;37-39

" If you **love** your father and mother more than
you **love** me, you are not worthy of being mine; or if
you **love** your son or daughter more than me, you

LOVE/LOYALTY

MATTHEW 19;37-39 cont'd

Are worthy of being mine. If you refuse to take up your cross and follow me, you are not worthy of being mine. I f you cling to your life, you will lose it, but if you give it up for me you will save it." said Jesus Christ

M

MAN-MADE   MARK 8;33

Jesus turned and looked at his disciples and said, " Satan, get behind me! You are looking at this only from a human, **man-made** point of view and not from God's." said Jesus Christ   also see LAWS

MANAGEMENT   LUKE 16;1-12

Jesus now told this story to his disciples: "A rich man hired an accountant to handle his affairs, but soon a rumor went around that the accountant was thoroughly dishonest.

"So his employer called him in and said, 'What's this I hear about you stealing from me? Get your report in order, for you are dismissed.'"

"The accountant thought to himself. 'Now what? I'm through here and I haven't the strength to go out and dig ditches, and I am too proud to beg? I know just the thing! And then I'll have plenty of friends to take care of me when I leave!

" So he invited each one who owed money to his

MANAGEMENT   LUKE 18;1-12 cont'd
employer to come and discuss the situation, He
asked the first one, ' how much do you owe him?'

'My debt is 850 gallons of olive oil,' the man
replied. 'Yes, here is the contract you signed,' the
accountant told him. 'Tear it up and write another
one for half that much!'

" 'And how much do you owe him?' he asked the
next man. 'A thousand bushels of wheat,' was his
reply. ' Here,' the accountant said, 'take your note
and replace it with one for only 800 bushels!'

" The rich man had to admire the rascal for being
so shrewd. And it is true that the citizens of this
world are more clever in dishonesty than the godly
are. But shall I tell you to act that way, to buy
friendship through cheating? Will this ensure your
entry to an everlasting home in heaven? *No!* For
unless you are honest in the small matters, you
won't be in the large ones. If you cheat even a
little, you won't be honest with greater
responsibilities. And if you are untrustworthy about
worldly wealth, who will trust you with the true
riches of heaven? And if you are not faithful with
other people's money, why should you be entrusted
with money of your own?" said Jesus Christ

MARRIAGE MATTHEW19;4-12

"Don't you read the Scriptures?" he replied. "In
them it is written that at the beginning, God created

MARRIAGE MATTHEW 19;4-12 cont'd
man and woman, and that man should leave his
father and mother and forever unite with his wife.
The two shall become one- no longer two, but one!
And no man may divorce what God has joined
together.

{ "Then why, "they asked, "did Moses say a
man may divorce his wife by merely writing her a
letter of dismissal?}

Jesus replied, "Moses did that in recognition of
your hard and evil hearts, but it was not what God
had originally intended. And I tell you this, that
anyone who divorces his wife, except for
fornication, and marries another commits adultery."

{Jesus' disciples then said to him," If that is how
it is, is it better not to marry?"}

"Not everyone can accept this statement." Jesus
said. Only those who God helps. Some are born
without the ability to **marry,** and some are disabled
by men, and some refuse to **marry** for the sake of
the Kingdom of Heaven. Let anyone who can,
accept my statement." said Jesus Christ

MATTHEW 22; 29-30

But Jesus said, "Your error is caused by your
ignorance of the Scriptures and of God's power! For
in the resurrection there is no **marriage;** everyone is
an angel in Heaven." said Jesus Christ

MARRIAGE   MARK 10;3-12

" What did Moses say about divorce?" Jesus asked them, "And why did he say that? Jesus asked. " I'll tell you why- it was a concession to your hard hearted wickedness. For from the very first He made man and woman to be joined together permanently in **marriage;** therefore a man is to leave his father and mother and he and his wife are to be united so they are no longer two, but one. And no man may separate what God has joined together.

Later when he was alone with his disciples they brought up the subject again.

He told them, " When a man divorces his wife to **marry** someone else, he commits adultery against her. And if a wife divorces her husband and **remarries,** she, too, commits adultery." said Jesus Christ

MARRY/WEDDINGS/END TIMES   MATTHEW 24;38

"The world will be at ease- banquets and parties and **weddings-** just as it was in Noah's time before the sudden coming of the flood; people wouldn't believe what was going to happen until the flood actually arrived and took them all away. So shall my coming be. " said Jesus Christ

LUKE 17; 26-27

" When I return, the world will be as indifferent to God as the people were in Noah's day. They ate

MARRY/WEDDINGS/END
TIMES   LUKE 17; 26-27cont'd

and drank and married- everything just as usual right up to the day Noah went into the ark and the flood came and destroyed them all." said Jesus Christ   LUKE 20; 34-35

Jesus replied, "**Marriage** is for people here on earth, but when those who are counted worthy of being raised from the dead get to Heaven, they do not marry. And they will never die again; in these respects they are like angels, and are sons of God, for they are raised up in a new life from the dead." said Jesus Christ

MARTHA see PRIORITIES

MASTER

MATTHEW10;24-25

"A student is not greater than his teacher. A servant is not greater than his **master**. The student shares his teacher's fate. The servant shares his master's. said Jesus Christ

MATTHEW 23;10

"And don't be called **'Master,'** for only One is your master, even the Messiah." said Jesus Christ

JOHN 13;12-17

After washing their feet, he put on his robe again and sat down and asked. "Do you understand what I was doing? You call me '**Master**' and 'Lord' and you do well to say it is true, And since I am the Lord

MASTER   JOHN 13;12-17cont'd

and Teacher, have washed your feet, you ought to wash each other's feet. I have given you an example to follow; do as I have done to you. How true it is that a servant is not greater than his **master.** Nor the messenger more important than the one who sends him. You know these things-now do them! That is the path of blessing." said Jesus Christ

MASTERS/MONEY

MATTHEW 6;24

" You cannot serve two **masters:** God and money. For you will hate one and love the other, or else the other way around." said Jesus Christ

LUKE 16;13

"For neither you nor anyone else can serve two **masters.** You will hate one and show loyalty to the other, or else the other way around-you will be enthusiastic about one and despise the other. You cannot serve both God and money." said Jesus Christ

MERCY

MATTHEW 5;6-10

"Happy are those who long to be just and good, for they shall be completely satisfied. Happy are the kind and **merciful,** for they shall be shown **mercy.**

MERCY   MATTHEW 5;6-10 cont'd

Happy are those whose hearts are pure for they shall see God. Happy are those who strive for peace-they shall be called the sons of God. Happy are those who are persecuted because they are good, for the Kingdom of Heaven is theirs." said Jesus Christ

MARK. 5;19

" Go home and tell your friends." he told him, "and tell them what wonderful things God has done for you; how **merciful** He has been." said Jesus Christ

LUKE 6;36-38

" Try to show as much compassion as your Father does. Never criticize or condemn-or it will come back on you. Go easy (have **mercy)** on others; then they will do the same for you. For if you give, you will get! Your gift will return to you in full and overflowing measure, pressed down, shaken together to make room for more, and running over. Whatever measure you use to give-large or small-will be used to measure what is given back to you." said Jesus Christ

MERCY/MESSED UP

MATTHEW 9;12-13

"Because people who are well don't need a doctor! It's the sick people who do !"was Jesus' reply. Then he added, "Now go away and learn the meaning of this verse of Scripture,

MERCY/MESSEDUP

MATTHEW 9;12-13 cont'd

" ' It isn't your sacrifices and your gifts I want- I want you to be **merciful.** For I have come to urge sinners, not the self-righteous back to God.'" Said Jesus Christ

MATTHEW 12;7

"But if you had known the meaning of this Scripture verse, 'I want you to be **merciful** more than I want your offerings,' you would have not condemned those that are not guilty." said Jesus Christ

MATTHEW 23;23-24

" Yes, woe upon you Pharisees, and you other religious leaders-hypocrites! For you tithe down to the last mint leaf in your garden, but ignore the important things like justice and **mercy** and faith. Yes, you should tithe, but you shouldn't leave the more important things undone. Blind guides! You strain out a gnat and swallow a camel." said Jesus Christ

See GOOD SAMARITAN

MILLSTONE/ MIRACLES

MARK 9;39-42

38[One of his disciples, John, told him one day, " Teacher, we saw a man using your name to cast out demons; but we told him not to, for he wasn't one of our group."]

MILLSTONE/MIRACLES

MARK 9;39-42 cont'd

"Don't forbid him!" Jesus said. "For no one doing **miracles** in my name will quickly turn against me. Anyone who isn't against us is for us. If anyone as much as gives you a cup of water because you are Christ's-I say this to you solemnly-He won't lose his reward. But if someone causes these little ones who believe in me to Jose faith- it would be better for that man if a huge **millstone** were tied around his neck and he were thrown into the sea" said Jesus Christ

MIRACLES   (see also BREAD, HEALING, LAZARUS)

MATTHEW 7;22

"At the Judgment, many will tell me, 'Lord, Lord, we told others about you and used your name to cast out demons and do many other great **miracles.'** but I will reply, 'You have never been mine. Go away for your deeds are evil." said Jesus Christ   MATTHEW 11;21-24

" Woe to you Chorazin, and woe to you, Bethsaida! For if the **miracles** I did in your streets had been done in wicked Tyre and Sidon their people would have repented Jong ago in shame and humility. Truly, Tyre and Sidon will be better off on Judgment Day than you! And Capemum, though highly honored, shall go down to hell! For if the

MIRACLES (see also BREAD, HEALING, LAZARUS)

MATTHEW 11;21-24 cont'd
marvelous **miracles I** did in you had been done in Sodom, it would still be here today. Truly, Sodom will be better off at Judgment Day than you." said Jesus Christ

MATTHEW 12;39
But Jesus replied, "Only an evil, faithless nation would ask for a **miraculous** sign; and none will be given except what happened to Jonah the prophet! For as Jonah was in the great fish for three days and three nights, so, I, the Messiah, shall be in the heart of the earth for three days and three nights." said Jesus Christ   MATTHEW 24;24
"For false christs shall arise and false prophets, and will do wonderful **miracles** so that if it were, even God's chosen would be deceived. See I have warned you!" said Jesus Christ

MARK 13;22
"For there will be many messiahs and false prophets who will do wonderful **miracles** that would deceive, if possible, even God's children. Take care! I've warned you!" said Jesus Christ

JOHN 4; 48
Jesus asked, "Won't any of you believe in me unless I do more and more miracles? Said Jesus Christ

MIRACLES (see also BREAD, HEALING, LAZARUS)

JOHN 10;25-30,32, 37,38

"I have already told you, and you don't believe me." replied Jesus. The proof is in the **miracles** I do in the name of the Father. But you don't believe me because you are not part of my flock. My sheep recognize my voice, and I know them, and they follow me. I give them eternal life and they shall never perish. No one shall snatch them away from me, for my Father has given them to me, and he is more powerful than anyone else, so no one can kidnap them from me. I and the Father are one."

32 Jesus said, "At God's direction I have done many a **miracle** to help the people. For which one are you killing me?" said Jesus Christ

37-38 "Don't believe me unless I do **miracles** of God. But if I do, believe them even if you don't believe me. Then you will become convinced that the Father is in me and I in the Father." said Jesus Christ   JOHN 14;10-11

"Don't you believe that I am in the Father and the Father is in me? The words I say are not my own but are from my Father who lives in me. Just believe it- that I am in the Father and the Father is in me. Or else believe it because of the mighty **miracles** you have seen me do." said Jesus Christ

MIRACLES (see also BREAD, HEALING
    LAZARUS)

JOHN 15; 24-25

"If I hadn't done such mighty **miracles** among
them they would not be counted guilty. But as it is,
they saw **miracles** and yet they hated both of us- me
and my Father. This has fulfilled what the prophets
said concerning the Messiah, 'They hated me
without reason.'" said Jesus Christ

**** JOHN 20;30 (Jesus did NOT speak
the following words, but they are written and
give reader insight about the record of
miracles.)

30 { Jesus' disciples saw him do many other
miracles besides the ones told about in this book,
but these are recorded so that you will believe he is
the Messiah, the Son of God, and believing in him,
you will have life.}

MISSION   LUKE 4; 18,19 21

"The Spirit of the Lord is upon me; He has
appointed me to preach Good News to the poor; He
sent me to heal the brokenhearted and to announce
to captives they shall be released and the blind shall
see, that the downtrodden shall be freed from their
oppressors, and that God is ready to give blessings
to all who come to Him.

21 Then he added, "These Scriptures came true
today!" said Jesus Christ

MOON
MATTHEW 24;29

"Immediately after the persecution of those days the sun will be darkened and the **moon** will not give light, the stars will seem to fall from the heavens, the powers overshadowing the earth will be convulsed. " said Jesus Christ

MARK 13;24

"After the tribulation ends, then the sun will grow dim and the **moon** will not shine, and the stars will fall- the heavens will convulse." said Jesus Christ

MOUNTAIN/ MUSTARD SEED
MATTHEW 17;17,20-21

"Because of your little faith, "Jesus told them. "For if you had faith even as small as a tiny **mustard seed** you could say to this **mountain,** 'Move!' and it would go far away. Nothing would be impossible." said Jesus Christ

MARK 11;22-25

In reply Jesus said to his disciples. "If you only have faith in God-this is the absolute truth- you can say to this **Mount** of Olives, 'Rise up and fall into the Mediterranean' and your command will be obeyed. All that is required is that you believe and have no doubt! Listen to me! You can pray for *anything* and *if you believe, you have it,* it's yours! But when you pray, first forgive anyone you are holding a grudge against, so that your Father in Heaven will forgive you too. " said Jesus Christ

MOURN   MATTHEW 5;4-5

"Humble men are very fortunate!" he told them, " for the Kingdom of Heaven is given to them. Those who **mourn** are fortunate! For they shall be comforted. The meek and lowly are fortunate! For the whole world belongs to them. " said Jesus Christ   MATTHEW 9;15

" Should the bridegroom's friends **mourn** and go without food while he is still with them?" Jesus asked. "But the time is coming when I will be taken from them. Time enough for them to refuse to eat." said Jesus Christ

MURDER/MURDERER(S)
MATTHEW 5;21-22

"Under the law of Moses, the rule was, ' Do not **murder** or you must die.' But I have added to that rule, and tell you that if you are only *angry,* even in your own home, you are in danger of judgment! If you call your friend an idiot, you are in danger of being brought before the court. And if you curse him, you are in danger of the fires of hell." said Jesus Christ

MATTHEW 15; 19-20

"For from the heart come evil thoughts, **murder,** adultery, fornication, theft, lying and slander. These are what defile: but there is no spiritual defilement from eating without first going through ceremonial hand washing!" said Jesus Christ

MURDER/MURDERER(S)

JOHN 8;42-45

Jesus told them, " If that were so, then you would love me, for I have come to you from God. I am not here on my own, but He sent me. Why can't youunderstand what I am saying? It is because you are prevented from doing so! For you are children of your father the devil and you love the evil things he does. He was a murderer from the beginning and ahater of truth-there is not one iota of truth in him.

When he lies, it is perfectly normal; for he is the father of liars. And so when I tell you the truth, you naturally don't believe it." said Jesus Christ

MUSTARD SEED (also see FAITH and MOUNTAIN)

MATTHEW 13;30-32

" The Kingdom of Heaven is like a tiny **mustard seed** planted in a field. It is the smallest of all **seeds,** but becomes the largest of plants and grows into a tree where birds can find shelter."said Jesus Christ

MARK 4;30-31

Jesus asked, " How can I describe the Kingdom of God? What story shall I use to illustrate it? It is like a tiny **mustard seed**! Though this is one of the smallest of **seeds**, yet it grows to be one of the largest plants, with long branches where birds can build their nests and be sheltered." said Jesus Christ

MUSTARD SEED (also see FAITH and
   MOUNTAIN)

LUKE 13; 18-19

Now he began teaching them again about the
Kingdom of God: "What is the Kingdom like?" he
asked. "how can I illustrate it? It is like a tiny
mustard **seed** planted in a garden soon to grow into
a tall bush, and the birds live among its branches."
said Jesus Christ

LUKE 17;6

"If your faith were only the size of a mustard
seed, "Jesus answered, "it would be large enough
to uproot that mulberry tree over there and send it
hurtling into the sea! Your command would bring
immediate results!" said Jesus Christ

N

NAME   MATTHEW 18;20

"For where two or more gather in my **name**, I
will be right there among them." said Jesus Christ

MATTHEW 28;19

"Therefore go and make disciple in all nations,
baptizing them in the **name** of the Father and of the
Son and the Holy Spirit and teach these new
disciples to obey al the commands I have given you;
and be sure of this- that I am with all the way until
the end of the world." said Jesus Christ

N

NAME   JOHN 5;41-42

"Your approval or disapproval means nothing to me, for I know so well, you don't have God's love within you. I know because I have come to you representing my Father, in His **name,** and you refuse to welcome me, though you readily receive those who aren't sent from Him, but represent only themselves! No wonder you can't believe! For you gladly honor each other, but you don't care about the honor that comes only from God!" said Jesus Christk   JOHN 12;27-28

"Now my soul is deeply troubled. Shall I pray, 'Father save me from what lies ahead?' But that is the very reason I came! Father, bring honor and glory to your **name."** said Jesus Christ

JOHN 14; 12-13

" In solemn truth I tell you, anyone believing in me shall do the same miracles I have done, even greater ones, because I am going to be with my Father. You can ask Him for anything, using my **name** and I will do it for this praise to the Father because of what I, the Son, will do for you. Yes, ask anything using my **name** and I will do it!" said Jesus Christ   JOHN 15;16

" You didn't choose me! I chose you! I appointed you to go and produce lovely fruit always, so that no matter what you ask for from the Father, using my **name,** He will give it to you." said Jesus Christ

NAME   JOHN 16;23

"At that time you won't need to ask me for anything, for you can go directly to the Father and ask Him and He will give you what you ask for because you use my **name.** You haven't tried this before, but begin now. Ask, using my **name,** and you will receive and your cup of joy will overflow." said Jesus Christ

NARROW   MATTHEW 7;13-14

"Heaven can be entered only through a **narrow** gate! The highway to hell is broad, and its gate wide enough for all the multitudes who choose its easy way. But the Gateway to Life is small and the road **narrow** and few will ever find it. " said Jesus Christ

LUKE 13;24

And he replied, "The door to Heaven is **narrow** work hard to get in, for the truth is that many will try to enter but when the head of the house has locked the door, it will be too late. Then if you stand outside knocking and pleading, "Lord , open the door for us,' he will reply, 'I don't know you.' " said Jesus Christ

NATION(S)

MATTHEW 24;14

"And the Good News about the Kingdom shall be preached throughout the whole world, so that all **nations** will hear it and finally the end will come." said Jesus Christ

178 N

NATION(S)   MATTHEW 25;32

"And the **nations** shall be gathered before me. And I will separate the people as a shepherd separates sheep from goats, and place the sheep at my right hand and the goats at my left." said Jesus Christ   MATTHEW 28;19

"Therefore go and make disciples in all **nations** baptizing them in the name of the Father and the Son and the Holy Spirit..." said Jesus Christ
MARK 11;17

He told them, "It is written in the Scriptures, 'My Temple is to be a place of prayer for all **nations,**' but you have turned it into a den of robbers." said Jesus Christ

NATIONS and NEAR
LUKE 21; 25-28

"Then there will be strange events in the skies- warnings, evil omens and portents in the sun, moon and stars ; down on earth **nations** will be in turmoil perplexed by roaring seas and strange tides. The courage of many people will falter because of a fearful fate they see coming upon the earth, for the stability of the very heavens will be broken up. Then the peoples of the earth shall see me, the Messiah, coming in a cloud with power and great glory. So when all these things begin to happen, look up! For your salvation is **near.**" said Jesus Christ

NEAR LUKE 10;8-9

"If a town welcomes you, follow these two rules;
(1) Eat whatever is set before you.

(2) Heal the sick: as you heal them, say, 'The Kingdom of God is very **near** you now.'" said Jesus Christ

NEED(S), NEEDED, NEEDY
MATTHEW 6;1-4,8

"TAKE CARE! Don't do your good deeds publicly, to be admired, for then you will lose your reward from your Father in Heaven. When you give to the **needy,** don't shout about it as the hypocrites do-blowing trumpets in the synagogues and streets to call attention to their acts of charity! I tell you in all earnestness, they have received all the reward they will ever get. But when you do kindness to someone , do it secretly- don't tell your left hand what the right hand is doing. And your Father who knows all your secrets will reward you. " said Jesus Christ

8   "Remember your Father knows exactly what you **need** before you even ask Him!"

MARK 2;17

When Jesus heard what they were saying, he told them, "Sick people **need** the doctor, not the healthy ones! I haven't come to tell the good people to repent, but the bad ones." said Jesus Christ

NEED(S), NEEDED,NEEDY
LUKE 12;30

" All mankind scratches for daily bread, but your heavenly father knows your **needs**. He will always give you what you need from day to day if you will make the Kingdom of God your primary concern. " said Jesus Christ   JOHN 13;10

Jesus replied, " One who has bathed all over **needs** only to have his feet washed to be entirely clean. Now you are clean-but that isn't true of everyone here." said Jesus Christ

NEGLECT (ED   LUKE 11;42

"But woe to you Pharisees! For though you are careful to tithe even to the smallest part of your income, you **neglect** the love and justice of God. You should tithe, yes, but you should not leave these other things undone." said Jesus Christ

NEIGHBOR (S)   MATTHEW 19;19

And Jesus replied, "Don't kill, don't commit adultery, don't steal, don't lie, honor your father and your mother and love your **neighbor** as you love yourself."said Jesus Christ

MARK 12;31

"The second is: 'You must love your **neighbor** as much as yourself. No other commandments are greater than these." said Jesus Christ

LUKE 10;27

"It says, "he replied, "that you must love the

NEIGHBOR (S)   LUKE 10;27 cont'd
Lord your God with all your heart, and with all
your soul, and with all your strength, and all your
mind. And you must love your **neighbor** as much as
you love yourself." said Jesus Christ

NETWORK (description)
           JOHN 15; 1-17
"I am the true Vine and my Father is the Gardener.
He lops off every branch that doesn't produce. And
he prunes those branches that bear fruit for even
larger crops. He has already tended you by pruning
you back for greater strength and usefulness by
means of commands I gave you. For a branch can't
produce fruit when severed from the vine. Nor can
you be fruitful apart from me."
    "Yes. I am the Vine; you are the branches.
Whoever lives in me and I in him shall produce a
crop of fruit. For apart from me you can't do a
thing. If anyone separates from me, he is thrown
away like a useless branch, withers and is gathered
into a pile with the others and burned. But if you
stay in me and obey my commands, you may ask
any request you like, and it will be granted! My true
disciples produce bountiful harvests. This brings
great glory to my Father.
    'I have loved you even as the father has loved
me. Live within my love. When you obey me you
are living in my love, just as I obey the Father and

182 N

NETWORK (description)

JOHN 15;1-17 cont'd

live in His love. I have told you this so you can be filled with joy. Yes, your cup will overflow! I demand that you love each other as much as I love you. And here is how to measure it-the greatest love is shown when a person lays down his life for his friends; and you are my friends if you obey me. I no longer call you slaves (employees); now you are my friends, proved by the fact that I told you everything the Father told me." said Jesus Christ

NEVER   MARK 3;29

"I solemnly declare that any sin of man can be forgiven, even blasphemy against me, but blasphemy against the Holy Spirit can **never** be forgiven, it is an eternal sin. "said Jesus Christ

MARK 4;11-12

He replied, " You are permitted to know some truths about the Kingdom of God that are hidden to those outside the Kingdom:

> 'Though they see and hear, they
> will **never** understand or turn
> to God, or be forgiven for
> their sins.'

But if you can't understand this simple illustration, what will you do about all the others I am going to tell?" said Jesus Christ

NEVER   LUKE 21;33

"I solemnly declare to you that when these things happen, and the end of this age has come. And though all heaven and earth shall pass away, my words will **never** pass away." said Jesus Christ

JOHN 6;35-40

Jesus replied, "I am the Bread of Life. No one coming to me will ever be hungry again. Those believing in me will **never** thirst. But the trouble is, as I have told you before, you haven't believed even though you've seen me. But some will come to me- those the Father has given me- and I will **never, never** reject them." said Jesus Christ

JOHN 10;28

'I give them eternal life and they shall **never** perish. No one shall snatch them away from me. " said Jesus Christ

JOHN 11;26

" He is given eternal life for believing in me and shall **never** perish. Do you believe this, Martha?" said Jesus Christ

NEW   MATTHEW 13;52

Then he added, "Those experts in the Jewish law who are now my disciples have double treasures- for the Old Testament as well as from the **New."** said Jesus Christ

NEW LUKE 22;20

After supper he gave them another glass of wine saying, "This wine is the token of God's **new** agreement to save you- an agreement sealed with the blood I shall pour out to purchase back your souls." said Jesus Christ

JOHN 13;34

"And so I am giving a **new** commandment to you now- love each other as much as I love you. Your strong love for each other will prove to the world you are my disciples."said Jesus Christ

NONE MATTHEW 12;39-40

But Jesus replied, "Only an evil faithless nation would ask for further proof; and **none** will be given except what happened to Jonah the prophet! For as Jonah was in the great fish for three days and three nights, so I, the Messiah, shall be in the heart of the earth three days and three nights." said Jesus Christ

JOHN 17;9-12

" My plea is not for the world but for those You have given me because they belong to You. And all of them, since they are mine, belong to You; and You have given them back to me with everything else of Yours, *so they are my glory!* Now I am leaving the world, leaving them behind, and coming to You. Holy father keep them in your care-all those You have given me- so that they will be united just as we are, with **none** missing. During my

NONE   JOHN 17; 9-12 cont'd

"time here I have kept safe within your family all of these that you gave me. I guarded them so that **no one** perished, except the son of hell as the Scriptures foretold." said Jesus Christ

NOW   JOHN 5; 25

"And I solemnly declare that the time is coming-in fact it is here **now,** when the dead shall hear my voice-the voice of the Son of God-and those who listen shall live. The Father has life in Himself, and has granted His Son to have life in himself, and to judge the sins of all mankind because he is the Son of Man. Don't be so surprised! Indeed the time is coming when all the dead in their graves shall hear the voice of God's Son and shall rise again-those who have done good, to eternal life; and those who have continued in evil, to judgment." said Jesus Christ

JOHN 13;18-19

"I am not saying these things to all of you; I know so well each one of you I chose. The Scripture declares. 'One who eats supper with me will betray me,' and this will come true. I tell you this **now** so when it happens, you will believe in me." said Jesus Christ

JOHN 13;36

And Jesus replied, "You can't go with me **now;** but you will follow me later." said Jesus Christ

NOW   JOHN 16;12

"Oh, there is so much more I want to tell you, but you can't understand it **now.**" said Jesus Christ

NULLIFY   MATTHEW 15;5-6

" But you say, 'Even if your parents are in need, you may give their support money to the church instead. And so by your man-made rule, you **nullify** a direct command of God to honor and care for your parents." said Jesus Christ

NUMBER (ED)   LUKE 12;6-7

"What is the price of five sparrows? A couple of pennies? Not much more than that. Yet God does not forget a single one of them. And He knows the **number** of hairs on your head! Never fear, you are far more valuable to Him than a whole flock of sparrows." said Jesus Christ

NURSING   LUKE 21;22-23

"For those will be the days of God's judgment, and the words of the ancient Scriptures written by the prophets will be abundantly fulfilled. Woe to expectant mothers in those days and those with tiny **nursing** babies. For there will be great distress upon this nation and wrath upon the people. " said Jesus Christ

OBEY   MATTHEW 19;17

"When you call me good you are calling me God," Jesus replied, "for God alone is truly good. But to answer your question, you can get to Heaven if you **obey** the commandments." said Jesus Christ

MATTHEW 29;19-20

"Therefore go and make disciples in all nations, baptizing them in the name of the Father, the Son and the Holy Spirit, and then teach these new disciples to **obey** all the commands I have given you; and be sure of this- I am with you always until the end of the world." said Jesus Christ

LUKE 11;28

He replied, " Yes, but even more blessed are all who hear the Word of God and **obey** it." said Jesus Christ   JOHN 14; 15,21

15"If you love me, **obey** me; and I will ask the Father and He will give you another Comforter, and he will never leave you. He is the Holy Spirit, the Spirit who leads to all truth. The world at large cannot receive him, for it isn't looking for him and doesn't recognize him. But you do, for he lives with you now and someday shall be in you, "said Jesus Christ

21 "The one who **obeys** me is the one who loves me; and because he loves me, my Father will love him; and I will too, and I will reveal myself to him." said Jesus Christ

188 O

OBEY JOHN 14; 24-26

" Anyone who doesn't **obey** me doesn't love me. And remember, I am not making up this answer to your question! It is the answer given to me by the Father who sent me. I am telling you these things now while I am still with you. But when the Father sends the Comforter instead of me- and by the Comforter I mean the Holy Spirit- he will teach you much, as well as remind you of everything else I have told you." said Jesus Christ

OFFER /OFFERING(S)
MATTHEW 5; 23-24

" So if you are standing before the altar in the Temple **offering** sacrifice to God, and suddenly you remember that a friend has something against you, leave your sacrifice there beside the altar and go apologize and be reconciled to him, and then come and **offer** your sacrifice to God.." said Jesus Christ

ONE MARK 10;7-9

" For from the very first He made man and woman to be joined together permanently in marriage; therefore and man is to leave his father and mother, and he and his wife are united so that they are no longer two but **one.** And no man may separate what God has joined together." said Jesus Christ

MARK 10;21

Jesus felt genuine love for this man as he looked at him. "You lack only **one** thing," he told him,

ONE   MARK 10;21 cont'd

"go and sell all you have and give the more to the poor-and you shall have treasure in Heaven-and come, follow me." said Jesus Christ

[Then the man's face fell, and he went sadly away, for he was very rich.]

MARK 12; 29-30

Jesus replied, "The **one** that says, 'Hear, O Israel! The Lord our God is the **one** and only God. And you must love Him with all your heart and soul and mind and strength." said Jesus Christ

LUKE 10;42

But the Lord said to her, "Martha, dear friend, you are so upset over all these details! There is really only **one** thing worth being concerned about. Mary has discovered it-I won't take that away from her!" said Jesus Christ   JOHN 3;16-17

"For God loved the world so much that He gave His **one** and only Son so that anyone who believes in him shall not perish but have eternal life. God did not send His Son into the world to condemn it, but to save it." said Jesus Christ

JOHN 10;16

"I have other sheep, too, in another fold. I must bring them also. They will heed my voice; there will be **one** flock with **one** Shepherd."said Jesus Christ

JOHN 10;30

"I and the Father are **one**. "said Jesus Christ

190   O

ONE AGAINST ONE
MATTHEW 18;15-18

" If **one** brother sins **against** you, go to him privately with his fault. If he listens and confesses it, you won back a brother. But if not, then take one or two others with you and go back to him again proving everything you say by these witnesses. If he still refuses to listen, take your case to the church, and the verdict favors you, but he won't accept it, then the church should excommunicate him. And I tell you whatever you bind on earth is bound in Heaven, and whatever you free on earth will be freed in Heaven. " said Jesus Christ

ONE PERSON   LUKE 15;7

"Well, in the same way Heaven will be happier over **one lost sinner** who returns to God than over ninety-nine others who haven't strayed away!" said Jesus Christ

OPEN (ED)   MATTHEW 13;35

" I will **open** my mouth in parables; I will explain mysteries hidden since the beginning of time." said Jesus Christ   LUKE 11;9-10

"And so it is with prayer-keep on asking and you will keep on getting; keep on looking and you will keep on finding; knock and the door will be **opened**. Everyone who asks, receives; all who seek, find and the door is **opened** to everyone who knocks" said Jesus Christ

OPPRESSED/ OPPRESSORS
LUKE 4;19-19

"The Spirit of the Lord is upon me; He has appointed me to preach the Good News to the poor; He has sent me to heal the broken hearted and to announce to captives they shall be released and the blind shall see, that the **downtrodden (oppressed)** shall be freed from their **oppressors** and that God is ready to give blessing to all who come to Him." said Jesus Christ

ORPHANS   JOHN 14;18

"No, I will not abandon you or leave you as **orphans** in the storm- I will be gone from the world, but I will still be present with you. For I will live again- and you will too. When I come back to life again, you will know that I am in my Father and you are in me, and I in you." said Jesus Christ

OTHER(S)
MATTHEW 7;2

"For **others** will treat you as you treat them." said Jesus Christ

MATTHEW 7;12

"Do for **others** what you want them to do for you. This is the teaching of the laws of Moses in a nutshell." said Jesus Christ

LUKE 6;31

"Treat **others** as you want them to treat you." said Jesus Christ

OTHER (S)   LUKE I 7;34-36

"That night two men will be asleep in the same room. One will be taken and the **other** left. Two women will be working together at household tasks; one will be taken and the **other** left; so it will be with men working in the fields." said Jesus Christ

OVERCOME   MATTHEW 16;18

" You are Peter, a stone: and upon this rock I will build my church and the powers of hell shall not **overcome** it." said Jesus Christ

JOHN 16;33

"I have told you this so that you will have peace of heart and mind. Here on earth you will have many trials and sorrows; but cheer up, for I have **overcome** the world." said Jesus Christ

OVERFLOW (see JOY) LUKE 6;45

"A good man produces good deeds from a good heart. An evil man produces evil deeds from his hidden wickedness. Whatever is in your heart **overflows** into your speech." said Jesus Christ

OVERWHELMED   MATTHEW 26;38

"My soul is **overwhelmed** with horror and sadness to the point of death...stay here...stay awake with me." said Jesus Christ

OWN   JOHN 7;16

So Jesus said to them ."I'm not teaching you my **own** thoughts, but those of God who sent me." said Jesus Christ

OWN   JOHN 10;18

"The Father loves me because I lay down my life that I may have it back again. No one can kill me without my consent- but I lay it down on my **own** accord. For I have the right and the power to lay it down when I want to and also the right and the power to take it again. For the Father has given me this right." said Jesus Christ

OWNER   MATTHEW 24;43

"Just the **owner** of the house can prevent trouble from thieves by keeping watch for them, so you can avoid trouble by always being ready for my unannounced return." said Jesus Christ

P

PAGAN   MATTHEW 6;7-8

"Don't recite the same prayer over and over as the **pagans** do, who think prayers are answered only by repeating them again and again. Remember your Father knows exactly what you need before you ask Him."said Jesus Christ

MATTHEW 6;31-32

" So don't worry about having enough food and clothing. Why be like the **pagans?** For they take pride in all these things and are deeply concerned about them. Father already knows perfectly well that

PAGAN   MATTHEW 6;31-32 cont'd

you need them and He will give them to you if you give Him first place in your life." said Jesus Christ

PARABLES   MATTHEW 13;35

"For it had been prophesied, "I will talk in **parables;** I will explain mysteries hidden since the beginning of time.'" said Jesus Christ

LUKE 8;10

He replied, "God has granted you to know the meaning of these **parables,** for they tell a great deal about the Kingdom of God. But these crowds hear the words and do not understand, just as ancient the prophets predicted." said Jesus Christ

PARTYING   MATTHEW 24;45-51

"Are you a wise and faithful servant of the Lord? Have I given you the task of managing my household, to feed my children day by day? Blessings on you if l return and find you faithfully doing your work. I will put such faithful ones in charge of everything I own.

"But if you are evil and say to yourself, 'My Lord won't be coming for a while, and begin oppressing your fellow servants and **partying** and getting drunk, your Lord will arrive unannounced and unexpected and severely whip you and send you off to the judgment of the hypocrites. There will be weeping and gnashing of the teeth." said Jesus Christ

PEACE MATIHEW 5;9

"Happy are those who strive for **peace**- they shall be called the true sons of God."

MATTHEW 10;34-38

" Don't imagine that I came to bring **peace** to the earth! No, rather, a sword. I have come to set man against his father and daughter against her mother, and a daughter-in-law against her mother-in-law- a man's worst enemies will be right in his own home! If you love your father and mother more than you love me, you are not worthy of being mine; if you love your son or your daughter more than you love me, you are not worthy of being mine. If you refuse to take up your cross and follow me, you are not worthy of being mine." said Jesus Christ

MARK. 9;50

"Live in **peace** with each other." said Jesus Christ LUKE7;50

A Jesus said to the woman, "Go in **peace,** your faith has saved you." said Jesus Christ

LUKE 19;42-44

"Eternal **peace** was within your reach and you turned it down," he wept, "and now it is too late. Your enemies will pile up earth against your walls and encircle you and close in upon you, and crush you to the ground, and your children with you; your enemies will not leave one stone upon another- for you have rejected the opportunity God has given

196

P

you." said Jesus Christ

JOHN 14;27

"I am leaving you a gift-**peace** of mind and heart! And the peace I give is not fragile like the **peace** the world gives. So don't be troubled or afraid." said Jesus Christ

JOHN 16;33

"I have told you all this so that you will **peace** of heart and mind. Here on Earth you will have many trials and sorrows; but cheer up, for I have overcome the world." said Jesus Christ

PERFECT   MATTHEW 19;21

Jesus told them, " If you want to be **perfect,** go and sell everything you have and give it to the poor, and you will have treasuré in Heaven; come and follow me." said Jesus Christ

PERISH   LUKE 13;3

"And don't you realize that you also will **perish** unless you leave your evil ways and turn to God? " said Jesus Christ

JOHN 3;16

" For God so loved the world that He gave His only Son so that anyone who believes in him shall not **perish** but have eternal life." said Jesus Christ

JOHN 19; 28-30

"I give them eternal life and they shall never **perish**. No one can snatch them away from me, for

PERISH JOHN 10;28-30 cont'd
my Father has given them to me, and He is more
powerful than anyone else, so none can kidnap them
from me. I and the Father are one." said Jesus Christ

PERSECUTE, (D), PERSECUTION
MATTHEW 5;10-12

"Happy are those who are **persecuted** for the
Kingdom of Heaven is theirs. When you are reviled
and **persecuted** and lied about because you are my
followers-wonderful! Be happy about it! Be very
glad! For a tremendous award awaits you up in
heaven. And remember, ancients prophets were
persecuted too." said Jesus Christ

MATTHEW 5;44

"But I say, ' Love your enemies! Pray for those
who **persecute** you!" said Jesus Christ

MATTHEW 13;20-21

"The shallow rocky soil represents the heart of a
man who hears the message with great joy, but he
doesn't have much depth in his life, and the seeds
don't root very deeply, and after a while when
trouble comes and **persecution** begins because of
his beliefs, his enthusiasm fades and he drops out."
said Jesus Christ

LUKE 21;12

"But before all this occurs, there will be a time
of special **persecution,** and you will be dragged into
synagogues and prisons and before kings and

PERSECUTION   LUKE 21;12 cont'd
governors for my name sake. But as a result, the
Messiah will be widely known and honored." said
Jesus Christ

JOHN 15;20

"Do you remember what I told you? A slave isn't
greater than his master! So since they **persecuted**
me, they will **persecute** you. And if they listened to
me, they will listen to you." said Jesus Christ

PETER   (at the Heaven's gate symbolism)

MATTHEW 16;18

"You are **Peter,** a stone; upon this rock I will
build my church; and all the powers of hell shall not
prevail against it. And I will give you the keys to the
Kingdom of Heaven; whatever doors you lock on
Earth shall be locked in Heaven; and whatever
doors you open shall be open in heaven!" said Jesus
Christ

PLACE   JOHN 14;2

"Let not your heart be troubled. You are trusting
God, now trust in me. There are many homes up
where my Father lives, and I am going to prepare a
place for your coming." said Jesus Christ

PLEASURES   LUKE 8;14

"The seed among the thorns represents those
who listen and believe God's words but whose faith
afterwards is choked out by worry and riches and
the responsibilities and **pleasures** of life. And so

PLEASURES   LUKE 8;14cont'd

they are never able to help anyone else believe the Good News" said Jesus Christ

POOR   (see also **PERFECT**)

MATTHEW 1;5

" ....and tell him about me preaching the Good News to the **poor.** Then give them this message, 'Blessed are those who don't doubt me." said Jesus Christ

LUKE 4;18

"The Spirit of the Lord is upon me; He has appointed me to preach the Good News to the **poor."** said Jesus Christ

LUKE 6;20

Then he turned to his disciples and said, " What happiness there is for you who are **poor,** the Kingdom of God is yours." said Jesus Christ

JOHN 12;8

Jesus replied, " Let her alone. She did this in preparation for my burial. You can always help the **poor,** but I won't be with you very long." said Jesus Christ

POPULAR, POPULARITY (Social Status)

JOHN 5;41-44

" Your approval or disapproval means nothing to me, for as I know so well, you don't have God's love within you. I know because I have come to you representing my Father and you refuse to welcome

POPULAR, POPULARITY (Social Status)
JOHN 5;41-44 cont'd
 me, though you readily enough receive those who
aren't sent from Him, but represent only
themselves! No wonder you can't believe! For you
gladly honor each other, but you don't care about
the honor that comes from the only God." said Jesus
Christ

POWER (also see LORD'S PRAYER and
CHRIST'S PRAYERS)
MATTHEW 22;29-30
 "Your error is caused by your ignorance of the
Scriptures and God's **power!**" said Jesus Christ
MATTHEW 24;30
 "And the last signal of my coming will appear in
the heavens and there will be deep mourning all
around the earth. And the nations of the world will
see me arrive in the clouds of heaven, with **power**
and great glory." said Jesus Christ
MARK 13;26-27
 "Then all of mankind will see me, the Messiah,
coming in the clouds with great **power** and glory.
And I will send out the angels to gather together my
chosen ones from all over the world-from the
farthest bounds of earth and heaven." said Jesus
Christ
LUKE 8;46
 "No, it was someone who deliberately touched

POWER   LUKE 8;46 cont'd

me, for I felt the healing **power** go out from me"
said Jesus Christ

LUKE 10;19-20

"And I have given you authority over the **power**
of the enemy, and to walk among serpents and
scorpions and to crush them. Nothing shall injure
you! However, the important thing is not that
demons obey you, but that your names are registered
as citizens of heaven." said Jesus Christ

LUKE 21;27

"Then the peoples of the earth will see me
coming in a cloud with **power** and glory." said
Jesus Christ

LUKE 24;49

"And now I will send the Holy Spirit upon you,
just as my Father promised. Don't begin telling
others yet- stay here in the city until the Holy spirit
comes and fills you with **power** from Heaven." said
Jesus Christ   JOHN 19;11

" You would have no **power** at all over me unless
it were given to you from above. So those that
brought me here have the greater sin." said Jesus
Christ

PRACTICE   (see also HYPOCRITES,OBEY)

MATTHEW 7;24-25

" All who listen to my instructions and put them
into **practice** are wise, like a man who builds his

PRACTICE (also see HYPOCRITES, OBEY)

MATTHEW 7;24-25 cont'd

house on solid rock. Though the rain comes in torrents, and the floods rise and the storm winds beat against his house, it won't collapse for it is built on rock." said Jesus Christ

MATTHEW 23;2-5

" You would think these Jewish leaders and Pharisees were Moses, the way they keep making up new laws! And of course, you should obey their every whim! It may be all right to do what they say, but above anything else, don't follow their example! For they don't **practice what they preach.** They load you with impossible demands that they themselves don't even try to keep. Everything they do is for show." said Jesus Christ

PRAISE   MATTHEW 5;15-16

"Don't hide your light! Let it shine for all; let your good deeds show for all to see, so that they will **praise** your heavenly Father." said Jesus Christ

MATTHEW 21;16

"Don't you ever read the Scriptures? For they say, 'Even the little babies shall **praise** Him!" said Jesus Christ

PRAY,PRAYER (S) (also see LORD'S PRAYER

and CHRIST'S PRAYERS)

MATTHEW 6: 5-6

"And now about **prayer.** When you **pray,** don't

P 203

PRAY,PRAYERS (see also LORD'S
PRAYER and CHRIST'S
PRAYERS)

MATTHEW 6;5-6 cont'd

be like hypocrites who pretend to **pray** publicly on
street comers and synagogues where everyone can
see them. Truly, that is all the reward they will ever
get. But when you **pray,** go away by yourself, all
alone, and shut the door behind you and **pray** to
your Father, who knows your secrets and will
reward you." said Jesus Christ

MATTHEW 6;7-8

"Don't recite the same **prayer** over and over as
the heathen do, who think their **prayers** are only
answered by repeating them again and again.
Remember your Father knows exactly what you
need even before you ask Him!" said Jesus Christ

PREACH (ED) (ING)

(see also GOOD NEWS,PRACTICE, POOR)

MATTHEW 10;7

"As you go, **preach** this message, that the
Kingdom of Heaven is near." said Jesus Christ

MARK.13;10

" This is your opportunity to **preach** the Good
News. And the Good News must be **preached** to
every nation before the end time finally comes."
said Jesus Christ

PREACH (ING) (ED)
(also see GOOD NEWS, PRACTICE, POOR)
LUKE 24;46-48

"Yes, it was written long ago that the Messiah must suffer and die and rise again from the dead on the third day; and that the message of salvation should be taken from Jerusalem and preached to all the nations: there is forgiveness of sins for all those who turn to me. *You have seen these prophecies come true.* " said Jesus Christ

PREPARE   MATTHEW 11;10

"Yes, he is more than just a prophet. For John is the man mentioned in the Scriptures-a messenger to precede me, to announce my coming and prepare people to receive me." said Jesus Christ

MATTHEW 25;34

"Then, I, the King, shall say to those at my right, 'Come, blessed of my Father. Into the Kingdom prepared for you since the founding of the world.'" said Jesus Christ   JOHN 14;2

"There are many homes up there where my Father lives, and I am going to prepare them for your coming." said Jesus Christ

PRESENCE   JOHN 8;38

" I am telling you what I saw in the presence of my Father. But you are following the advice of *your* father." said Jesus Christ

P   205

PRESENCE   JOHN 17;5

"And now, Father, reveal my glory as I stand in your **presence**, the glory we shared before the world began." said Jesus Christ

PRETEND   LUKE 7; (29-30) 31-32

{And all who heard John preach-even the most wicked of them-agreed that God's requirements were right, and they were baptized by him. All, that is except the Pharisees and the teachers of Moses' Law. They rejected God's plan for them and refused baptism by John.}

"What can I say about such men? "Jesus asked. "With what shall I compare? They are like a group of children who complain to their friends. 'You don't like to play **pretend** "wedding" and 'You don't like to play pretend "funeral!" For John the Baptist used to go without food and never took a drop of liquor all his life and you said, 'He must be crazy!' But if I eat my food and drink my wine and you say, 'What a glutton Jesus is! And he drinks! And he has the lowest sort of friends.' But I am sure you can always justify your inconsistencies." said Jesus Christ

PRINCE   JOHN 12;31-32

"" The time of judgment for the world has come-and the time when Satan, the **prince** of this world, will be cast out. And when I am lifted up onto the cross, I will draw everyone to me." said Jesus Christ

P

PRINCE   JOHN 14;30-31

"I don't have much more time to talk to you, for the evil **prince** of this world approaches. He has no power over me, but I will freely do what the Father requires of me so that the world will know that I love the Father. Come, let's get going." said Jesus Christ   JOHN 16;9-11

" The world's sin is unbelief in me; there is righteousness available because I go to the Father and you shall see me no more; the **prince** of this world has been condemned." said Jesus Christ

PRIORITIES   LUKE 10;41-42

But the Lord said to her, "Martha, dear friend, you are so upset over all of these details! There is really only one thing that is worth being concerned about. Mary has discovered it-and I won't take that away from her." said Jesus Christ

PROMISE (S)(ED)   LUKE 24;49

"And now I will send the Holy Spirit upon you, just as my Father **promised.** Don't begin telling others yet-stay here in the city until the Holy Spirit comes and fills you with power from heaven. "said Jesus Christ

PROPHECY,PROPHESIES,PROPHESIED
PROPHETS   MATTHEW 5;17-19

" Don't misunderstand why I have come here-it isn't to cancel the laws of Moses and the warnings of the **prophets.** No, I have come to fulfill them

P   207

PROPHECY, **PROPHESIES,PROPHESIED**
PROPHETS   MATTHEW 5;17-19 cont'd
and make them all come true. With all the
earnestness I have I say: Every law in the Book will
continue until its purpose is achieved and so if
anyone breaks even the least commandment, and
teaches others to, he shall be least in the Kingdom
of Heaven. But those who teach God's laws *and
obey them* shall be great in the Kingdom of
Heaven." said Jesus Christ

                    MATTHEW 7;15
  "Beware of false **prophets** who come disguised
as harmless sheep, but are wolves and will tear you
apart. You can detect them by the way they act, just
like you can identify a tree by its fruit." said Jesus
Christ   MATTHEW 7;22-23
  "At the Judgment, many will tell me, 'Lord, Lord
did we not **prophecy** in your name and use your
name to cast out demons and do many other great
miracles? But I will reply, 'You have never been
mine. Go away for your deeds are evil.'" said Jesus
Christ

                    MATTHEW 10;41
  "If you welcome a **prophet** because he is a man
of God, you will be given the same reward a
prophet gets. And if you welcome good and godly
men because of their godliness, you will be given a
reward like theirs" said Jesus Christ

P

PROPHECY, PROPHESIES,PROPHESIED
PROPHETS   MATTHEW 11;9-10

"Or a **prophet** of God? Yes, he is more than just a **prophet.** For John the Baptist is the man mentioned in the Scriptures to precede me. To announce my coming and prepare people to receive me." said Jesus Christ

MATTHEW 22;37-40

Jesus replied, "Love the Lord with all you heart, soul and mind. This is the first and greatest commandment. The second most important is 'Love your neighbor as much as you love yourself.' all the other commandments and all the demands of the **prophets** stem from these two laws. And are fulfilled if you obey them. Keep only these and you will find that you obey all others," said Jesus Christ

MATTHEW 24;23-25

"Then if anyone tells you. ' The Messiah has arrived at such and such a place, or has appeared here or there,' don't believe it! For false Christs shall arise and false **prophets** will do wonderful miracles so that if it were possible God's chosen ones would be deceived. See, I have warned you." said Jesus Christ   LUKE 4;24

"But solemnly I declare to you that no **prophet** is accepted in his own home town." said Jesus Christ

LUKE 6; 22-24

"What happiness it is when others hate you and

PROPHECY, PROPHESIES,PROPHESIED
PROPHETS   LUKE 6; 22-24 cont'd

exclude you and insult you and smear your name because you are mine! When that happens, rejoice! Yes, leap for joy! For you will have a great reward waiting for you in heaven. And you will be in good company-the ancient **prophets** were treated that way too!" said Jesus Christ

LUKE 10; 23-24

Then, turning to the twelve disciples he said quietly, "How privileged you are to see what you have seen. Many a **prophet** and king of old has longed for these days, to see and hear what you have seen and heard!" said Jesus Christ

LUKE 11;46-49

"Yes," Jesus said, "the same horrors await you! For you crush men beneath impossible religious demands- demands that you yourselves would never think of trying to keep. Woe to you! For you are exactly like your ancestors who killed the **prophets** long ago. Murderers! You agree with your fathers that what they did was right- you would have done the same yourselves.

"This is what God says about you: ' I will send **prophets** and apostles to you, and you will kill some and chase away others'" said Jesus Christ

LUKE 16;31

"But Abraham said, If they won't listen to Moses

PROPHEC(S)Y, PROPHESIES,PROPHESIED
PROPHETS   LUKE 16;31 cont'd
and the **prophets,** they won't listen even though
someone rises from the dead;'" said Jesus Christ
                    LUKE 24;25-26
   Then Jesus said to them, " You are such foolish,
foolish people! You find it so hard to believe all that
the **prophets** wrote in the Scriptures! Wasn't it
clearly predicted by the **prophets** that the Messiah
would have to suffer all of these things before
entering his glory?" said Jesus Christ
                    LUKE 24; 44-45
   Then he said, " When I was with you before,
don't you remember my telling you that everything
written about me by Moses and the **prophets** and in
Psalms must all come true?" {Then he opened their
minds to understand the last of these many
Scriptures}   said Jesus Christ

PROSPEROUS /PROPHETS
                    LUKE 6;24-26
   "But , oh, the sorrows that await the rich. For
they have only their happiness down here. They are
fat and **prosperous** now, but a time of awful hunger
is before them. And what sadness is ahead for those
that praised by crowds- for false **prophets** have
always been praised." said Jesus Christ

PROTECT,(ED) (S) PROTECTION
JOHN 17;6-26

"I have told these men all about You. They were in the world, but then You gave them to me. Actually they were always Yours and You gave them to me; and they have obeyed You. Now that everything I have is a gift for You, for I have passed them the commands You gave me; they accepted them and know of certainty that I came to earth from You, and they believe you sent me.

"My plea is not for the world but for those You have given me because they belong to You. And all of them, since they are mine, belong to You; and You have given them back to me with everything else of Yours, *and so they are my glory!* Now I am leaving the world and leaving them behind, and coming to You. Holy Father **keep them in Your own care**-all of those You have given me- so that they will be united just as we are with none missing. During my time here **I have kept safe within Your family** all of these You gave me. I guarded them so that no one perished, except the son of hell as Scriptures foretold.

"And now I am coming to You. I have told them many things while I was with them so that they would be filled with my joy. I have given them Your commands. And the world hates them because they don't fit in with it, just as I don't. I'm not

212 P

PROTECT, (ED) (S) PROTECTION
JOHN 17;6-26 cont'd
asking You to take them out of the world, but **keep them safe** from Satan's power. They are not part of this world any more than I am. Make them pure and Holy through teaching of Your Word of Truth. As You sent me into the world, I am sending them into the world, and I consecrate myself to meet their need for growth in truth and holiness.

"I am not praying for these alone but also for future believers who will come to me because of the testimony of these. My prayer for them is that they will be of one heart and mind just as You and I are, Father- that just as You are in me and I am in You, so they will be in us and the world will believe You sent me.

" I have given them the glory You gave me- the glorious unity of being one, as we are- I in them and You in me, all being perfected into one- so that the world will know You sent me and will understand that You love them as much as You love me. Father I want them with me-those that You have given me-so they can see my glory because You loved me before the world began!

"O righteous Father, the world doesn't know You, but I do; and these disciples You sent me. And I have revealed You to them and will keep on

P

213

JOHN 17;6-26 cont'd

PROTECT, (ED) (S) PROTECTION

revealing You so that the mighty love You have for me may be in them, and I in them" said and prayed Jesus Christ

PUNISH, (ED), (MENT)

MATTHEW 25;45-46

"And I will answer, 'When you refused to help the least of these my brother, you were refusing to help me.'

"And they shall go away into eternal **punishment;** but the righteous into everlasting life." said Jesus Christ

MARK 12;38-40

"Beware of the teachers of religion! For they love to wear robes of the rich and scholarly, and have everyone bow to them as they walk through the markets. They love to sit in the best seat in the synagogues, and at places of honor at banquets-but they shamelessly cheat widows out of their homes and then to cover up the kind of men they really are, they pretend to be pious by praying long prayers in public. Because of this, their **punishment** will be greater." said Jesus Christ

P

PUNISH, (ED), (MENT)
LUKE 12;48

"But anyone who is not aware that he is doing wrong will be **punished** only lightly. Much is required from those who much is given, for their responsibility is greater." said Jesus Christ

LUKE 21;22-24

"For those will be days of God's judgment, and the words of **punishment** of the ancient Scriptures written by the prophets will be abundantly fulfilled. Woe to expectant mothers in those days, and those with tiny babies. For there will be great distress upon this nation and wrath upon its people." said Jesus Christ

PURE   MATTHEW 5;8

"Blessed are those whose hearts are **pure,** for they shall see God." said Jesus Christ

Q

QUESTIONS?   MARK 11;29,30,33

Jesus replied, "I'll tell you if you answer one **question!** What about John the Baptist? Was he sent by God or not? Answer me!"

[they couldn't]

33 To which Jesus replied, "Then I won't answer your **question** either!" said Jesus Christ

QUIET   MARK 4;39

Then he rebuked the wind and said to the sea, " **Quiet** down!" {And the wind fell and there was great calm.} said Jesus Christ

MARK 6;31-32

Then Jesus suggested, " Come with me by yourselves to a **quiet** spot." said Jesus Christ

LUKE 20;40

He replied, "If they keep **quiet,** the stones along the road will burst into cheers!" said Jesus Christ

R

RAIN   MATTHEW 5;45

"In that way you will be acting as true sons of your Father in Heaven. For He gives His sunlight to both the evil and the good, and sends **rain** on the just and the unjust. If you love only those who loveyou, what good is that? Even scoundrels do thatmuch. If you are friendly only to your friends, howare you different from anyone else? Even heathen do that. But you are to be perfect even as your Father in Heaven is perfect." said Jesus Christ

MATTHEW 7;24-25

" All those who listen to my instructions and follow them are wise, like a man who builds his house on solid rock. Though the **rain** comes in torrents, and floods rise and the storm winds beat

RAIN   MATTHEW 7; 24-25 cont'd
against his house, it won't collapse, for it is built on rock." said Jesus Christ

RAISE, (ED) (ES), RISE (N),
MATTHEW 17;23

{One day while they were still in Galilee,} Jesus told them, "I am going to be betrayed into the power of those who kill me, and on the third day I will be **raised** to life again." said Jesus Christ

LUKE 7;21-23

" Go back to John and tell him all that you've seen and heard here today: how those who were blind can see. The lame are walking without a limp. The lepers are completely healed. The deaf can hear again. The dead are **raised** back to life. And the poor are hearing the Good News. And tell him,' Blessed is the one who does not lose his faith in me.'" said Jesus Christ

LUKE 16;31

"But Abraham said, 'If they won't listen to Moses and the prophets, they won't even listen even though someone **rises** from the dead.'" said Jesus Christ   LUKE 18;32-33

"I will be handed over to the Gentiles to be mocked and treated shamefully and spat upon, and lashed and killed. And on the third day, I will **rise** again." said Jesus Christ

RAISE, (ED) (ES), RISE (N),

JOHN 2;19-22

"All right!, Jesus replied, "This is the miracle I will do for you: Destroy this sanctuary and in three days I will **rise** it up!" said Jesus Christ
20-22 { "What!" they exclaimed. "It took us forty six years to build this Temple, and you can do it in three days?" } [But by "this sanctuary" he meant his body. After he came back to life again, the disciples remembered him saying this and realized that what he had quoted from the Scriptures really did refer to him, and had all come true!]

JOHN 5;19-21

Jesus replied, " The Son of God can do nothing by himself. He does only what he sees the Father doing, and in the same way. For the Father loves the Son and tells him everything He is doing: and the Son will do far more awesome miracles than this man's healing. He will even **raise** from the dead anyone he wants to just as the Father does." said Jesus Christ   JOHN 5;28-29
"Don't be so surprised! Indeed the time is coming when all the dead in their graves shall hear the voice of God's Son and shall rise again-those who have done good, to eternal life; and those who have continued in evil to judgment." said Jesus Christ

JOHN 6;39

"And it is the will of God, that I should not lose

RAISE, (ED) (ES), RISE (N),

JOHN 6;39 cont'd

even one of all those He has given me, but I should **raise** them to eternal life on the Last Day." said Jesus Christ

RANSOM   MATTHEW 20;28

" Your attitude must be like my own, for I, the Messiah, did not come to be served, but to serve and to give my life as **ransom** for many," said Jesus Christ

MARK 10;45

"For even I, the Messiah, am not here to be served, but to help others, and give my life as **ransom** for many." said Jesus Christ

RAPTURE   MATTHEW 24;37-42

" The world will be at ease- banquets and parties and weddings-just as it was in Noah's time before the sudden coming of the flood; people wouldn't believe what was going to happen until the flood actually arrived and took them all away. So shall my coming be.

"Two men will be working together in the fields, and **one will be taken, the other left.** Two women will be going about their household tasks; **one will be taken, the other left.**

" So be prepared, for you don't know what day your Lord is coming." said Jesus Christ

R   219

READER   MATTHEW 24; 15-18

"So, when you see the horrible thing told about by Daniel standing in the Holy place, let the **reader** understand, then those in Judea must flee into the Judean hills. Those on their porches must not even go back inside and pack before they flee. Those in the fields must not even return home for theirclothes." said Jesus Christ

MARK 13;14

"When you see the horrible thing standing in the Temple-**reader** pay attention!-flee, if you can to theJudean hills. Hurry! If you are on your rooftop porch, don't even go back into your house. If you are out in the fields, don't even return for your money or clothes." said Jesus Christ

READING   MARK 12;10,24

Don't you remember **reading** this verse in the Scriptures?"

24 Jesus replied, " Your trouble is that you don't know the Scriptures and don't know the power of God." said Jesus Christ

READY   MATTHEW 24;43-51

"Just as a man can prevent trouble from thieves by keeping watch for them, you can avoid trouble by always being **ready** for my unannounced return.

"Are you a wise and faithful servant of the Lord? Have I given you the task of managing my household, to feed my children day by day?

READY   MATTHEW 24;43-51 cont'd

Blessings on you if I return and find you faithfully doing your work. I will put such faithful ones in charge of everything I own!

"But if you are evil and say to yourself, 'My Lord won't be corning for a while,' and begin oppressing your fellow servants, partying and getting drunk, your Lord will arrive unannounced and unexpected, and severely whip you and send you off to the judgment of the hypocrites; there will be weeping and gnashing of teeth." said Jesus Christ

LUKE 12;35-47

"Be prepared- all dressed and **ready-for** your Lord's return from the wedding feast. Then you will be **ready** to open the door and let him in the moment he arrives and knocks. There will be great joy for those who are **ready** and waiting for his return. He himself will seat them and put on a waiter's uniform and serve them as they sit and eat! He may come at nine o'clock at night- or even at midnight. But whenever he comes there will be joy for his servants who are **ready!**

"Everyone would be **ready** for him if they knew the exact hour of his return-just as they would be **ready** for a thief if they knew he was corning. So be **ready** all of the time. For ,I, the Messiah, will come when least expected. [Peter asked, "Lord, are you talking just to us or to everyone?]

R   221

READY   LUKE 12;35-47 cont'd

And the Lord replied, "I'm talking to any faithful, sensible man whose master gives him the responsibility of feeding the other servants. If his master returns and finds he has done a good job, there will be a reward-his master will put him in charge of all he owns.

" But if the man begins to think, 'My Lord won't be back for a long time,' and begins to whip the men and women he is supposed to protect, and to spend his time at drinking parties and drunkenness

well, his master will return without notice and remove him from his position of trust and assign him to the place of the unfaithful. He will be severely punished, for though he knew his duty, he refused to do it." said Jesus Christ

REAL , REALIZE JOHN 6;53-58

So Jesus said it again, " With all the earnestness I possess, I tell you this: Unless you eat the flesh of the Messiah and drink his blood, you cannot have eternal life within you. But anyone who does eat my flesh and drink my blood has eternal life, and I will raise him on the Last Day. For my flesh is the **real** food and my blood the **real** drink. Everyone who eats my flesh and drinks my blood is in me, and I in him. I live by the power of the living Father who sent me, and in the same way, those who partake of me shall live because of me! I am the true bread

R

REAL,REALLY,REALIZE

JOHN6;53-58 cont'd
from Heaven; and anyone who eats this Bread shall live forever and not die as your fathers did-though they ate bread from heaven." said Jesus Christ

JOHN 6; 59-60 {He preached this sermon in the Synagogue at Capernaum } 60 [Even his disciples said, "This is very hard to understand. Who can tell what it means?]

JOHN 13;7
Jesus replied, "Do you not **realize** now why I am doing it ; some day you will." said Jesus Christ

JOHN 13;38
Jesus answered, " Will you **really** lay down your life for me? No- three times before the cock crows tomorrow morning, you will deny that you even know me!" said Jesus Christ

REAP (ER) (S)   LUKE 12;24

"Look at the ravens-they don't plant or **reap** or have barns or store away their food, and yet, they get along all right-for God feeds them. And you are far more important than any birds!" said Jesus Christ   JOHN 4;35-38

"Do not think the work of harvesting will not begin until the summer ends four months from now? Look around you! Vast fields of human souls are ripening all around us, and are ready for **reaping. The reapers** will be paid good wages and

REAP (ER) (S)   JOHN 4;35-38 cont'd
will be gathering eternal souls into the granaries of
Heaven! What joys await the sower and the **reaper**
both together! For it is true that one sows and the
other one **reaps**. I sent you to **reap** where you didn't
sow; others did the work, and you received the
harvest." said Jesus Christ

REASON   JOHN 12;27

"Now my soul is deeply troubled. Shall I pray,
'Father, save me from what lies ahead'? **But** that is
the very **reason** why I came! Father bring glory and
honor to your name." said Jesus Christ

JOHN 15;25

" This has fulfilled what the prophets said
concerning the Messiah, 'They hated me without
reason.'" said Jesus Christ

JOHN 18;37

"Yes," Jesus said. "I was born for that **reason.**
And I came to bring truth to the world. All who
truth are my followers." said Jesus Christ

REBELLION   MARK 14;48-49

Jesus asked them, " Am I some dangerous robber
leading a **rebellion,** that you come at me like this,
armed to the teeth to capture me? Why didn't you
arrest me at the Temple? I was there teaching every
day. But these things are happening to fulfill the
prophecies about me." said Jesus Christ

RECEIVE (S) (ED)

MATTHEW 6;2

"Take care! Don't do your good deeds publically, to be admired, for then you will lose reward from your Father in Heaven. When you give a gift to a beggar, don't shout about it as the hypocrites do-blowing trumpets in the synagogues and streets to call attention to their acts of charity! I tell you in all earnestness, they have **received** all the reward they will ever get but when you do a kindness to someone, do it secretly- don't tell your left hand what you right hand is doing. And your Father who knows all your secrets, will reward you." said Jesus Christ

MATTHEW 10;8

"Heal the sick, raise the dead, cure the lepers and cast out demons. Give as freely as you have **received!**" said Jesus Christ

MARK 10;15

"I tell you as seriously as I know how that anyone who refuses to **receive** the Kingdom of God like a little child will never be allowed into His Kingdom." said Jesus Christ

MARK 10;29-30

And Jesus replied, "Let me assure you that no one has ever given up anything-home, brothers, sisters, mother, father, children or property-for love of me and to tell others about the Good News, who won't **receive** a hundred times over, homes,

R 225

RECEIVE(S) (ED) MARK 10;29-30 cont'd brothers, sisters, mothers, children and land-with persecutions! All these will be his here on earth, and in the world to come he shall have eternal life." said Jesus Christ

MARK 11;24-25

"Listen to me! You can pray for anything, and if you believe that you have **received** it, its yours! But when you are praying, first forgive anyone you are holding a grudge against, so that your Father in Heaven will forgive your sins too." said Jesus Christ

LUKE 11;10

" And so it is with prayer-keep on asking and you will keep getting; keep on looking and you will keep finding; knock and the door will be opened. Everyone who asks, **receives;** all who seek, find; and the door is opened to everyone who knocks." said Jesus Christ

JOHN 16;24

"You haven't tried this before, but begin now. Ask using my name, and you will **receive** and your cup of joy will overflow." said Jesus Christ

JOHN 20;22

Then he breathed into them and told them, **"Receive** the Holy Spirit." SAID Jesus Christ

RECOGNIZE, RECOGNITION

MATTHEW 7;16

" You can detect them by the way they act, just as you can **recognize** a tree by its fruit." said Jesus Christ

RECONCILED   MATTHEW 5;23-24

"So if you are standing before the altar in the Temple, offering a sacrifice to God, and suddenly remember that a friend has something against you, leave your sacrifice there beside the altar and go apologize and be **reconciled** to him, and then come and offer your sacrifice to God." said Jesus Christ

REDEEM (ER), REDEMPTION

LUKE 21;25-28

"Then there will strange events in the skies- warnings, evil omens and portents in the sun, moon and stars; and down here on earth the nations will be perplexed by the roaring seas and the strange tides. The courage of many people will falter because of the fearful fate they see coming upon the earth, for the stability of the very heavens will be broken up. The peoples of the earth shall see me, the Messiah, coming in a cloud with power and great glory. So when all these things happen, stand straight and look up! For your **redemption,** (salvation) is near." said Jesus Christ

REJECT , REJECTING

LUKE 10;16

" Then he said to the disciples, "Those who welcome you are welcoming me. And those who **reject** you are **rejecting** me. And those who **reject** me are **rejecting** God who sent me." said Jesus Christ   JOHN 12;48

"But all who **reject** me and my message will be judged at the Day of Judgement by the truths I have spoken!" said Jesus Christ

REJOICE(S), REJOICING

LUKE 6;22-23

"What happiness it is when others hate you and exclude you and smear your name because you are mine! When that happens, **rejoice!** Yes, leap for joy! For you will have a great reward in Heaven. And you will be in good company-the ancient prophets were treated that way too!" said Jesus Christ

LUKE 10; 19-20

"And I have given you authority over all the power of the Enemy, and to walk among serpents and scorpions and crush them. Nothing shall injure you! However, the important thing is not that demons obey you, but that you **rejoice** because names are registered as citizens of Heaven" said Jesus Christ

REJOICE,REJOICING

LUKE 15;6-9

"When you arrived you would call together your friends and neighbors to **rejoice** with you because your lost sheep was found.

" Well in the same way Heaven there will be more **rejoicing** over one lost sinner who returns to God than over ninety-nine others who haven't turned away!

"Or take another illustration: A woman has ten valuable silver coins and loses one. Won't she light a lamp and look in ever comer of her house and sweep every nook and cranny until she finds it? And won't she call in her friends to **rejoice** with her? In the same way there is joy in the presence of angels of God when one sinner repents?" said Jesus Christ

REMAIN

JOHN 15;4-9

" Take care to **remain** in me, and let me **remain** in you. For a branch can't produce fruit when it is severed from the vine. Nor can you be fruitful apart from me.

" Yes, I am the Vine; you are the branches. Whoever **remains** in me and I in him shall produce a large crop of fruit. For apart from me, you can't do a thing. If anyone separates from me, he is thrown away like a useless branch and withers, and is gather into a pile a burned. But if you **remain** in me and obey my commands, you may ask any request

REMAIN JOHN15; 4-8 cont'd

you like, and it will be granted! My true disciples produce bountiful harvests! This brings great glory to the Father." said Jesus Christ

RENT ,LEASE MATTHEW 21;33-44

"Now listen to this story; A certain landowner planted a vineyard with a hedge around it, and built a platform for the watchman, then leased the vineyard to some farmers on a sharecrop basis, and went away to live in another country."

"At the time of grape harvest he sent his agents to the farmers to collect his share. But the farmers attacked his men, beat one and killed one and stoned another."

"Then he sent a larger group of his men to collect for him, but the results were the same. Finally the owner sent his son, thinking surely they would respect him."

"But when the farmers saw the son coming they said among themselves, 'Here comes the heir to the estate, come let's kill him and get it for ourselves! So they dragged him out of the vineyard and killed him."

"When the owner returns what do you think he will do to those farmers?"

{The Jewish leaders replied, 'He will put them to a horrible death and **lease** the vineyard to others who will pay him promptly." }

RENT, LEASE   MATTHEW 23;33-44 cont'd

Then Jesus asked them, " Didn't you ever read the Scriptures: The stone rejected by the builders has been honored as the cornerstone; how remarkable! What an amazing thing the Lord has done?"

"What I mean is that the Kingdom of God shall be taken away from you and given to a nation that will give God a share of the crop. All who stumble on the rock of truth shall be broken, but those it falls on will be scattered like dust." said Jesus Christ

45[{When the chief priests and other Jewish leaders realized that Jesus was talking about them- they were the fanners in this story-they wanted to get rid of him, but they were afraid to because of the crowds, for they accepted Jesus as a prophet.]

(From C.C.- realize this is about us too. Are we in the crowd defending him? Are we giving God and His Son what they want as payment which is all the love of our heart, soul and mind? Or are we small minded and choosing to vanish like dust? All leases have an end date.)

REPAY   LUKE 6;34

"And you lend money only to those who can **repay** you, what good is that? Even the most wicked will lend to their own kind for full return!" said Jesus Christ

REPAY   LUKE 14;14

"Then at the Resurrection of the godly, God will reward you for inviting those who can't **repay** you." said Jesus Christ

REPENT   MATTHEW 4;17

From then on, Jesus began to preach, **"Repent,** turn from sin and turn to God for the Kingdom of Heaven is near." said Jesus Christ

LUKE 13;3

"Not at all! And don't you realize that you will also perish unless you **repent** and leave your evil ways and turn to God?" said Jesus Christ

LUKE 17;3

"Rebuke your brother if he sins, and forgive him if he **repents** and says he is sorry. Even if he is wrong seven times a day and each time turns to you and asks for forgiveness, forgive him.." said Jesus Christ   LUKE 24; 46-49

And he said, "Yes, it was written long ago that he Messiah must suffer and die and rise again on the third day; and that the message of salvation should be taken from Jerusalem to all nations: *There is forgiveness of sins for all who* **repent** *and turn to me.* You have seen these prophecies come true.

" And now I will send the Holy Spirit upon you, just as my Father promised. Don't begin telling others yet-stay here in the city until the Holy Spirit comes and fills you with the power of Heaven." said

Jesus Christ (cont'd)

RESIST   MATTHEW 5;39-42

"But I say: Don't **resist** violence! If you are slapped on one cheek, turn the other too. If you are ordered to court, and your shirt is taken from you, give your coat too. If the military demand that you carry their gear for a mile, carry it two. Give to those who ask, and don't turn away from those who want to borrow." said Jesus Christ

LUKE 21; 14-15

"Therefore, don't be concerned about how to answer charges against you, for I will give you the right words and such logic that none of your opponents will be able to **resist.**" said Jesus Christ

REST   MATTHEW 11;29-30

"Come to me and I will give you **rest-all** of you who work so hard beneath a heavy yoke. Wear my yoke- for it fits perfectly-and let me teach you: for I am gentle and humble and you shall find **rest** for your souls; for I give you only light burdens." said Jesus Christ

MARK 6;31

Then Jesus suggested, "Let's get away from the crowds for a while and **rest.**" said Jesus Christ

RESURRECTION   PREDICTION

MATTHEW 17;22-23

One day while they were still in Galilee, Jesus told them, "I am going to be betrayed into the power

R   233

RESURRECTION PREDICTION
MATTHEW 17;22-23 cont'd
of those who kill me, and on the third day
afterwards I will be brought back to life again." said
Jesus Christ

RESURRECTION MATTHEW 22;31-32
"But now, as to whether there is **resurrection** of
the dead-don't you ever read the Scriptures? Don't
you realize God was speaking directly to you when
He said, 'I am the God of Abraham, Isaac and
Jacob'? So God is not a God of the dead, but of the
living. " said Jesus Christ

MARK 12;26-27
"But as to whether there will be a **resurrection-**
have you never read in the book of Exodus about
Moses and the burning bush? God said to Moses, 'I
am the God of Abraham, and I am the God of Isaac,
and I am the God of Jacob.'
"God was telling Moses that these men, though
dead for hundreds of years, were still very much
alive, for He would not have said, 'I am the God' of
those who do not exist! You have made a serious
error!" said Jesus Christ

LUKE 20;37-38
"But as to your real question-whether or not there
is a **resurrection-why,** even the writings of Moses
himself prove this. For when he describes how God
appeared before him in the burning bush, he speaks

RESURRECTION LUKE 20; 37-38 cont'd
of God as the God of Abraham, the God of Isaac
and the God of Jacob. To say that the Lord is some
person's God means the person is alive not dead! So
from God's point of view, all men are living." said
Jesus Christ

JOHN 11;25-26

Jesus told her, "I am the **resurrection** and the
life. Anyone who believes in me, even though he
dies like everyone else, shall live again. He is given
eternal life for believing in me and shall never
perish. Do you believe this..?" said Jesus Christ

RETURN   MATTHEW 24;46

"Blessings on you if I **return** and find you
faithfully doing your work. I will put such faithful
ones in charge of everything I own." said Jesus
Christ

LUKE 17;30

"Yes, it will be 'business as usual' right up to the
hour of my **return.** " said Jesus Christ

REVEAL(S),REVELATION(S
          MATTHEW 11;25-27

And Jesus prayed this prayer: " O Father, Lord of
Heaven and earth, thank you for hiding the truth
from those who think themselves so wise, and for
revealing it to the little children. Yes, Father, for it
pleased you to do it this way!"

"Everything has been entrusted to me by my

R   235

REVEAL(S},REVELATION(S}

MATTHEW 11;25-27 cont'd
Father. Only the Father knows the Son and the Father is only known by the Son and by those to whom the Son **reveals** Him." said Jesus Christ

REVOLUTIONS   LUKE 21;9

"And when you hear of wars and **revolutions** beginning don't panic. True, wars must come, but the end won't follow immediately- for nations will rise against nation and kingdom against kingdom, and there will be earthquakes and famines in manylands, and epidemics and terrifying things happening in the heavens." said Jesus Christ

REWARD   MATTHEW 5;11-12

" When you are reviled and persecuted and lied about because you are my followers-wonderful! Be happy about it! Be glad! For a tremendous **reward** awaits you up in Heaven." said Jesus Christ

MATTHEW 6;1
"Take care! Don't do your good deeds publically to be admired, for then you will lose your **reward** in Heaven." said Jesus Christ

MATTHEW 6;5-6
"And now about prayer, when you pray, don't be like hypocrites who pretend piety by praying publically on the street comers and in synagogues where everyone can see them. Truly, that is all the **reward** they will ever get! But when you pray, go

REWARD   MATTHEW 6;5-6 cont'd
away by yourself, all alone, and shut the door
behind you and pray to your Father secretly, and
your Father knows your secrets and will **reward**
you." said Jesus Christ

MATTHEW 10;41

"If you welcome a prophet because he is a man
of God, you will be given the same **reward** a
prophet gets." said Jesus Christ

MATTHEW 16; 27

"For, I, the Messiah, the Son of Mankind, shall
come with the angels in the glory of my Father to
judge and **reward** each person according to their
own deeds." said Jesus Christ

LUKE 6;22-23

"What happiness when others hate you and
exclude you and insult you and smear your name
because you are mine! When that happens, rejoice!
Yes, leap for joy! For you will have great **reward**
awaiting you in Heaven and you will be in good
company-the ancient prophets were treated like that
too." said Jesus Christ   LUKE 6;35

"Love your enemies! Do good to them! Lend to
them! And don't be concerned about the fact they
won't repay. Then your **reward** in Heaven will be
very great and you will be truly acting like the sons
of God for He is kind to the unthankful and to those
who are very wicked." said Jesus Christ

RICH(ES)   MATTHEW 19;21-24,26

Jesus told them, "If you want to be perfect, go and sell all your **riches,** everything you have and give the money to the poor, you will have treasure in Heaven; come follow me" {But when the young man heard this, he went away sadly, for he was very rich}

Then Jesus said to the disciples, "It is almost impossible for a **rich** man to get into the Kingdom of Heaven. I say it again-it is easier for a camel to go through an eye of a needle than for a **rich** man to enter the Kingdom of God!"

26 Jesus looked at them intently and said, "Humanly speaking, no one. But with God everything is possible." said Jesus Christ

MARK 10;21,23-25,27

Jesus felt genuine love for this man as he looked at him. "You lack only one thing," he told him; "go and sell your **riches** and all that you have and give the money to the poor-and you shall have treasure in Heaven.- and come, follow me.

23 Jesus watched him go, then turned around and said to his disciples, "It is almost impossible for the **rich** to get into the Kingdom of God!"

This amazed them, so Jesus said it again: " Dear children, how hard is it for those who trust in **riches** to enter the Kingdom of God. It is easier for a camel to go through the eye of a needle than for a **rich**

RICH(ES)   MARK   10;21,23-25,27 cont'd

man to enter the Kingdom of God!'

27 Jesus looked at them intently, then said, "Without God it is utterly impossible. But with God, everything is possible." said Jesus Christ

LUKE 6;24-25

"But, oh, what sorrows await the **rich.** For they have only their happiness down here. They are fat and prosperous now, but a time of awful hunger is before them. Their careless laughter now means sorrow then." said Jesus Christ

LUKE 8;14

" The seed among the thorns represents those who listen and believe God's words but whose faith afterwards is choked out by worry and **riches** and the responsibilities and the pleasures of life. And so they are never able to help anyone else believe the Good News." said Jesus Christ

LUKE 12;21

"Yes, every man is a fool who gets **rich** on earth and not in Heaven." said Jesus Christ

LUKE 16;19-23

"There was a certain **rich** man, "Jesus said, " who was splendidly clothed and lived each day in mirth and luxury. One day, Lazarus, a diseased beggar, was laid at his door. As he lay there longing

RICH(ES)   LUKE 16;19-23 cont'd
for scraps, the dogs licked his open sores. Finally
the beggar died and was carried by the angels to be
with Abraham in the place of the righteous dead.
The **rich** man also died and was buried, and his soul
went into hell. There, in torment, he saw Lazarus
in the far distance with Abraham." said Jesus Christ
                    LUKE 18;25,27
   Jesus watched him go and said to his disciples,
"How hard it is for the **rich** to enter the Kingdom
of God. It is easier for a camel to go through an eye
of a needle than for a **rich** man to enter the
Kingdom of God."
27 He replied, "God can do whatever men can't."
said Jesus Christ

RIGHT(CORRECT
                    JOHN 8;15-6
   "You pass judgment on me without knowing the
facts. I am not judging you now, but if l were, it
would be an absolutely **right** judgment in every
respect, for I have with me the Father who sent me"
said Jesus Christ   JOHN 18;37
   "You are **right** saying that I am a king. I was born
for that purpose. And I came to bring truth to the
world. All who love the truth are my followers."
said Jesus Christ

RIGHTEOUS   MATTHEW 5;45

"For He gives His sunlight to both evil and good and sends rain to the **righteous** and the **unrighteous** too . If you love only those who love you, what good is that? Even scoundrels do that much. If you are friendly only to your friends, how are you different from anyone else? Even the heathen do that. But you are to be perfect even as your Father in Heaven is perfect." said Jesus Christ

MATTHEW 13;43,49

"Then the **righteous** shall shine as the sun in the Father's Kingdom. Let those with ears listen!" 49 "That is the way it will be at the end of the world-the angels will come and separate the wicked from the **righteous,** casting the wicked into the fire; there will be weeping and gnashing of teeth. Do you understand?" said Jesus Christ

MATTHEW 25;46

"And they shall go away to eternal punishment; but the **righteous** to everlasting life." said Jesus Christ

MARK 2;17

When Jesus heard what they were saying, he told them, " Sick people need the doctor, not the healthy ones! I haven't come to tell the **righteous** to repent, but the bad ones." said Jesus Christ

RIGHTEOUSNESS JOHN 16;8-11

" And when the Comforter, Holy Spirit, has come he will convince the world of its sin, and of the availability of God's goodness, and of deliverance from judgment. The world's sin is unbelief in me; there is **righteousness** available because I go to the Father and you shall see me no more; there is deliverance from judgment because the prince of the world has already been judged." said Jesus Christ

RIPE(NED)(NING) MARK 4;26-29

"Here is another story illustrating what the Kingdom of God is like:

"A farmer sowed his field, and went away, and as days went by, the seeds grew and grew without his help. For the soil made the seeds grow. First a leaf - blade pushed through, and later the wheat heads formed and finally the grain **ripened,** and then the farmer came at once with his sickle and harvested it."   said Jesus Christ   JOHN 4;39

Then Jesus explained, "My nourishment comes from doing the will of God who sent me, and from finishing His work. Do you think the work of harvesting will not begin until the summer ends four months from now? Look around you! Vast fields of human souls are **ripening** all around us and ready now for reaping."   said Jesus Christ

(check out Revelation 14;15 Then the angel came from the temple and called out to him, "Begin to use the sickle, for the time has come for you to reap: the harvest is ripe on earth.)

242   R

ROAD   MATTHEW 7;13-14

"Heaven can be enter only through a narrow gate! The **road** to hell is broad, and its gate wide enough for all the multitudes to choose its easy way. But the gateway to life is small and the **road** narrow, only a few will ever find it. "said Jesus Christ

ROCK   MATTHEW 7;24

"All who listen to my instructions and follow them are wise, like a man who builds his house on solid **rock.** Though the rain comes in torrents, and flood rise and the storm winds beat against his house, it won't collapse for it is built on **rock."** said Jesus Christ

MATTHEW 16;18

" You are Peter, a stone and upon this **rock** I will build my church; and all the powers of hell shall not prevail against it." said Jesus Christ

ROOM   MATTHEW 6;6

"But when you pray, go into your **room** all alone and shut the door behind you. And pray to your Father secretly, and your Father, who knows your secrets will reward you." said Jesus Christ

ROOM   MARK 14;14-15

"At the house he enters, tell the man in charge, 'Our master sent us to see the **room** you have ready for us, where we will eat the Passover supper this evening!' He will take you upstairs to a large **room** all set up. Prepare our supper there." said Jesus Christ

LUKE 12;1-3

"But such hypocrites cannot be hidden forever. It will become as evident as yeast in dough.

"Whatever they have said in the dark shall be heard in the light, and what you have whispered in inner **rooms** shall be broadcast from the housetops for all to hear." said Jesus Christ

JOHN 8;37

"Yes, I realize you are descendants of Abraham! And yet some of you are trying to kill me because you my message can't find **room** in your hearts." said Jesus Christ   JOHN 14;1-4

"Let not your heart be troubled. You are trusting God, now trust in me. There are many homes and **rooms** up there where my Father lives, and I am going to prepare them for your coming. When everything is ready, then I will come and get you, so that you can always be with me where I am. If this weren't so important, I would plainly say so. And now you know where I am going and how to get there." said Jesus Christ

ROOT(S),(ED)   MATTHEW 3;10

"And even now the axe of God's judgment is poised at the **roots** to chop down every unproductive tree. They will be chopped and burned." said Jesus Christ

MATTHEW 13;20-21

"The shallow rocky soil represents the heart of the man who hears the message and receives it with full joy, but he doesn't have much depth in his life, and the seeds don't **root** very deeply, and after a while when trouble comes, or persecution begins because of his beliefs, his enthusiasm fades and he drops out." said Jesus Christ

MATTHEW 15;13

Jesus replied, "Every plant not planted by my Father shall be rooted up so ignore them. They are blind guides leading the blind, and both will fall into the ditch." said Jesus Christ
(I Timothy 6;10 The LOVE of money is the root of all kinds of evil.....This is not a quote of Christ. This was written by Paul. See what Christ said about listening to his DISCIPLES])

RUIN   MATTHEW 12;25

Jesus knew their thoughts and replied, " A divided kingdom ends in **ruin.** A city or home divided against itself cannot stand." said Jesus Christ

R   245

RULES   MARK 7;6-9

Jesus replied, " You bunch of hypocrites! Isaiah the prophet described you very well when he said, 'These people speak very prettily about the Lord but have no love for Him at all. Their worship is a farce, for they claim that God commands the people to obey their petty **rules.'** How right Isaiah was! For you ignore God's specific orders and substitute your own traditions. You are simply rejecting God's laws and trampling them under your feet for the sake of tradition." said Jesus Christ

LUKE 22;26

"But among you, the one who **rules** is like the one who serves. Out in the world the master sits at the table and is served by servants. But not here! For I am your servant." said Jesus Christ

RUMORS   MATTHEW 24; 4-6

Jesus told them, " Don't let anyone fool you. For many will come claiming to be the Messiah, and will lead many astray. When you hear of wars beginning and **rumors** of wars, this does not signal my return; these must come but the end is not yet. · The nations and the kingdoms will rise against each other and there will be famines and earthquakes in many places. But this will only be the beginning of horrors to come." said Jesus Christ

RUN , RUNNING   MATTHEW 6;31-33

" So don't worry at all about having enough food and clothing. Why be like the heathen? For they take pride in all these things and **run** after them and are deeply concerned about them. But your heavenly Father already knows perfectly well that you need them, and He will give them to you if you give Him first place in your life and live as He wants you to," said Jesus Christ

LUKE 17;23-24

"Reports will reach you that I am at this place or that. Do not go **running** off looking for these places. For when I return, you will know it beyond all doubt. It will as evident as the lightening that flashes across the skies." said Jesus Christ

RUST   MATTHEW 6;19

"Don't store up treasures here on earth where the moths and **rust** can destroy them or they can be stolen. Store them in Heaven where they will never lose their value, and are safe from thieves. If your profits are in Heaven, your heart will be there too." said Jesus Christ

S

SABBATH   MATTHEW 12;5-8

"And haven't you ever read the law of Moses how the priests on duty in the Temple may work on

S   247

SABBATH   MATTHEW 12;5-13 cont'd
the **Sabbath?** And truly, one is here who is greater than the Temple. But if you had known the meaning of the Scripture verse, 'I want you to be merciful more than I want your offerings,' you would not have condemned those who aren't guilty! For I, the Messiah, am master even of the **Sabbath.**
[Then he went over to the synagogue, and noticed a man with a deformed hand. The Pharisees asked Jesus,] {"Is it legal to work by healing on the **Sabbath"**}[They were of course, hoping he would say "Yes", so they could arrest him.]

    This was his answer. "If you had just one sheep and it fell into a well on the **Sabbath,** would you work to rescue it that day? Of course you would. And how much more valuable a person is than a sheep! Yes, it is right to do good on the **Sabbath."** then he said to the man, " Stretch out your arm" and he did and his hand became normal. said Jesus Christ   MARK 2;28

    "And, I, the Messiah, have authority even to decide what men do on **Sabbath** days!" said Jesus Christ   LUKE 6;8-9

    " Then Jesus said to the Pharisees and teachers of the Law, "I have a question for you. Is it right to do good on the **Sabbath** day or do harm? To save a life or destroy it?" said Jesus Christ

SABBATH   LUKE 14;3,5

Jesus said to the Pharisees with legal experts standing around, "Well, is it within the law to heal a man on the **Sabbath** day or not?"

5 " Which of you does not work on the **Sabbath?**" said Jesus Christ

SACRED   MATTHEW 7;6

"Don't give **sacred** things to depraved men. Don't give pearls to swine! They will trample the pearls and turn and attack you." said Jesus Christ

SACRIFICE (D) (S)   MATTHEW 9;13

Then he added, "Now go away and learn the meaning of this verse of Scripture.

'It isn't your **sacrifices** and your gifts I want. I want you to be merciful.'"
said Jesus Christ

SAFE   JOHN 17;12

"During my time here I have kept **safe** within your family all those you gave me. I guarded them so that not one perished., except the son of hell as the Scriptures foretold." said Jesus Christ

SALT   MATTHEW 5;13

" You are the **salt** of the earth, to make it tolerable. If you lose your flavor, what will happen to the world? And you, yourselves will be thrown out and trampled underfoot as worthless." said Jesus Christ

SALVATION, SAVED

MATTHEW 10;22

"Everyone shall hate you because you belong to me. But all of you who endure until the end shall be **saved**." said Jesus Christ

MATTHEW 16;25

"For anyone who keeps his life for himself shall lose it; and anyone who loses his life for me shall **save** it." said Jesus Christ

MATTHEW 24;13

"But those enduring until the end shall be **saved**." said Jesus Christ

LUKE 7;50

And Jesus said to the woman. "Your faith has **saved** you; go in peace." said Jesus Christ

LUKE 19;9-10

Jesus told them, "This shows that **salvation** has come to this home today. This man was one of the lost sons of Abraham, and I, the Messiah, have come to search for and **save** souls such as his." said Jesus Christ

SAME   MATTHEW 7;2

"For the **same** way you have judged others, you shall be judged." said Jesus Christ

SATAN   MATTHEW 4;10

" Get out of here, **Satan!**" Jesus told him. "The Scriptures say, 'Worship only the Lord God. Obey only Him."said Jesus Christ

SATAN   MATTHEW 12;25-30

Jesus knew their thoughts and replied, " A divided kingdom ends in ruin. A city or a home divided against itself cannot stand. And if Satan is casting out **Satan**, he is fighting himself, and destroying his own kingdom. And if, as you claim, I am casting out demons by invoking the powers of **Satan**, then what power do your people use when they cast them out? Let them answer your accusation! But I am casting out demons by the Spirit of God , then the Kingdom of God has arrived among you. One cannot rob **Satan's** kingdom without first binding **Satan**. Only then can his demons be cast out! Anyone who is not helping me is harming me." said Jesus Christ

MATTHEW 16;23

Jesus turned to Peter and said, "Get away from me , you **Satan**! You are a dangerous trap for me. You are thinking from merely a human point of view not from God's." said Jesus Christ

MARK. 4;15

" The hard pathway, where some seeds fell, represents the hard hearts of some of those who hear God's word; **Satan** comes and tries to make them forget it." said Jesus Christ

SATAN   LUKE 10;18

" Yes, "he told them. "I saw **Satan** falling from heaven in a flash of lightening!" said Jesus Christ

SATISFIED   LUKE 6;21

"What happiness there is for you who are hungry, for you are going to be **satisfied**." said Jesus Christ

SAVIOR (Christ referred to himself a the Messiah, Son of God and Son of Man...we call him Savior)

SAY, SAYING

MATTHEW 10;19-20

" When you are arrested, don't worry about what you **say** at your trial, for you will be given the right words at the right time. For it won't be you doing the talking, it will be the Spirit of your heavenly Father speaking through you." said Jesus Christ

MATTHEW 16;15

Then he asked them, " Who do you **say** I am?" said Jesus Christ

MARK 8;27

.... "Who do people think I am? What are they **saying** about me?" said Jesus Christ

JOHN 8;26

He replied, "I am the one I always claimed to be. I could condemn you for much and teach you much, but I won't, for I **say** only what I am told to by the one who sent me; and He is the Truth." said Jesus Christ

SAY, SAYING   JOHN 8;43

" Why can't you understand what I am **saying**? It is because you are prevented from doing so!" said Jesus Christ

SCATTER, (ED) (S) MATTHEW 26;31-32

Then Jesus told them, "Tonight you will all desert me. For it is written in the Scriptures that God will smite the Shepherd, and the sheep of the flock will be **scattered.** But after I have been brought back to life again, I will go to Galilee, and meet you there." said Jesus Christ

(see also SEEDS, SHEPHERD)

SCRIPTURES   MATTHEW 22;29

"Your error is caused by your ignorance of the **Scriptures** and of God's power!" said Jesus Christ

MARK 14;49

"But these things are happening because the **Scriptures** must be fulfilled." said Jesus Christ

LUKE 16;29

"But Abraham said, ' The **Scriptures** have warned them again and again. Your brothers can read them any time they want to." said Jesus Christ

LUKE 24;25-26

Then Jesus said to them, "You are such foolish, foolish people! You find it so hard to believe all that the prophets wrote in the **Scriptures**! Wasn't it clearly predicted by the prophets that the Messiah

SCRIPTURES   LUKE 24;25-26 cont'd
would have to suffer all these things before
entering his time of glory?" said Jesus Christ

JOHN 5;39

" You search the **Scriptures** for you believe
they give you eternal life. And the **Scriptures** point
to me! Yet, you won't come to me so that I can give
you life eternal!" said Jesus Christ

JOHN 10;34-36

"In your own law it says men are gods!" he
replied. "So if the **Scriptures** which cannot be
untrue, speak of those as gods to whom the message
of God came, do you call it blasphemy when the one
sanctified and sent into the world by the Father says,
I am the Son of God?' Don't believe me unless I do
miracles of God. But if I do, believe them even if
you don't believe me. Then you will become
convinced that the Father is in me and I in the
Father." said Jesus Christ

SEARCH   LUKE 15;8-10

"Or take another illustration: A woman has ten
valuable silver coins and loses one.. Won't she
light a lamp and **search** every corner of the house
and seek every nook and cranny until she finds it?
And won't she call her friends and neighbors to
rejoice with her? In the same way there is joy in
the presence of the angels of God when one sinner
repents." said Jesus Christ

254   S

SECRET (LY) (S) MATTHEW 6; 1-6

" Take care! Don't do your good deeds publically, to be admired, for then you will lose your reward from your Father in Heaven. When you give a gift to a beggar, don't shout about it as the hypocrites do-blowing trumpets in the synagogues and streets to call attention to their acts of charity! I tell you in all earnestness, they have received all the reward they will ever get. But when you do kindness to someone, do it **secretly**- don't tell your left hand what your right hand is doing. And your Father knows all secrets and will reward you.

" And now about prayer. When you pray, don't be like the hypocrites who pretend piety by praying publically on street corners and in synagogues where everyone can see them. Truly, that is all the reward they will ever get. But when you pray, go away by yourself, all alone in your room and shut the door behind you and pray to your Father **secretly**, and your Father who knows all your **secrets** will reward you." said Jesus Christ

MARK 4;11-12

"You are permitted to know some truths about the Kingdom of God that are **secrets** hidden from to those outside the Kingdom:

'Though they see and hear, they will not understand or turn to God or be forgiven for their sins.'" said Jesus Christ

SEE   MATTHEW 13; 12-17

" For to him who has more will more be given," he told them, " and he will have great plenty: but from him who has not, even the little he has will be taken away. That is why I use illustrations, so people will hear and **see** but not understand.

"This fulfils the prophecy of Isaiah:
'They hear, but don't understand;
They look, but don't **see**!
For their hearts are fat and heavy,
and their ears are dull, and they
have closed their eyes in sleep,
so they won't **see** and hear and
understand and turn to God
again and let me heal them.'"

"But blessed are your eyes, for they **see**; and your ears, for they hear. Many a prophet has longed to **see** what you have **seen** and hear what you have heard, but couldn't." said Jesus Christ

MARK 8;17-18

"No, it isn't it at all! Can't you understand? Are your hearts too hard to take it in? Your eyes are to **see** with-why don't you look? Why don't you open your ears to listen? Don't you remember anything at all?" said Jesus Christ   MARK 14; 62

Jesus said, "I am and you will **see** me sitting at the right hand of God and returning to earth in the clouds of Heaven." said Jesus Christ

SEE

" In just a little while, the world will not **see** me anymore, but I will still be present with you. For I will live again and so will you." said Jesus Christ

"In a little while, I will be gone and you will **see** me no more; but just a little while after that, you will **see** me again!" said Jesus Christ

SEED   ...see FAITH AND MUSTARD SEED

"This is its meaning; The **seed** is God's message to men," said Jesus Christ

Jesus replied that the time had come for him to return to his glory in Heaven and that, "I must fall and die like a kernel of wheat that falls into the furrows of the earth. Unless I die- I will be alone- a single **seed**. But my death will produce many new wheat kernels- a plentiful harvest of new lives. If you love your life down here-you will lose it. If you despise your life down here-you will exchange it for eternal glory." said Jesus Christ

SEEK   MATTHEW 7;7-8

"Ask, and you will be given what you ask for. **Seek**, and you will find. Knock and the door will be opened. For everyone who asks, receives. Anyone who **seeks**, finds. If you only knock, the door will open." said Jesus Christ

SEEN   JOHN 6;46

"No one actually sees Father, for only I have **seen** Him." said Jesus Christ

JOHN 14;9

Jesus replied, " Don't you even know who I am Philip, even after all this time I have been with you? Anyone who has **seen** me has seen the Father! So why are you asking to see Him? " said Jesus Christ

JOHN 20;29

Then Jesus told him, "You believe because you have **seen** me. But blessed are those who haven't **seen** me and believe anyway." said Jesus Christ

SELF   LUKE 9;24-25

" Whoever loses his life for my sake will save it, but whoever insists on keeping his life will lose it; and what profit is there in gaining the whole world when it means forfeiting one's **self**?" said Jesus Christ

SELF INDULGENCE MATTHEW 23;25-26

"Woe to you Pharisees, and you religious leaders -hypocrites! You are so careful to polish the outside of the cup, but inside you are foul with greed, extortion and **self-indulgence**. Blind Pharisees! First cleanse the inside of the cup, then the whole cup will be clean." said Jesus Christ

SEND, SENT,   MATTHEW 10;16

"I am **send**ing you out as sheep among the wolves." said Jesus Christ

SEND, SENT   MATTHEW 10;40

"Those who welcome you are welcoming me. And when they welcome me, they are welcoming God who **sent** me." said Jesus Christ

MATTHEW 24 ;30-31

"And the last signal of my coming will appear in the heavens and there will be deep mourning all around the earth. All nations in the world will see me arrive in the clouds of heaven with great power and glory. And I shall **send** forth my angels with the sound of a mighty trumpet blast, they shall gather my chosen ones from the farthest ends of the earth and heaven." said Jesus Christ

LUKE 4;18-19

" The Spirit of the Lord is upon me; He has appointed me to preach Good News to the poor; He has **sent** me to heal the brokenhearted and to announce that the captives shall be released and the blind shall see, that the downtrodden shall be freed from their oppressors, and that God is ready to give blessings to all who come to Him."said Jesus Christ

LUKE 11;49

" This is what God says about you: ' I will **send** prophets and apostles to you, and you will kill some of them and chase away others."'said Jesus Christ

JOHN 3;17

"God did not **send** His only Son into the world to condemn it, **but** save it." said Jesus Christ

S   259

SEND, SENT   JOHN 4;34

Then Jesus explained: "My nourishment comes from doing the will of God who **sent** me, and doing His work." said Jesus Christ

JOHN 5;24

"I say emphatically that anyone who listens to my message and believes in God who **sent** me has eternal life, and will never be damned for his sins, but already passed out of death into life." said Jesus Christ   JOHN 8;15-16

" You pass judgment on me without knowing the facts. I am not judging you now; but if I were, it would be an absolutely correct judgment in every respect, for I have with me the Father who **sent** me." said Jesus Christ   JOHN 9;4-5

"All of us must quickly carry out the tasks assigned to us by the one who **sent** me, for there is little time left before the night falls and all work comes to an end. But while I am still here in the world, I give it my light." said Jesus Christ

JOHN 14;26

"But when the Father **sends** the Comforter instead of me-and by the Comforter I mean the Holy Spirit-he will teach you much as well as remind you of everything I myself have told you." said Jesus Christ   JOHN 15;26

"But I will **send** you the Comforter- the Holy Spirit, the source of all truth." said Jesus Christ

SEND, SENT   JOHN 16;5-7

"But I am going away to the One who **sent** me; and none of you seems interested in the purpose of my going; none wonders why. Instead you are only filled with sorrow. But the fact of the matter is that it is best for you that I go away, for if I don't, the Comforter won't come. If Il do, he will- for I will **send** him to you." said Jesus Christ

JOHN 17;3

"And this is the way to eternal life- by knowing You, the only true God and Jesus Christ, the one You **sent** to earth!" said Jesus Christ

JOHN 17;18

"As You sent me into the world, I am sending them into the world, and I consecrate myself to meet their needs for growth in truth and holiness." said Jesus Christ   JOHN 20;21

He spoke to them again and said, "As the Father has **sent** me, even so I am sending you. Then he breathed on them and told them. 'Receive the Holy Spirit'." said Jesus Christ

SEPARATE   MATTHEW 19;4-6

"Don't you read the Scriptures?" he replied. "In them is written that at the beginning God created man and woman, and that he should leave his father and mother and be forever united with his wife. The two shall become one- no longer two but one! And no man should **separate** what God has joined

SEPARATE   MATTHEW 19;4-6cont'd
together." said Jesus Christ

MATTHEW 25;31-33

"But when I, the Messiah, shall come in my glory, and all the angels with me, then I shall sit upon my throne of glory. And all the nations will be gathered before me. And I will **separate** the people as a shepherd **separates** the sheep from the goats, and place the sheep at my right hand and the goats at my left." said Jesus Christ

SERVANT,SERVE,SLAVE

MATTHEW 20;25-28

But Jesus called them together and said, "Among the heathen kings are tyrants and each minor official lords over those beneath him. But among you it is quite different. Anyone wanting to be a leader among you must be your **servant**. And if you want to be right at the top, you must **serve like a slave.** Your attitude must be like my own, for I , the Messiah, did not come to be **served**, but to **serve** and give my life as ransom for many." said JesusChrist   MARK 10;42-45)

" As you know, the kings and the great men of the earth lord it over the people; but among you it is different. Whoever wants to great among you must be your **servan**t. And whoever wants to be greatest must be the **slave** to all. For even I, the Messiah, am not here to be **served**, but to help others and give

SERVANT,SERVE,SLAVE

MARK 10;42-45cont'd

my life as ransom for many." said Jesus Christ

MATTHEW 24;45

"Are you a wise and faithful **servant** of the Lord?" said Jesus Christ

LUKE 16;13

"For neither you nor anyone else can **serve** two masters. You will hate one and show loyalty to the other, or else the other way around-you will be enthusiastic about one and despise the other. You cannot **serve** both God and money." said Jesus Christ

LUKE 22; 25-26

Jesus told them, "In this world the kings and the great men order their **slaves** around, and the **slaves** have no choice but to like it! But among you, the one who **serves** you best will be your leader. Out in the world the master sits at the table and is **served** by his **servants**, but not here! For I am your **servan**t." said Jesus Christ

JOHN 8;30-32 34-36

"You are truly my disciples if you live as I tell you to, and you will know the truth and the truth will set you free......

34 "You are the **slaves** of sin, every one of you. And **slaves** don't have rights, but the Son has every right there is!" said Jesus Christ

SERVANT, SERVE, SLAVE
JOHN 12;26

"If any man wants to be my disciple, tell them to come and follow me, for my **servants** must be where I am. And if they follow me, my Father will honor them."said Jesus Christ

SEVEN   MATTHEW 18;22

{Peter came to him and asked, "Sir, how often do I forgive a brother who sins against me? **Seven** times?"}

"No!" Jesus replied, "**seventy** times **seven**!" said Jesus Christ

(**seven** is viewed as representing "all" "no limit")

SEX   MATTHEW 15;19

"From the heart come evil thoughts of murder, adultery, formication, theft lying and slander. These are what defile..." said Jesus Christ

MARK 7;20-23

And then he added, "It is the thought-life that pollutes. For from within, out of men's hearts, come evil thoughts of lust, theft, murder, adultery, wanting what belongs to others, wickedness, deceit, lewdness envy, slander, pride, and all other folly. All these vile things come from within; they are what pollute and make you unfit for God." said Jesus Christ

SHAME (From C.C....Christ did not focus on shame. He was about love, forgiveness and sharing information to save us..so we could choose to change and accountability if we never did.)

MARK. 8;38

"And anyone who is **ashamed** of me and my message in these days of unbelief and sin, I , the Messiah, will be **ashamed** of him when I return in the glory of the Father and the Holy angels." said Jesus Christ

SHARE   LUKE 3;11

"If you have two coats, "he replied, "give one to the poor. If you have extra food, give it away to those that are hungry" said Jesus Christ

SHEEP, SHEPHERD (also see **SEPARATE**)

MATTHEW 7;15

"Beware of false teachers who come to you disguised as harmless **sheep,** but are wolves and will tear you apart." said Jesus Christ

MATTHEW 10;16

"I am sending you out as **sheep** among wolves." said Jesus Christ   MATTHEW 26;31-32

Then Jesus said to them, "Tonight you will desert me. For it is written in the Scriptures that God will smite the **Shepherd,** and the **sheep** of the flock will be scattered. But after I have been brought back to life again I will go to Galilee, and meet you there." said Jesus Christ

S 265

SHEEP, HERD
(see SEPRATE MATTHEW 25;32)

LUKE 15;3-7

So Jesus used this illustration, "If you had a hundred **sheep** and one of them strayed away and was lost in the wilderness wouldn't you leave the ninety-nine others to go out and look for the lost one until you found it? And then you would joyfully carry it home on your shoulders. When you arrived you would call together your friends and neighbors to rejoice with you because your lost **sheep** was found?

"Well, in the same way Heaven will be happier over one lost sinner that returns to God than ninety-nine others who haven't strayed away." said Jesus Christ   JOHN 10;1-16

"Anyone refusing to walk through the gate into a **sheepfold**, who sneaks over the wall must surely be a thief! For the **shepherd** comes through the gate. The gatekeeper opens the gate for him, and the sheep hear the voice and come to him; and he calls his own **sheep** by name and leads them out. He walks ahead of them; and they follow him, for they recognize his voice. They won't follow a stranger but will run from him, for they don't recognize his voice.

{6 Those who heard Jesus use this illustration

SHEEP, SHEPHERD   JOHN 10;1-16 cont'd
didn't understand what he meant, so he explained it
to them}

   "I am the Gate for the **sheep**," he said, "All
others who came before me were thieves and
robbers. But the true sheep did not listen to them.

   Yes, I am the Gate. Those who come by way of
the Gate will be saved and go in and find green
pastures. The thief s purpose is to steal, kill and
destroy. My purpose is to give life to the fullest.

   "I am the Good **Shepherd.** The Good
Shepherd lays down his life for the sheep. A hired
man will run when he sees a wolf coming and will
leave the **sheep**, for they aren't his and he isn't
their **shepherd**. And so the wolf leaps on them
and scatters the flock. The hired man runs because
he is hired and has no real concern for the **sheep**.

   "I am the Good **Shepherd** and know my own
sheep, and they know me, just as my Father knows
me and I know the Father; and I lay down my life
for my **sheep**. I have other sheep too in another
fold. I must bring them also, and they will heed my
voice; there will be one flock with one **Shepherd**."
said Jesus Christ

SHINE (S), SHINING   MATTHEW 5;15-16

   "Don't hide your light! Let it **shine** for all;   let

SHINE(S), SHINING MATTHEW 5; 15-16
your good deeds glow for all to see and they will
praise your heavenly Father." said Jesus Christ
MATTHEW 13;43
"Then the righteous shall **shine** like the sun in
the Father's Kingdom. Let all who have ears
listen!" said Jesus Christ LUKE 11;36
" If you are filled with light from within, with
no dark comers, then your face will **shine** too like
the light is beamed upon you." said Jesus Christ

SHORT, SHORTEN(ED) (S)
MATTHEW 24;22
"In fact, unless those days are **shortened**, all
mankind will perish. But they will be **shortened** for
the sake of God's chosen people." said Jesus Christ
MARK 13;20
"And unless the Lord **shortens** that time of
calamity, not a soul on the earth will survive. But
for the sake of the chosen ones, He will limit those
days." said Jesus Christ
JOHN 7;33
"I am with you only for a **short** time. Then I shall
return to the one who sent me. You will search for
me, but not find me. And you won't be able to come
where I am!" said Jesus Christ

SICK (see also HEALING)
LUKE 5;31
Jesus answered them, "It is the **sick** who need a

SICK   LUKE 5;31

doctor, not those in good health. My purpose is to invite sinners to turn from their sins, not to spend time with those who think themselves already good enough." said Jesus Christ

                   JOHN 11;4

"The purpose of his **sickness** is not death, but the Glory of God. I, the Son of God, will receive glory from the situation." said Jesus Christ

SIDE   JOHN 18;37

... "Yes," Jesus said, "I was born for that purpose. And I came to bring Truth to the world. Everyone on the **side** of the Truth listens and are my followers." said Jesus Christ

SIGN(S) (see also END TIMES)

                   MATTHEW 16;2-4

"He replied, "You are good at reading the weather **signs** of the skies-red sky tonight means fair weather tomorrow; red sky in the morning means foul weather all day- but you can't read the obvious **signs** of the times! This evil, unbelieving nation is asking for some strange **sign** in the heavens, but no further proof will be given except the miracle that happened to Jonah." said Jesus Christ   MATTHEW 24;4-8

Jesus told them, "Don't let anyone fool you. For many will come claiming to be the Messiah and lead many astray. When you hear of wars

SIGN(S) (see also END TIMES)

MATTHEW 24;4-6 cont'd

beginning, and rumors of wars this does not **signal** my return; these must come but the end is not yet. The nations and the kingdoms of the earth shall rise against each other and there will be famines and earthquakes in many places. But this will only be the beginning of the horrors to come." said Jesus Christ

MATTHEW 24;24

"For false christs shall arise, and false prophets, and will do wonderful **signs** and miracles so that if were possible, even God's chosen ones would be deceived. See I have warned you." said Jesus Christ

MATTHEW 24;30-31

"And then at last the **sign** of my coming will appear in the heavens and there will deep mourning all around the earth. And the nations of the world will see me arrive in the clouds of heaven, with power and great glory. And I shall send forth my angels with the sound of a mighty trumpet blast, and they shall gather my chosen ones from the farthest ends of the earth and heaven." said Jesus Christ

MARK 8;12

He sighed deeply when he heard this and he said, "Certainly not. How many more **signs** and miracles do you people need?" said Jesus Christ

SIGN(S) (see also END TIMES ,TERRORS)
MARK 13;21-23

"And if anyone tells you, 'This is the Messiah,' or ' That one is,' don't pay any attention. For there will be many false Messiahs and false prophets who will do wonderful signs and miracles that would deceive if possible, God's own children. Take care! I have warned you!" said Jesus Christ

SIN (what to think about sin...separating from God)   MATTHEW 5;29-30

" So if your eye-even if it is your best eye!- causes you to lust and **sin**, gouge it out and throw it away.Better for part of you to be destroyed than for all of you to be cast into hell. And if your hand- even your right hand causes you to **sin**, cut it off and throw itaway. It is better than finding yourself in hell." said Jesus Christ MATTHEW 6;14

"...and forgive our **sins** as we have forgiven those who have **sinned** against us." said Jesus Christ
MATTHEW 18;6

"But if any of you cause one of these little ones who trust me to lose faith and **sin**, it would be better for you to have a rock tied to your neck and thrown into the sea." said Jesus Christ

SIN (what to think about sin.. separating from God)

MARK 3;28-29

"I solemnly declare that any sin of man can be forgiven, even blasphemy against me, but blasphemy against the Holy Spirit can never be forgiven. It is an eternal sin." said Jesus Christ

MARK 9;43-44

"If your hand sins, cut it off. Better to live forever with one hand than to be throw into the unquenchable fires of hell with two! If your foot sins and carries you toward evil, cut it off ! Better to be lame and live forever than have two feet to carry you into hell." said Jesus Christ

LUKE 17;1-3

"There will always be temptation to sin. "Jesus said one day to his disciples, "but, woe to the man who does the tempting. If he were thrown into the sea with a huge rock tied around his neck, he would be far better off than facing the punishment in store for those who harm the little children's souls. I am warning you!

"Rebuke your brother if he sins, and forgive him if he is sorry." said Jesus Christ

JOHN 8;7

"All right, hurl the stones at her until she dies. But only he who has never sinned may throw the first stone." said Jesus Christ

272   S

SIN (what to think about sin...separating from God)

JOHN 8;34-36

Jesus replied, "You are slaves to sin, every one of you. And slaves don't have rights, but the Son has every right there is! So if the Son sets you free, you indeed will be free-" said Jesus Christ

JOHN 8;46-47

" Which one of you can truthfully accuse me of one single sin? No one! and since I am telling you the truth, why don't you believe me? Anyone whose Father is God listens gladly to the words of God. Since you don't, it proves you aren't His children.' said Jesus Christ

JOHN 16;9-11

" The world's sin is unbelief in me; there is righteousness available because I go to the Father and you shall see me no more; there is deliverance from judgment because the prince of this world has already been judged. " said Jesus Christ

SINS (our choice of thoughts and /or words and/or actions that separates us From God)

SKIES, SKY   MARK 13; 24-25

"After the tribulation ends, then the sun will grow dim and the moon will not shine, and the stars will fall from the sky-the heaven will convulse. " said Jesus Christ

(see END TIMES, SIGNS and others)

S   273

SLANDER   MATTHEW 15;19-20

"For from the heart comes evil thoughts, murder, adultery, fornication, theft lying and **slander.** These are what defile; there is no spiritual defilement from eating without first going through the ritual of ceremonial hand washing." said Jesus Christ

SLOW   LUKE 24;25

Then Jesus said to the people, " You are such foolish, foolish people! Your heart is so **slow** to believe all that the prophets wrote in the Scriptures! Wasn't it clearly predicted that the Messiah would have to suffer all these things before he entered his time of glory?" said Jesus Christ

SON (used throughout the Bible especially the New Testament and interchanged with Messiah)

MATTHEW 8;20

But Jesus said, " Foxes have dens and birds have nests, but I, the **Son** of Man, have no home of my own- no place to lay my head." said Jesus Christ

MATTHEW 11;27

"Everything has been entrusted to me by my Father. Only the Father knows the **Son,** and the Father is only know by the **Son** and by those to whom the **Son** reveals him." said Jesus Christ

MATTHEW 16;27

"For I, the **Son** of Mankind, shall come with my angels in the glory of my Father and judge each person according to his deeds." said Jesus Christ

SON   MARK 8;38

"And anyone who is ashamed of me and my message in these days of unbelief and sin , I, the **Son** of Man will be ashamed of him when I return in the glory of my Father, with the holy angels." said Jesus Christ

MARK 13;32

"However, no one, not even the angels in Heaven, nor I the **Son,** knows the day or the hour when these things will happen; only the Father knows. And since you don't know when it will happen, stay alert. Be on the watch for my return." said Jesus Christ

MARK 14;62

" I am the **Son** of Man and you will see me sitting at the right hand of God, and returning to earth in the clouds in Heaven." said Jesus Christ

LUKE 12; 8-9

" And I assure you this: I, the **Son** of Man, will publicly honor you in the presence of God's angels if you publicly acknowledge me here on earth as your Friend. **But** I will deny before the angels those who deny me here among men. " said Jesus Christ

LUKE 18;6-8

Then the Lord said, " If even an evil judge can be worn down like that, don't you think that God will surely give justice to His people who plead with Him day and night? Yes, He will answer them

SON   LUKE 18;6-8 cont'd

quickly! But the question is: When I, the **Son** of Man return, how many will I find who have faith and are praying?" said Jesus Christ

LUKE 18; 31-33

Gathering the Twelve around him he told them, "As you know, we are going to Jerusalem. And when we get there, all the predictions of the ancient prophets concerning the **Son** of Man will come true. I will be handed over to the Gentiles to be mocked and treated shamefully and spat upon, and lashed and killed. And on the third day I will rise again?" said Jesus Christ

LUKE 19;9-10

Jesus told them, " This shows that salvation has come to this home today. This man was one of the lost sons of Abraham and I, the **Son** of Man, have come to search for and save souls such as his." said Jesus Christ   JOHN 3; 10-17

Jesus replied, " You, a respected Jewish teacher, and yet you don't understand these things? I am telling you what I know and what I have seen- and yet you don't believe. me. But if you don't believe me when I tell you about such things as these that happen here among men how can you possibly believe ifI tell you what is going on in Heaven? For only I , the Messiah, the **Son** of Man, have come to earth and will return to Heaven again. And

SON   JOHN 3; 10-17 cont'd

as Moses in the wilderness lifted up a bronze image of a serpent on a pole, even so, I must be lifted up upon a pole, so that everyone who believes in me will have eternal life. For God loved the world so much that He gave His only **Son** so that anyone who believes in Him shall not perish but have eternal life. God did not send His **Son** into the world to condemn it, but to save it." said Jesus Christ   JOHN 5;19-21

Jesus replied, "The **Son** can do nothing by himself He does only what he sees the Father doing, in the same way. For the Father loves the **Son,** and tells him everything He is doing and the **Son** will do far more awesome miracles than this man's healing. He will even raise from the dead anyone he wants to as the Father does." said Jesus Christ   JOHN 6;38-40

" For I have come here from Heaven to do the will of God who sent me, not to have my own way. And this is the will of God that I should not lose even one of all those that He has given me, but I should raise them to eternal life on the Last Day. For it is my Father's will that everyone who sees His **Son** and believes in him should have eternal life-that I should raise them at the Last Day." said Jesus Christ

SON   JOHN 11;4

But when Jesus heard about it he said, "The purpose of his illness is not death, but for the glory of God. I, the **Son** of God will receive glory from this situation," said Jesus Christ

JOHN 13;31-33

"My time has come; the glory of God will soon surround me and the **Son** of Man glorified and receive great praise because of all that happens to me. And God will give me His own glory, and this is so very soon. Dear, dear children, how brief are these moments before I must go away and leave you! Then even though you search for me, you cannot come to me- just as I told the Jewish leaders.

"And so I am giving a new commandment to you now- love each other as much as I love you. Your strong love for each other will prove to the world that you are my disciples." said Jesus Christ

JOHN 17;1-5

When Jesus had finished saying all these things, he looked up to Heaven and said, "Father the time has come. Reveal the glory of Your **Son** so that he can give glory back to you. For you have given him authority over every man and woman in all the earth. He gives eternal life to each You have given him. And this is the way to have eternal life-by knowing you, the only true God and Jesus Christ, the one You sent to earth! I brought You glory by

278   S

SON   JOHN 17;1-5 cont'd
doing everything You told me to. And Father reveal my glory as I stand in Your presence, the glory we shared before the world began." said Jesus Christ

SONS   MATTHEW 5;8-10
"Happy are those whose hearts are pure, for they shall see God. Happy are those who strive for peace- they shall be called the **sons** of God. Happy are those who are persecuted because they are good, for the Kingdom of Heaven is theirs." said Jesus Christ

     MATTHEW 13;37-39
"All right, "said Jesus. "I am the farmer who sows the choice seed. The field is the world, and the seed represents the **sons** and daughters of the Kingdom; the thistles are the people belonging to Satan. The enemy who sowed the thistles among the wheat is the devil; the harvest is the end of the world, and the reapers are the angels." said Jesus Christ

     LUKE 6;35
"Love you *enemies!* Do good to *them!* Lend to *them!* And don't be concerned about the fact they won't repay. Then your reward in heaven will be very great, and you will be truly acting like **sons** of God, for He is kind to the *unthankful* and to those who are *very wicked.* " said Jesus Christ

SONS   JOHN 12;35-36

Jesus replied, "My light will shine out for you just a little while longer. Walk in it while you can, and go where you want before darkness falls, for then it will be too late for you to find your way. Make use of the Light while there is still time; then you will become **sons** of light." said Jesus Christ

SOUL (S)   MATTHEW 10;28

"Don't be afraid of those who can kill only your bodies-but can't touch your **souls!** Fear only God who can destroy both your body and **soul** in hell."said Jesus Christ

MATTHEW 11;29-30

"Come with me and I will give you rest- all of you who work so hard beneath a heavy yoke. Wear my yoke- for it fits perfectly- and Jet me teach you; for I am gentle and humble. And you shall find rest for your **souls;** for I give you only light burdens." said Jesus Christ

MATTHEW 16; 24-26

Then Jesus said to his disciples, "If anyone wants to be a follower of mine, Jet him deny himself and take up a cross and follow me. For anyone whokeeps his life for himself shall lose it; anyone wholoses his life for me shall find it again. What profitis there if you gain the whole world- and Jose your **soul,** your eternal life?" said Jesus Christ

SOUL(S)   MARK 8;36-38

"And how does a man benefit if he gains the whole world and loses his **soul** in the process? For is anything worth more than his **soul?** And anyone who is ashamed of me and my message in these days of unbelief and sin, I, the Messiah will be ashamed of him when I return in the glory of my Father, with the holy angels. " said Jesus Christ

SPARROW(S)   MATTHEW 10;29

"Not one **sparrow,** What do they cost? Two for a penny? can fall to the ground without your Father knowing it. And the very hairs on your head are all numbered, so don't worry! You are more valuable to Him than many **sparrows!"** said Jesus Christ

LUKE 12;6-7

" What is the price of five **sparrows?** A couple of pennies? Not much more than that. Yet God does not forget a single one of them. And He knows the number of hairs on your head! Never fear, you are more valuable to Him than a flock of **sparrows."** said Jesus Christ

SPEAK,SPEAKING,SPEAKS

MATTHEW 10;19-20

"When you are arrested, don't worry about what to say at your trial. For you will be given the right words at the right time. For it won't be you doing the talking- it will be the Spirit of your Heavenly father **speaking** through you!" said Jesus Christ

SPEAK, SPEAKING,
SPEAKS   MATTHEW 12;31-32

"Even blasphemy against me or any other sin can be forgiven-all except one; **speaking** against the Holy Spirit shall never be forgiven in this world or the world to come." said Jesus Christ

MARK 7;6-8

Jesus replied. "You bunch of hypocrites! Isaiah the prophet described you very well when he said, 'These people **speak** very prettily about the Lord but they have no love for Him at all. Their worship is a farce, for they claim that God' commands the people to obey their petty rules.' How right Isaiah was! For you ignore God's specific orders and substitute your own traditions." said Jesus Christ

MARK 12;35-37

... "Why do your religious teachers claim that the Messiah must be a descendant of King David? For David himself said- and the Holy Spirit was **speaking** through him when he said it- 'God said to my Lord, sit at my right hand until I make your enemies your footstool.' Since David called him his Lord, how can he be his son? " said Jesus Christ

LUKE 6;43-45

" A good man produces good deeds from a good heart. And an evil man produces evil deeds from his hidden wickedness. Whatever is in the heart overflows into what he **speaks.**" said Jesus Christ

SPEAK, SPEAKING, SPEAKS   JOHN 12;49-50

"For I do not **speak** on my own accord, but I have told you what the Father said to tell you. And I know His instructions lead to eternal life; so whatever He tells to say, I say!" said Jesus Christ

SPECK (see BOARD)

SPIRIT (S) (Spirit and spirituality are used throughout the Bible . These are quotes telling us what it is. See also HOLY SPIRIT, SPEAK)

MATTHEW   12;43-45

" The evil nation is like a man possessed by a demon. For if the demon leaves, it goes into the deserts for a while, seeking rest but finding none. Then it says, 'I will return to the man I came from. So it returns and finds the man's heart clean but empty! The demon finds seven other **spirits** more evil than itself, all enter the man and live within him. And he is worse off than before." said Jesus Christ

MATTHEW 26;41

"Keep alert and pray. Otherwise temptation will overpower you. For the **spirit** is indeed willing but the body is weak." said Jesus Christ

LUKE 4;18-19

" The **Spirit** of the Lord is upon me; He has appointed me to preach the Good News to the poor; He sent me to heal the brokenhearted and to

SPIRIT (S) (Spirit and spirituality are used throughout the Bible . These are quotes telling us what it is.) (See also HOLY SPIRIT, SPEAK)

LUKE 4;18-19 cont'd

announce that captives shall be released and the blind shall see and the downtrodden shall be freed from their oppressors, and God is ready to give blessings to all that come to Him." said Jesus Christ

LUKE 11;13

"And even if sinful persons like yourselves give children what they need, don't you realize that your Heavenly Father will do at least as much , and give the Holy **Spirit** to those who ask Him?" said Jesus Christ   LUKE23;46

Then Jesus shouted, "Father, I commit my **spirit** unto You."(and with those words he died)

JOHN 3; 5-8

Jesus replied, "What I am telling you so earnestly is this; Unless one is born of water and the **Spirit,** he cannot enter the Kingdom of God. Men can only reproduce human life, but the Holy **Spirit** gives new life from Heaven; so don't be surprised at my statement that you must be born again! Just as you hear the wind but can't tell where it comes from or where it will go next, so it is with the **Spirit.** We do not know on whom he will next bestow life from Heaven." said Jesus Christ

284   S

SPIRIT (S) (Spirit and spirituality are used throughout the Bible . These are quotes telling us what it is.) (See also HOLY SPIRIT, SPEAK)

JOHN 4;21-23

Jesus replied, "The time is coming ma'am, when we will no longer be concerned about whether to worship the Father here or in Jerusalem. For it is not where we worship that counts, but how we worship- is our worship **spiritual** and real? Do we have the Holy **Spirit's** help? For God is **Spirit,** we must have His help to worship as we should. The Father wants this kind of worship from us." said Jesus Christ

JOHN 6;61-64

Jesus knew within himself that his disciples were complaining and said to them, "Does this offend you? Then what will you think if you see me, the Messiah, return to Heaven again? Only the Holy **Spirit** gives eternal life. Those born only once with physical birth, will never receive this gift. But now I have told you how to get this true **spiritual** life. But some of you don't believe me."(For Jesus knew from the beginning who didn't believe and knew the one who would betray him.)   said Jesus Christ

JOHN 7; 37-39

On the last day of the climax of the holidays Jesus shouted to the crowds, "If anyone is thirsty, lethim come to me and drink. For the Scriptures declare that the rivers of living water shall flow

S   285

SPIRIT (S)   (Spirit and spirituality are used throughout the Bible . These are quotes telling us what it is.) (See also HOLY SPIRIT, SPEAK)

JOHN 7; 37-39 cont'd

from the inmost being of anyone who believes in me. {He was speaking of the Holy **Spirit,** who would be given to everyone believing in him; but the **Spirit** had not yet been given, because Jesus had not returned to his glory in Heaven}

JOHN 9:39

Then Jesus told him, "I have come into the world to give sight to those who are **spiritually** blind and to show who think they see that they are blind." said Jesus Christ   JOHN 14;15-17

If you love me, obey me; I will ask the Father to and He will send you another Comforter, He will never leave you. He is the Holy **Spirit.** The world at large cannot receive him, for it isn't looking for him and doesn't recognize him. But you do, for he lives with you now and someday shall be in you." said Jesus Christ   JOHN 14;26

"But when the Father sends the Comforter instead of me- and by the Comforter I mean the Holy **Spirit-** he will teach you much, as well as remind you of everything myself have told you." said Jesus Christ   JOHN 15;26-27

"But I will send you the Comforter- the Holy **Spirit,** the source of all Truth. He will come to you

SPIRIT (S) (Spirit and spirituality are used throughout the Bible . These are quotes telling us what it is.) (See also HOLY SPIRIT, SPEAK)

JOHN 15;26-27 cont'd

from the Father and will tell you about me. And you also must tell everyone about me because you have been with me from the beginning." said Jesus Christp   JOHN 16;13

"When the Holy **Spirit,** who is Truth, comes, he shall guide you into all Truth, for he will not be presenting his own ideas, but will be passing on what he has heard. He will tell you about the future." said Jesus Christ

STAND   MATTHEW 10;22

"Brother shall betray brother to death, and fathers will betray their own children. And children will rise against their parents and cause their deaths. Everyone shall hate you because you belong to me. But all of you who **stands** firm until the end shall be saved." said Jesus Christ   LUKE 21;16-19

"Even the closest to you-your parents, brothers, sisters, relatives and friends will betray you and have you arrested; and some of you will be killed. And everyone will hate you because you are mine and are called by my name. But not a hair on your head will perish! For if you **stand** firm, you will win your souls." said Jesus Christ

STAND JOHN 16;11

"The world's sin is unbelief in me; there is righteousness available because I go to the Father and you shall see me no more; there is deliverance from judgment because the prince of this world stands condemned." said Jesus Christ

STARS MARK 13;24-25

"After the tribulation ends, then the sun will grow dim and the moon will not shine, and the stars will fall-the heavens will convulse." said Jesus Christ

STEAL MATTHEW 6;19-21

"Don't store up treasures here on earth where they can erode away or thieves can steal them. Store them in Heaven where they will never lose their value, and are safe from thieves. If your profits are in heaven your heart will be there too." said Jesus Christ MATTHEW 19;18

And Jesus replied, "Don't kill, don't commit adultery, don't steal, don't lie, honor your father and mother and love your neighbor as yourself!" said Jesus Christ JOHN 10;10

"The thief s purpose is to steal, kill and destroy. My purpose is to give life in all its fullness."said Jesus Christ

STONE,(S) MATTHEW 7;9-11

"If a child asks his father for a loaf of bread will he be given a stone instead? If he asks for a fish will he be given a poisonous snake? Of course not! And

STONE, (S)   MATTHEW 7;9-11 cont'd
if you hardhearted sinful men know how to give good gifts to your children, won't your Father in Heaven even more certainly give good gifts to those who ask for them?" said Jesus Christ

MATTHEW 23;37-39

" O Jerusalem, Jerusalem the city that kills prophets and **stones** all those God has sends to her! How often have I wanted to gather your children together as a hen gathers her chicks beneath her wings, but you wouldn't let me. And now your house left yo you is desolate. For I tell you this, you will never see me again until you are ready to welcome the one sent to you from God." said Jesus Christ   MATTHEW 24;2

But he told them, "All of these buildings will be knocked down, with not one **stone** left on top of another." said Jesus Christ

MARK 12;10

"Don't you remember reading the Scriptures? The Rock the builders threw away became the cornerstone the most honored **stone** in the building! This is the Lord's doing and an amazing thing to see." said Jesus Christ   MARK 13;2

Jesus replied, "Yes, look! For not one **stone** will be left upon another, except as ruins." said Jesus Christ

STONE, (S)   LUKE 19;40

Jesus replied, "If they keep quiet, the **stones** along the road will burst into cheers." said Jesus Christ   LUKE 20;17-18

Jesus looked at them and said, "Then what does the Scripture mean where it says, ' The **Stone** rejected by the builders was made the cornerstone? Whoever stumbles over that **Stone** shall be broken; and those on whom it falls will be crushed to dust, " said Jesus Christ   JOHN 8; 7

"All right, hurl the **stones** at her until she dies. But only he who never sinned may throw the first!" said Jesus Christ   JOHN 10;32

Jesus said, "At God's direction I have done many a miracle to help the people. For which one are you **stoning** me?" said Jesus Christ

STOP   JOHN 5;14

... "Now you are well; **stop** sinning as you did before, or something even worse may happen to you." said Jesus Christ   JOHN 6; 43-46

But Jesus replied, "**Stop** grumbling among yourselves about my saying that. For no one can come to me unless the Father who sent me draws them to me, and at the Last Day I will cause all such to rise again from the dead. As it is written in the Scriptures. They shall all be taught of God. Those the Father speaks to, who learn the Truth from Him, will be attracted to me. Not that anyone can see the

STOP   JOHN 6;43-46 cont'd

Father, for only I have seen Him." said Jesus Christ

JOHN 7;24

"**Stop** judging by mere appearances, and you will see that I am right." said Jesus Christ

JOHN 20;27

Then he said to Thomas, " Put your finger into my hands. Put your hand into my side. **Stop** doubting and believe!" said Jesus Christ

STRENGTH   MARK 12;29-30

Jesus replied, "The one that says. 'Hear, O, Israel! The Lord our God is the one and only God. And you must love Him with all your heart and soul and mind and **strength**. " said Jesus Christ

STRENGTHEN   LUKE 22;32

"..but I have pleaded in prayer for you that your faith would not completely fail. So when you have repented and turned to me again, **strengthen** and build up the faith of your brothers." said Jesus Christ

STROKE   MATTHEW 5;18

" I tell you the Truth, until Heaven and Earth disappear, not the smallest letter, not the least **stroke** of a pen, will by any means disappear from the Law until everything is accomplished. " said Jesus Christ   LUKE 16;17

"It is easier for Heaven and Earth to disappear than for the least **stroke** of a pen to drop out of the Law." said Jesus Christ

STUMBLE,(S)STUMBLING

MATTHEW 16;23

Jesus turned to Peter and said, "Get away from me, you Satan!. You are a **stumbling** block to me. You are thinking merely from a human point of view, and not from God's." said Jesus Christ

JOHN 11;9-11

Jesus replied, "There are twelve hours of daylight every day, and during every hour of it a man can walk safely and not **stumble.** Only at night is there danger of a wrong step because of the dark,... Our friend Lazarus has gone to sleep, but now I will go and awaken him!" said Jesus Christ

STUPIDITY , (FOOLS, FOOLISHNESS)

LUKE 11;39-41

Then Jesus said to them, "You Pharisees wash the outside, but inside you are still dirty-full of greed and wickedness! Fools! What **stupidity!** Didn't God make the inside as well as the outside? Purity is the best demonstrated by generosity. "said Jesus Christ

LUKE 24;25-26

Then Jesus said to them, "You are such foolish, foolish people! What **stupidity!** You find it so hard to believe all the prophets wrote in the Scriptures! Wasn't it clearly predicted by the prophets that the Messiah would have to suffer all these things before entering his time of glory?" said Jesus Christ

SUFFER , SUFFERING LUKE 22;15

" I have looked forward to this hour with deep longing, anxious to eat this Passover meal with you before my **suffering** begins. For I tell you now that I won't eat it again until what it represents has occurred in the Kingdom of God." said Jesus Christ

LUKE 24;26

" Wasn't it clearly predicted that the Messiah would have to **suffer** all these thing s before entering his time of glory?" said Jesus Christ

LUKE 24;43-48

Then he said, "When I was with you before, don't you remember my telling you that everything written about me by Moses and the prophets and in the Psalms must all come true?"{ Then he opened their minds so they understood all the Scriptures!} And he said, " Yes, it is written long ago that the Messiah must **suffer** and die and rise again from the dead on the third day; and the message of salvation should be taken from Jerusalem to all nations: *There is forgiveness of sins for all who turn to me.* You have seen these prophecies come true." said Jesus Christ

SULFUR, SULPHUR , BRIMSTONE

LUKE 17;28-30

"And the world will be as it was in the days of lot: people went about their daily business- eating and drinking, buying and selling, farming and

SULFUR, SULPHUR , BRIMSTONE
LUKE l7;28-30

building-until the morning Lot left Sodom. The fire and brimstone (sulfur) rained down from Heaven and destroyed them all. Yes, it will be business as usual' right up to the hour of my return." said Jesus Christ

SUN, SUNLIGHT (see also SHINE)
MATTHEW 5;45

"In that way you will be acting like true sons of your Father in Heaven. For He gives sunlight to both the evil and the good. And sends rain on the just and the unjust too." said Jesus Christ

MARK 13;24-25

"After the Tribulation ends, then the sun will grow dim and the moon will not shine, and the stars will fall- the heavens will convulse."said Jesus Christ

SURROUND
LUKE 21;20-21

"But when you see Jerusalem surrounded by armies, then you will know that the time of destruction has arrived. Then let the people of Judea flee to the hills. Let those in Jerusalem try to escape, and those outside the city must not attempt to return." said Jesus Christ

SURVIVE
MARK 13;20

"And unless the Lord shortens that time of calamity, not a soul on earth will survive. But for

SURVIVE   MARK 13;20 cont'd

the sake of His chosen ones, He will limit those days." said Jesus Christ

SWALLOW   MATTHEW 23;24

"Blind guides! You strain out a gnat and **swallow** a camel!" said Jesus Christ

SWEAR   MATTHEW 5;34-37

"But I say: Don't make any vows! And even to say, ' By heavens!' is a sacred vow to God, for the heavens are God's throne. And if you say,' By the earth!' it is a sacred vow, for the earth is His footstool! And don't **swear!** ' By Jerusalem!' for Jerusalem is the capital of a great King. Don't even **swear,** ' By my head!' for you can't turn one hair white or black. Say just a simple, 'Yes, I will' or 'No, I won't.' your word is enough. To strengthen your words with a vow shows that something is wrong." said Jesus Christ

SWORD   MATTHEW 10;34

" Don't imagine that I came to bring peace to the earth! No, rather a **sword.** I have come to set man against his father and daughter against her mother, and a daughter-in -law against her mother-in -law- a man's worst enemies will be right in his own home." said Jesus Christ

SWORD   MATTHEW 26;52

"Put away your sword," Jesus told him, "those who fight with the sword will die by the sword." said Jesus Christ   MARK 14;48

Jesus asked them. "Am I some dangerous robber, that you come at me like this with your swords and your clubs armed to the teeth to capture me? Why didn't you arrest me at the Temple? I was there teaching every day. But these things are happening to fulfill the prophecies about me." said Jesus Christ

T

TAKEN, TAKE(S) MATTHEW 13;12

"For to him who has, more will be given," he told them, "and he will have great plenty; but from him who has not, even the little he has will be taken away. That is why I use these illustrations, so people will see and hear but not understand." said Jesus Christ   MATTHEW 24;40

"Two men will be working in the fields and the one will be taken and the other one left. Two women will be going about their household tasks; one will be taken and the other one left." said Jesus Christ

TAKEN, TAKE(S) MATTHEW 26;39

He went forward a little and fell face downward on the ground and prayed, "My Father! If it is possible, Jet this cup be **taken** away from me. But I want Your will be done, not mine."said Jesus Christ   MARK 4;15

"The farmer I talked about is anyone who tries to bring the God's message to others, trying to plant good seeds within their lives. The hard pathway, where some seeds fell, represents the hard hearts of some who hear God's message; Satan comes at once and **takes** away the words to make them forget." said Jesus Christ   LUKE 6;30-31

" Give what you have to anyone who asks for it; and when things are **taken** away from you, don't worry about getting them back. Treat others as you would have them treat you."said Jesus Christ {LUKE 6; 31...above...is the Golden Rule}
JOHN 10;18

"No one can kill me without my consent- I lay down my life voluntarily. For I have the right and the power to lay it down when I want to and the power to **take** it again." said Jesus Christ

TALK(S)   MATTHEW 12; 33-37

A tree is identified by its fruit, a tree from a select variety produces good fruit and poor varieties don't. You brood of snakes! How could evil men like you **talk** about what is good and right? For a man's

TALK(S)   MATTHEW 12;33-37 cont'd
heart determines his speech. A good man's speech
reveals his treasures within him. An evil hearted
man is filled with venom and his speech reveals it.
And I tell you this, that you must give account on
judgment Day for every idle word you speak. You
words now reflect your fate then: either you will be
justified by them or you will be condemned." said
Jesus Christ

TAUGHT, TEACH (ES) (ER(S) (ING)
MATTHEW 5;19
"And so if anyone breaks the least of the
commandments and **teaches** others to do so, he
shall be least in the Kingdom of Heaven. But those
who **teach** God's laws and obey them shall be great
in the kingdom of Heaven." said Jesus Christ

MATTHEW 10;24
"A student is not greater than his **teacher."** said
Jesus Christ   MATTHEW 13;52
Then he added, " Those **teachers** of Jewish law
who are now my disciples have double treasures-
from the Old Testament as well as the New!" said
Jesus Christ

MATTHEW 15;9
"These people say they honor me, but their
hearts are faraway. Their worship is worthless, for
they **teach** their man-made laws instead of those
from God. "said Jesus Christ

TAUGHT, TEACH (ES) (ER) (S) (ING)
MATTHEW 28;18-20

He told his disciples, "I have been given all authority in Heaven and Earth. Therefore go and make disciples in all nations, baptizing them in the name of the Father and of the Son and of the Holy Spirit, and **teach** these new disciples to obey all commands I have given you; and be sure of this- I am with you always, even until the end of the world." said Jesus Christ

MARK 12;38-40

"Beware of **teachers** of religion! For they love to wear the robes of the rich and scholarly, and to have everyone bow to them as they walk through the markets. They love to sit in the best seats in the synagogues, and the places of honor at banquets- but they shamelessly cheat widows out of their homes and then to cover up the kind of men they really are, they pretend to be pious by praying long prayers in public. Because of this their punishment will be greater." said Jesus Christ

LUKE 6;40

"How can a student know more than his **teacher?** But if he works hard he may learn as much.." said Jesus Christ   LUKE 12;12

"...for the Holy Spirit will **teach** you the right words to say even as you are standing there." said Jesus Christ

T   299

TAUGHT, TEACH (ES) (ER(S) (ING)
LUKE 20;46

"Beware of these **teachers** of religion, for they love to parade in dignified robes and be bowed to by people as they walk along the street. And how they love seats of honor in the synagogues and religious festivals! But even while they are praying long prayers with great outward piety, they are planning schemes to cheat widows out of their property. Therefore God's heaviest sentence awaits these men." said Jesus Christ

JOHN 6;45

"As it is written in the Scriptures, ' They shall be **taught** by God.' Those the Father speaks to, who learn the truth from Him, will be attracted to me." said Jesus Christ

JOHN 7;16-17

So Jesus told them, "I'm not **teaching** you my own thoughts, but those of God who sent me. If any of you really determines to do God's will, then you will certainly know whether my **teaching** is from God or merely my own ." said Jesus Christ

JOHN 13;13-13-14

" You call me 'Master and Lord' and you do well to say it for it is true. And since I, the Lord and **Teacher,** have washed your feet you ought to wash each other's feet. I have given you an example to follow to do as I have done to you" said Jesus Christ

300   T

TAUGHT, TEACH (ES) (ER(S) (ING)
JOHN 14;24-26

"Anyone who doesn't obey me doesn't love me. And remember, I am not making up the answer to your question! It is the answer given to me by the Father who sent me. I am telling you these things while I am still here with you. But when the Father sends the Comforter- and by the Comforter I mean the Holy Spirit-he will **teach** you much as well as remind you of everything I, myself have told you." said Jesus Christ

TAX(ES), COLLECTORS
MATTHEW 5; 46

" If you love only those who love you, what good is that? Even **tax collectors** do that much. If you arefriendly to only your friends, how different are you from anyone else? Even the heathen do that! But you are to be perfect even as your Father is perfect!" said Jesus Christ

MATTHEW 11;19

"And I, the Messiah, feast and drink, and you complain that I am a glutton and a drinking man and hang around **tax collectors** and sinners! But brilliant men like you can justify every inconsistency!" said Jesus Christ

T   301

TAX(ES), COLLECTORS
MATTHEW 17;25-27

..."What do you think, Peter? Do kings levy taxes against their own people or conquered foreigners?"

{"Against the foreigners." Peter replied}

" Well then," Jesus said, "the citizens are free! However we don't want to offend them, so go down to the shore and throw in a line, and open the mouth of the first fish you catch. You will find a coin to cover the taxes for both of us; and take it and pay them." said Jesus Christ

MATTHEW 22; 17-21

{"Now tell us if it is right to pay taxes to the Roman government or not."}

But Jesus knew what they were after. " You hypocrites!" he exclaimed. " Who are you trying to fool with your trick questions? Here, show me a coin. [and they handed him a penny]

"Whose picture is stamped on it? He asked them. "And whose name is beneath the picture?" {"Caesar's" they replied}

"Well, then," he said, "give it to Caesar if it is his and give to God everything that belongs to God." said Jesus Christ'

MARK 12;15-17

{"Now tell us if it is right to pay taxes to Rome or not,"} Jesus saw their trick and said, " Show me a coin and I'll tell you. Whose picture and title are on

TAX(ES), COLLECTORS

MARK 12;15-17cont'd

this coin?...All right," he said, "if it his, give it to him. But everything that belongs to God must be given to God!" said Jesus Christ

LUKE 18; 10-14

[Then he told this story to some who boasted about their virtue and scorned (put down) everyone else]

"Two men went into the Temple to pray. One was a proud, self-righteous Pharisee, and the other a cheating tax collector. The proud Pharisee 'prayed' this prayer, 'Thank God, I am not a sinner like everyone else, especially like that tax collector over there! For I never cheat, I don't commit adultery, I go without food twice a week, and I give God a tenth of everything I earn.'

"But the corrupt tax collector stood at a distance and dared to not even lift his eyes to Heaven as he prayed, but beat upon his chest in sorrow, exclaiming, "God be merciful to me, a sinner. I tell you this sinner, not the Pharisee returned home forgiven! For the proud shall be humbled, but the humble shall be honored." said Jesus Christ

TEMPLE   MATTHEW 12;6

"And truly the one is here who is greater than the Temple," said Jesus Christ

TEMPLE   JOHN 2; 14-16

{In the **Temple** are he saw merchants selling cattle, sheep and doves for sacrifices, and money changers behind the counters. Jesus made a whip from some ropes and chased them all out, and drove out the sheep and the oxen scattering the money changers' coins all over the floor and turning over the tables! Then going over to the men selling doves, he told them,} "Get these things out of here! Don't turn my Father's house into a market!" said Jesus Christ   JOHN 2;19

"All right, "Jesus replied, "this is the miracle I will do for you: Destroy this sanctuary **(temple)** and in three days I will raise it up!" said Jesus Christ 21[But by this "sanctuary" **(temple)** he meant his body. After he came back to life again, the disciples remembered him saying this and realized that what he had quoted from the Scriptures really did refer to him, and all had come true!]

TEMPT, (ATION), (ED), (ER), (ING), (S)
MATTHEW 26;41

"Keep alert and pray. Otherwise **temptation** will over power you. For the spirit is indeed willing, but how weak the body is!" said Jesus Christ
MARK 14;38

"Watch with me and pray lest the **Tempter** over power you. For though the spirit is willing the body is weak." said Jesus Christ

TEMPT, (ATION), (ED), (ER), (ING), (S)
LUKE 22;40, 46

Then he told them, " Pray God that you will not be overcome by **temptation**" said Jesus Christ 46 "Asleep!" he said "Get up! Pray God that you will not fall when you are **tempted!**" said Jesus Christ.

(also see PRAYERS)

TERROR (S)   (see also SIGNS)
LUKE 21; 8-33

He replied, " Don't let anyone mislead you. For many will come announcing themselves as the Messiah, and saying 'The time has come.' But don't believe them! And when you hear of wars and insurrections beginning, don't panic. True, wars must come, but the end won't follow immediately- for nation will rise against nation and kingdom against kingdom, and there will be great earthquakes and famines in many lands, and epidemics and terrifying things happen in the heavens.

"But before all this occurs, there will be a time of special persecution, and you will be dragged into synagogues and prisons and before kings and governors for my name's sake. But as a result, the Messiah will be widely known and honored. Therefore don't be concerned about how you

T   305

TERROR (S)   (see also SIGNS)

LUKE 21; 8-33 cont'd

answer charges against you, for I will give you the right words with such logic that none of your opponents will be able to reply! Even those closest to you- your parents, your brothers, your sisters, relatives and friends will betray you and have you arrested; and some of you will be killed. And everyone will hate you because you are mine and are called by my name. But not a hair on your head will perish! For if you stand firm, you will win your souls.

"But when you see Jerusalem surrounded by armies, then you will know the time of destruction has arrived. Then let the people of Judea flee to the hills. Let those in Jerusalem try to escape, and those outside the city must not try to return. For those will be the days of God's judgment, and the words of the ancient Scriptures written by the prophets will be abundantly fulfilled. Woe to expectant mothers in those days and those with tiny babies. For there will be great distress upon the nation and wrath upon its people. They will be brutally killed by enemy weapons and sent away as exiles and captives to all nations of the world; and Jerusalem shall be conquered and trampled down by the Gentiles until the period of Gentile triumph ends in God's good time.

TERROR (S) (see also SIGNS)

LUKE 21; 8-33 cont'd

"Then there will be strange events in the skies- warnings, evil omens and **potents** in the sun, moon and stars; and down here on earth nations will be perplexed by roaring seas and strange tides. The courage of many will falter because of the fearful fate they see coming upon the earth, for the stability of the very heavens will be broken up. Then the people of the earth shall see me, the Messiah, coming in a cloud with power and great glory. So when all of these things begin to happen, stand straight and look up! For your salvation is near.

Then he gave them this illustration; "Notice a fig tree, or any other tree. When the leaves come out, you know without being told that summer is near. It is the same way when you see these events taking place that I have described you can be just as sure the Kingdom of God is near.

"I solemnly declare to you that when these things happen, the end of the age has come. And though all heaven and earth shall pass away, yet my words remain forever true." said Jesus Christ

TEST (ING)   LUKE 4;12

Jesus replied, "The Scriptures also say, ' Do not put the Lord your God to a foolish **test**." said Jesus Christ

TEST (ING)   LUKE 8;13

"The stony ground represents people who enjoy listening to sermons, but somehow the message never really gets through to them and doesn't take root and grow. They know the message is true, and sort of believe for a while; but in times of **testing** and the hot winds of persecution blow, they lose interest and fall away." said Jesus Christ

TESTIFY (ED) (ES) **(MONY)**

MATTHEW 15;19

" But evil words come from an evil heart, and defile the man who says them. For from the heart comes evil thoughts, murder, adultery, fornication, theft, lying and **false testimony** and slander. These are what defile; but there is no defilement from eating without first going through ceremonial hand washing !" said Jesus Christ

MATTHEW 24; 14

"And the Good News will be preached throughout the whole world as a **testimony** so that all nations will hear it, and then, the end will finally come. "said Jesus Christ

JOHN 5;24-47

" I say emphatically that anyone who listens to my message and believes in God who sent me has eternal life and will never be damned for his sins, but already has passed out of death into life. And I solemnly declare that the time is coming, in fact it is

TESTIFY (ED) (ES) (MONY)

JOHN 5; 24-47 cont'd

here, when the dead shall hear my voice- the voice of the Son of God- and those who listen shall live. The Father has life in Himself, and has granted His Son to have life in himself, and to judge the sins of all mankind because he is the Son of Man. Don't be surprised! Indeed the time is coming when all the dead in their graves shall hear the voice of God's Son and rise again-those who have done good to eternal life; and those who have continued to do evil to judgment.

"But I pass no judgment without consulting the Father, I judge as I am told. And my judgment is absolutely fair and just, for it is according to the will of God who sent me and is not merely my own.

"When I make claims about myself they aren't believed, but someone else, yes, John the Baptist, is **testifying** for me too. You have gone out to listen to his preaching, I can assure you all he says is true! But the truest witness I have is not from man, though I have reminded you about John's witness so that you believe in me and be saved. John shone brightly for a while, and you benefited and rejoiced, but I have a greater witness than John. I refer to the miracles I do; these have been assigned to me by the Father, and they prove the Father has sent me. And

TESTIFY (ED) (ES) (MONY)

JOHN 5; 24-47 cont'd

the Father Himself has also **testified** about me, although not appearing to you personally, or speaking to you directly. But you are not listening to Him, for you refuse to believe me-the one sent to you with God's message.

"You search the Scriptures, for you believe they give you eternal life. And the Scriptures point to me! Yet, you won't come to me so that I can give
. you this life eternal."

"Your approval of disapproval means nothing to me, for as I know so well, you don't have God's love within you. I know because I have come to you representing my Father and you refuse to welcome me, though you readily enough receive those who aren't sent from Him, but represent only themselves! No wonder you can't believe! For you gladly honor each other, but you don't care about the honor that comes from God!

"Yes, it is I who will accuse you of this to my Father-Moses will! Moses on whose laws you set your hopes for heaven. For you have refused to believe Moses. For he wrote about me, but you refuse to believe him, so you refuse to believe in me. And since you don't believe what he wrote, no wonder you don't believe in me either" said Jesus Christ

310   T

TESTIFY (ED) (ES) (MONY)
JOHN 7;7

Jesus replied, "It is not the right time for me to go now. But you can go anytime and it will make no difference, for the world can't hate you, but it does hate me, because I testify that it does evil! You go on, I'll come later." {So he remained in Galilee} said Jesus Christ

JOHN 8;17

" Your laws say that if two men testify on something that has happened, their witness is accepted as fact. Well, I am one witness and my Father who sent me is the other." said Jesus Christ

JOHN 15;26-27

"But I will send you the Comforter- the Holy Spirit, the source of all truth. He will come to you from the Father and will tell you all about me. And you also must testify to everyone about me, because you have been with me from the beginning." said Jesus Christ

THANKS   JOHN 11;41-43

So they rolled the stone aside. Then Jesus looked up to the heaven and said, "Father, thank you for hearing me. You always hear me, of course, but I said it because all these people standing here will believe You sent me." Then he shouted, "Lazarus come out!" said Jesus Christ

THEFT,THIEF, THIEVES, (see also
STEAL &THINK & THOUGHT &
TREASURE)   MATTHEW 15;19-20

"For from the heart comes evil thoughts, murder,
adultery, fornication, theft, lying, and slander.
These are what defile; but there is no spiritual
defilement from eating without first going through
the ritual of ceremonial hand washing." said Jesus
Christ   LUKE 12;39-40

"Everyone should be ready for him if they knew
the exact hour of his return-just as they would be
ready for a thief if they knew he was coming. So be
ready all of the time. For , I, the Messiah, will come
when least expected." said Jesus Christ

JOHN 10;10

"The thief's purpose is to steal, kill and destroy.
My purpose is to give life in all its fullness." said
Jesus Christ

THING(S)   MATTHEW 19; 26

Jesus looked at them intently and said, "Humanly
speaking, no one, but with God all things are
possible" said Jesus Christ   MARK 10;21

Jesus felt genuine love for this man as he looked
at him and said, "There is only one thing you lack.
Go and sell everything you have and give the money
to the poor- and you shall have treasure in heaven-
and come follow me." said Jesus Christ

THING(S)   LUKE 6;45

"A good man brings good **things** out of a good heart. And evil man produces evil **things** from his hidden wickedness. Whatever is in the heart overflows into the speech." said Jesus Christ

LUKE 9;22

He gave them strict orders not to speak about this to anyone. "For , I, the Messiah, must suffer many **things,**" he said, "and be rejected by Jewish leaders-the elders, chief priests, and teachers of the law-and be killed and three days later I will come back to life again!" said Jesus Christ   LUKE 10;21-22

Then he was filled with joy of the Holy Spirit and said, "I praise You, O Father, Lord of Heaven and Earth, for hiding these **things** from the intellectuals and worldly wise and revealing them to those trusting as little children. Yes, thank you Father for that is the way You wanted it. I am an Agent of my Father in everything and no one really knows the Son except the Father, and no one really knows the Father except the Son and those to whom the Son chooses to reveal Him." said Jesus Christ

LUKE 10;42

But the Lord said to her, " Martha, dear friend, you are so upset over these details! There is really only one **thing** worth being concerned about. Mary has discovered it-I won't take that away from her!" said Jesus Christ

T 313

THING(S) JOHN 14;12-13

"In solemn truth I tell you; anyone believing in me shall do the same miracles I have done, and even greater ones. Because I am going to be with the Father. You can ask Him for **anything,** using my name, and I will do it, for this will bring praise to the Father because of what I, the Son will do for you. Yes, ask **anything,** using my name and I will do it!" Jesus Christ

THINK, THOUGHT

MATTHEW 22;42

Then surrounded by Pharisees he asked the question, "What do you **think** about the Messiah? Whose son is he?" said Jesus Christ

MARK 7;20-23

And then he added, "It is the **thought-life** that pollutes. For from within, out of men's hearts, come evil thoughts of lust, theft, murder, adultery, wanting what belongs to others, wickedness, deceit, lewdness, envy, slander, pride and all other folly. All of these vile things come from within; they are what pollute you and make you unfit for God." said Jesus Christ

THREE MATTHEW 12; 39-40

"Only an evil, faithless nation would ask for more proof, and none will be given except what happened to Jonah the prophet! For Jonah was in a great fish for **three** days and **three** nights, so I, the Messiah

THREE   MATTHEW 12;39-40 cont'd

will be in the earth for **three** days and **three** nights."
said Jesus Christ   MATTHEW 18;20

"For where two or **three** gather together because they are mine, I will be right among them." said Jesus Christ   MATTHEW 26;34

Jesus told him, "The truth is that this very night, before the cock crows at dawn, you will deny me **three** times." said Jesus Christ

MARK 14;30

"Peter," Jesus said, "before the cock crows a second time tomorrow morning you will deny me **three** times." said Jesus Christ

JOHN 2;19-22

"All right," Jesus replied, "this is the miracle I will do for you: Destroy this sanctuary and in **three** days I will raise it up!" said Jesus Christ
21-22{"What!" they exclaimed. "It took forty-six years to build this Temple and you will raise it in three days?}] [But by "this sanctuary" he meant his body. After he came back to life again, the disciples remembered him saying this and realized that what he had quoted from the Scriptures really did refer to him and had all come true!]

TIMES   MATTHEW 16;2-4

He replied, " You are good at reading the weather signs of the skies-red sky tonight means fair weather tomorrow, red sky in the morning meant foul

T 315

TIMES MATTHEW 16;2-4 cont'd
weather all day-but you aren't reading the obvious
signs of the **times!** This evil unbelieving nation is
asking for some strange sign in the heavens but no
further proof will be given except what happened to
Jonah," {Then Jesus walked out on them} said
Jesus Christ MATTHEW 18;21-22
{Then Peter came to him and asked," Sir, how
often must I forgive a brother who sins against me?
Seven times?"}"No!", Jesus replied, "seventy
times seven!"said Jesus Christ MARK 4;8
"But some of the seeds fell on good soil and
yielded thirty **times** as much as he planted-some of
it even sixty or a hundred **times** as much! If you
have ears listen!" said Jesus Christ
MARK 14;30
"Peter," Jesus said, "before the cock crows a
second time tomorrow morning you will deny me
three **times."** said Jesus Christ
LUKE 17;4
"Rebuke your brother if he sins and forgive him
if he is sorry. Even if he is wrong seven **times** a day
and each time turns to you and asks for forgiveness,
forgive him." said Jesus Christ

TODAY LUKE 23;43
And Jesus replied, "**Today** you will be with me
in paradise. This is a solemn promise" said Jesus
Christ

TOMORROW   MATTHEW 6;34

" So don't be anxious about **tomorrow.** God will take care of your **tomorrow** too. Live one day at a time." said Jesus Christ

TOOTH   MATTHEW 5;38-39

"The Law of Moses says, 'If a man gouges out another's eye, he must pay for it with his own eye. If a **tooth** gets knocked out, knock out the **tooth** of the one who did it. But I say; Don't resist violence! If you are slapped on the cheek, turn the other one too.!" said Jesus Christ

TORTURE (D)   MATTHEW 18;34

"Then the angry king sent the man to the **torture** chamber until he paid every penny due, so shall my heavenly Father do to you if you refuse to truly forgive your brothers." said Jesus Christ

TOUCH (ED), (ES)   MARK 5;30, 34

"Who **touched** my clothes?" asked Jesus.

34 " Daughter your faith has made you well; go in peace healed of your disease." said Jesus Christ

TRADITION(S)   MARK 7;6-8 ,13

Jesus replied, "You bunch of hypocrites! Isaiah described you very well when he said, 'These people speak very prettily about the Lord but they have no love for Him at all. Their worship is a farce, for they claim God's commands the people to obey their petty rules.' How right Isaiah was! For you ignore God's specific orders and substitute your

TRADITION(S)   MARK 7;6-8 ,13 cont'd
own **tradition.** You are simply rejecting God's
Laws for your own **tradition.''** 13 "And so you
break the law of God in order to protect your man-
made **tradition.** And this is only one example,
there are many others." said Jesus Christ

TRAMPLE (D) (ING) MATTHEW 5;13-16
 "You are the world's seasoning, to make it
tolerable. If you lose your flavor, what will happen
to the world? And you yourselves will be thrown
out and **trampled** underfoot as worthless. You are
the world's light- a city on a hill, glowing in the
night for all to see. Don't hide your light! Let it
shine for all; let your good deeds glow for all to see,
so they will praise your heavenly Father." said Jesus
Christ   MATTHEW 7;6
 " Don't give holy things to depraved men. Don't
give pearls to swine! They will **trample** the pearls
and turn and attack you." said Jesus Christ
                        LUKE 10;18-20
 "Yes," he told them, " I saw Satan falling from
Heaven as a flash of lightening! And I have given
you authority over all the power of the Enemy, and
to walk among the serpents and scorpions
trampling them. Nothing shall injure you!
However, the important thing is not that demons
obey you, but that your names are registered as
citizens of Heaven." said Jesus Christ

TRAMPLE (D) (ING)   LUKE 21;24

"They will be brutally killed by enemy weapons, or sent away as exiles and captives to all nations of the world; and Jerusalem will be conquered and **trampled** down by Gentiles until the period of Gentile triumph ends in God's good time." said Jesus Christ

TRAVEL   MATTHEW 23;15

"Yes, woe to you hypocrites. For you **travel** to all lengths to make one convert, and then turn him into twice the son of hell that you are yourselves." said Jesus Christ

TREASURE (D), (S)   MATTHEW 6;19-21

"Don't store up **treasure** here on earth where they can erode away or may be stolen. Store them in Heaven where they will never lose their value, and are safe from thieves. If your profits are in Heaven your heart will be too." said Jesus Christ

MATTHEW 13;44

" The Kingdom of Heaven is like a **treasure** a man discovered in a field. In his excitement, he sold everything he owned to get enough money to buy the field- and get the **treasure** too!" said Jesus Christ   MATTHEW 19; 21-24

Jesus told him, "If you want to be perfect, go and sell everything you have and give the money to the poor, you will have **treasure** in Heaven; and come follow me. {But when the young man heard this, he

TREASURE (D), (ES)   MATTHEW 19; 21-24
went away sadly as he was very rich.}

Then Jesus said to his disciples, "It is almost impossible for a rich man to enter the Kingdom of Heaven. I say it again, it is easier for a camel to go through the eye of a needle than a rich man to enter the Kingdom of God!" said Jesus Christ

LUKE 12;33

"Sell what you have and give to those in need. This will fatten your purse in Heaven! And the purses in Heaven have no rips or holes in them. Your **treasures** there will never disappear; no thief can steal them; no moth can destroy them. Wherever your **treasure** is, there your thoughts and heart will be also." said Jesus Christ

TREAT(ED),(S),(MENT) MATTHEW 18;35

"So shall my heavenly Father **treat** each of you if you truly refuse to forgive your brothers." said Jesus Christ

LUKE 6;22-23

"What happiness when others hate you and exclude you and insult you and smear your name because you are mine! When that happens rejoice! Yes, leap for joy! For you will have great reward awaiting you in Heaven! And you will be in good company- the ancient prophets were **treated** that way too!" said Jesus Christ

TREAT (ED), (S), (MENT)

JOHN 15;16-27 &
JOHN 16;1-4

"You didn't choose me, I chose you! I appointed you to go out and produce lovely fruit always, so that no matter what you ask in my name, He will give it to you. I demand that you love one another, for you get enough hate from the world! But then, it hated me before it hated you. The world would love you if you belonged to it; but you don't- for I chose you to come out of the world, and so it hates you. Do you remember what I told you? A slave isn't greater than his master! So since they persecuted me, naturally they will persecute you. And if they had listened to me, they would listen to you. The people of the world will persecute you because you belong to me, for they don't know God who sent me."

"They would not be guilty if I had not come and spoken to them. But now they have no excuse for their sin. Anyone hating me is also hating my Father. If I hadn't done such mighty miracles among them they would not be counted guilty. But as it is, they saw these miracles and yet they hated both of us- me and my Father. This has fulfilled what the prophets said concerning the Messiah. 'They hated me without reason.'"

TREAT (ED), (S), (MENT)
JOHN 15;16-27 &

JOHN 16;1-4   cont'd

"But I will send you the Comforter- the Holy Spirit, the source of all truth. He will come to you from the Father and will tell you about me. And you also must tell everyone about me, because you have been with me from the beginning." said Jesus Christ

JOHN 16;1-4 "I have told you these things so that you won't be staggered by all that lies ahead. For you will be excommunicated from the synagogues, and indeed the time is coming when those who choose to kill you will think they are doing God a service. This is because they have never known the Father or me. Yes, I am telling you these things now so that when they happen you will remember I warned you. I didn't tell you earlier because I was going to be with you a little while longer." said Jesus Christ

TREE   MATTHEW 3;10

" And even know God's axe is poised to chop down every unproductive **tree**. They will be chopped and burned." said Jesus Christ

MATTHEW 12;33

"A **tree** is identified by its fruit. A **tree** from a select variety produces good fruit, poor varieties don't. You brood of snakes! How could evil men like you speak what is good and right?" said Jesus Christ

TRIALS   LUKE 22;28-30

"Nevertheless, because you have stood by me in these times of terrible **trials,** and because my Father has granted me a Kingdom, I, here and now, grant you the right to eat and drink at my table in that Kingdom, and you will sit on thrones and judge the twelves tribes of Israel." said Jesus Christ

TRIBES   MATTHEW 19;28-30

And Jesus replied, "When, I, the Messiah, shall sit upon my glorious throne in the Kingdom, you disciples shall certainly sit on the twelve thrones judging the twelve **tribes** of Israel. And anyone who gives up his home, brothers, sisters, father ,mother, wife, children improper to follow me, shall receive

a hundred times as much in return, and shall have eternal life. But many of you who are first now will be last then; some who are last now will be first then." said Jesus Christ

TROUBLE (D), (S)   JOHN 14;1-4

" LET NOT YOUR HEART be **troubled.** You are trusting God, now trust in me. There are many homes up where my Father lives and I am going to prepare them for your coming. When everything is ready, then I will come and get you, so that you can always be with me where I am. If this weren't not so, I would tell you plainly. And you know where I am going and how to get there." said Jesus Christ

T   323

TROUBLE (D), (S)   JOHN 14;27-29

"I am leaving you with a gift-peace of mind and heart! And the peace I give isn't fragile like the peace the world gives. So let not you heart be **troubled** or afraid. Remember what I told you- I am going away, but I will come back to you again. If you really love me, you will be very happy for me, for now I can go to the Father, who is greater than I am. I have told you these things so that you will believe in me." said Jesus Christ

JOHN 16;33

"Do you finally believe this? Jesus asked. "But the time is coming-in fact it is here- when you will be scattered, each one returning to his own home, leaving me alone. Yet, I will not be alone, for the Father is with me. I have told you this so that you will have peace of heart and mind. Here on earth you will have many **troubles,** trials and sorrows; but cheer up, for I have overcome the world." said Jesus Christ

TRUE, TRUTH   LUKE 16;11-12

"And if you are untrustworthy about worldly wealth, who will trust you with the **true** riches of Heaven? And if you are not faithful with other people's money, why should you be trusted with money of your own? " said Jesus Christ

JOHN 3;21

"But whoever lives by the **Truth** will gladly

TRUE, TRUTH　　　JOHN 3;21 cont'd

come to the light to let everyone see that they are doing what God wants them, to." said Jesus Christ

JOHN 4;23-24

"The time is coming, in fact has now come, when the **true** worshipers will worship the Father in spirit and **Truth** for they're the kind of worshipers the Father seeks. God is Spirit, and His worshipers must worship Him in Spirit and in **Truth.**" said Jesus Christ　　　JOHN 5;31-34

"When I make these claims about myself, they aren't believed, but someone else, yes, John the Baptist, is making these claims too. You have gone out ot listen to his preaching, and I can assure you that all he says about me is **true!** But the **truest** witness I have is not from man, though I have reminded you about John's witness so that you will believe in me and be saved." said Jesus Christ

JOHN 6;32-33

Jesus said, " Moses didn't give it to them. My Father did. And now He offers you **true** bread from Heaven. The **true** bread is a Person- the one sent by God from Heaven, and he gives life to the world." said Jesus Christ　　　JOHN 7;18

"Anyone presenting his own ideas is looking for praise for himself, but anyone seeking to honor the one who sent him is a good and **true** person. "said Jesus Christ

T   325

TRUE, TRUTH,   JOHN 7;28

So Jesus, in a sermon in the Temple, called out, " Yes, you know me and where I was born and raised, but I am representative of one you don't know, and He is **Truth.** I know him because I was with Him and He sent me to you." said Jesus Christ

JOHN 8;32

Jesus said to them, " You are truly my disciples if you live as I tell you to, and you will know the **Truth** and the **Truth** will set you free." said Jesus Christ   JOHN 8; 40-46

{ The people replied, "We were not born out of wedlock-our true father is God Himself."}

Jesus told them, " If that were so, then you would love me, for I have come to you from God. I am not here on my own, but He sent me. Why can't you understand what I am saying? It is because you are prevented from doing so! For you are the children of your father the devil and you love the evil thing he does. He was a murderer from the beginning and a hater of **truth-** there is not one iota of **truth** in him. When he lies it is perfectly normal; for he is the father of liars. And so when I tell you the **Truth,** you just naturally don't believe." said Jesus Christ

JOHN 14;6

Jesus told him, "I am the Way- yes, and the **Truth** and the Life. No one can get to the Father except by means of me. If you had known who I am,

TRUE, TRUTH   JOHN 14;6 cont'd
then you would have known who the Father is.
From now on you know Him- and have seen me."
said Jesus Christ   JOHN 14;15-17

   "If you love me obey me; and I will ask the
Father and He will give you another Comforter, and
he will never leave you. He is the Holy Spirit and
the Spirit who leads to all **Truth.** The world at large
cannot receive him, for it isn't looking for him. But
you do, he with you now and someday shall be in
you." said Jesus Christ

                    JOHN 15;26-27
   "But I will send you the Comforter-the Holy
Spirit, the source of all **Truth.** He will come to you
from the Father and will tell you about me. And you
must also tell everyone about me, because you have
been with me from the beginning. "said Jesus
Christ   JOHN 16;13-14

   "When the Holy Spirit, who is **Truth,** comes, he
shall guide you into all **Truth,** for he is not
presenting his own ideas, but he will be passing on
what he has heard. He will tell you about the future.
He shall praise me and bring me great honor by
showing you me glory." said Jesus Christ

                    JOHN 17;1-4
   "When Jesus had finished saying all these things,
he looked up to Heaven and said, "Father the time
has come. Reveal the glory of your Son so that he

TRUE, TRUTH   JOHN   17;1-4 cont'd
can give glory back to you. For you have given him
authority over every man and woman in all the
earth. He gives eternal life to each one you have
given him. And this is the way to eternal life- by
knowing You, the only **True** God, and Jesus
Christ, the one you sent to earth! " said Jesus Christ

JOHN 17-16-17

" They are not part of this world any more than I
am. Make them pure and Holy through teaching
them your words of **Truth.** As You sent me into
this world, I am sending them into the world, and I
consecrate myself to meet their need for growth in
Truth and holiness." said Jesus Christ

JOHN 18;23

"If I lied, prove it,"Jesus replied. "Should you
hit a man for telling the **Truth?"** said Jesus Christ

JOHN 18;37

"Yes,"Jesus said. "I was born for that purpose.
And I came to bring **Truth** to the world. All who
love the **Truth** are my followers."said Jesus Christ

TRUST (ED),(ING),(S),(WORTHY) prefix un

LUKE 16; 8-12

"The rich man had to admire the rascal for being
so shrewd. And it is true that citizens of this world
are more clever in dishonesty than the godly are.
But shall I tell you to act that way, to buy friendship
through cheating? Will this ensure your entry to an

TRUST (ED) (ING), (S) (WORTHY) prefix un
LUKE 16; 8-12 cont'd

everlasting home in Heaven? No! For unless you are
honest in small matters, you won't be in large ones.
If you cheat even a little, you won't be honest with
greater responsibilities. And if you are
untrustworthy about worldly wealth, who will
trust you with the true riches of Heaven? And if
you are not faithful with other people's money, why
should you be **entrusted** with money of your own?"
said Jesus Christ

JOHN 12;36

" Put your **trust** in the light while there is still
time; then you will become light bearers," said
Jesus Christ

JOHN 14;1

"Let Not Your Heart Be Troubled. You are
trusting God, now **trust** in me. "said Jesus Christ

TURN, (ED)   MATTHEW 5; 38-39

"The law of Moses says, ' If a man gouges out
another's eye, he must pay with his own eye. If a
tooth gets knocked out, knock the tooth out of the
one who did it. But I say, don't resist violence! If
you are slapped on one cheek, **turn** the other too."
said Jesus Christ

MATTHEW 10; 34-36

"Don't imagine that I came to bring peace to the
world! No, rather a sword. I have come to **tum** man

TURN, (ED)   MATTHEW 10; 34-36 cont'd
against his father, and daughter against her mother, and daughter-in law against her mother-in law. A man's worst enemies will be right ion his own home." said Jesus Christ

LUKE 22;31-32

"Simon, Simon, Satan has asked to have you, to sift like wheat, but I have pleaded in prayer for you that your faith should not completely fail. So when you have repented and **turned** to me again, it will strengthen and build up the faith of your brothers. " said Jesus Christ

JOHN 16;20

Jesus realized they wanted to ask him so he said, "Are you asking yourselves what I mean? The world will greatly rejoice over what is going to happen to me, and you will weep. But your weeping shall suddenly be **turned** to wonderful joy when you see me again." said Jesus Christ

TWO   MATTHEW 6;24

"You cannot serve two masters: God and money. For you will hate on and love the other or the other way around," said Jesus Christ

MATTHEW 18;15-16

"If a brother sins against you, go to him privately and confront him with his fault. If he listens and confesses it, you have won back a brother, but if

TWO   MATTHEW 18;15-16 cont'd

not, take one or two others with you and go back to him again, proving everything you say by these witnesses. If he still refuses to listen, take your case to the church. If the church finds in your favor, but he won't accept it, he should be excommunicated. And I tell you this-whatever you bind on earth is bound in Heaven, and whatever you free on earth is free in Heaven." said Jesus Christ

MATTHEW 18;19-20

"I also tell you this- if **two** of you agree down here on earth concerning anything you ask for, my Father in Heaven will do it for you. For where two or three are gathered in my name, I will be right there among them." said Jesus Christ

MATTHEW 19;4-6

"Don't you read the Scriptures?, he replied. "In them it is written that in the beginning God created man and woman, and that a man should leave his father and mother, and be forever united with his wife. The two shall become one- no longer two, but one! And may no man divorce what God has joined together. "said Jesus Christ

LUKE 16;13

" For neither you nor anyone else can serve two masters. You will hate one and show loyalty to the other or the other way around- you will be enthusiastic about one and despise the other. You

TWO   LUKE 16;13 cont'd

cannot serve both God and money." said Jesus Christ   LUKE 17;35

"**Two** women will be working side by side doing household chores; one will be taken and the other one left behind. And so it will be also with men working in the fields." said Jesus Christ

LUKE 18; 10-14

"**Two** men went into the Temple to pray. One was a proud Pharisee, the other a cheating tax collector. The proud Pharisee 'prayed' this prayer. ' Thank God I am not a sinner like everyone else, especially that tax collector over there! For I never cheat, I don't commit adultery, I go without food twice a week, and I give God a tenth of everything I **earn.'**

"But the corrupt tax collector stood at a distance and dared not even to lift his eyes to Heaven as he prayed. He beat upon his chest in sorrow, exclaiming, 'God be merciful to me, a sinner!' I tell you this, this sinner, not the Pharisee, returned home forgiven! For the proud shall be humbled, but the humble shall be honored." said Jesus Christ

UNBELIEVER, UNBELIEVING

MATTHEW 17;17-18

" Oh, you stubborn, perverse, **unbelieving** generation! How long shall I bear with you? Bring him here to me! Said Jesus Christ [Then Jesus rebuked the demon from the boy and it left him, from that moment on, the boy was well.]

MARK 19;19

Jesus said , "Oh **unbelieving** generation! How much longer must I be with you until you believe? How much longer must I be patient with you? Bring the boy to me." said Jesus Christ

LUKE 9;41

" Oh you stubborn, **unbelieving** people! How long should I put up with you? Bring him to me." said Jesus Christ

UNDERSTAND (ING) (S)

MATTHEW 13;12-13

" For to him who has will more be given," he told them, " and he will have great plenty; but from him who has not, even the little he has will be taken away. That is why I use illustrations, so people will hear and see, but not **understand.**" said Jesus Christ

MATTHEW 13;23

"The good ground represents the heart of a man who listens to the message and **understands** it and goes out and brings thirty, sixty or even a hundred others into the Kingdom." said Jesus Christ

U   **333**

UNDERSTAND (ING) (S)

MATTHEW 24;14-17

"And the Good News about the Kingdom will be preached throughout the whole world, so that all nations will hear it and then finally the end will come.

" So when you see the abomination of desolation in the Holy Place, **understand** that those in Judea must flee to the Judean hills. Those on their porches must not even go inside to pack before they flee. Those in the fields must not return home for their clothes." said Jesus Christ

MARK 4;11-13

He replied, " You are permitted to **understand** some Truths about the Kingdom of God that are hidden to those outside the Kingdom. But if you can't **understand** this simple illustration, what will you do about all the others I am going to tell?" said Jesus Christ LUKE 12;55-57

" When the south wind blows you say, ' Today wil be a scorcher.' And it is. Hypocrites! You **understand** the sky well enough, but you refuse to notice the warning signs all around you about the crisis ahead. Why do you refuse to see for yourselves what is right??" said Jesus Christ

JOHN 8;26

He replied, "I am the one I have always claimed to be. I could condemn you for much and bring

334   U

UNDERSTAND (ING) (S)

JOHN 8;26

much **understanding** to you, but I won't for I say only what I am told to by the One who sent me; and He is Truth.." {But they still didn't understand he was talking about God.} said Jesus Christ

JOHN 13;7

Jesus replied, " You don't **understand** why I am doing it; some day you will." said Jesus Christ

JOHN 16;12-16

" Oh, there is so much more that I want to tell you, but you can't **understand** it now. When the Holy Spirit comes he will guide you to all Truth, for he will not be representing his own ideas but passing onto you what he has heard. He will tell you about the future," said Jesus Christ

JOHN 16;31-33

" Do you finally believe this?" Jesus asked. "But the time is coming -in fact it is here now- when you will be scattered, each one returning to his own home, leaving me alone. Yet, I will not be alone, for the Father is with me. I have told you all this so that you will **understand** and have peace of heart and mind. Here on earth you will have many trials and sorrows; but cheer up, I have overcome the world." said Jesus Christ

UNFRUITFUL   MARK 4;18-19

"The thorny ground represents the hearts of people who listen to the Good News and receive it, but all too quickly the attractions of this world and the delights of wealth, and the search for success and the lure of nice things come in and crowd out God's message from their hearts, so they become **unfruitful** and no crops are produced." said Jesus Christ

UNGRATEFUL   LUKE 6;35

"Love your *enemies!* Do good to them! Lend to them! And don't be concerned about the fact they won't repay you. Then your reward in Heaven will be very great, and you will truly be acting like sons of God; for He is kind to the **ungrateful** and to those who are wicked." said Jesus Christ

UNITY   JOHN 17;22-24

"I have given them the glory You gave me-the glorious **unity** of being one, as we are- I in them and You in me, all being perfected into one- so that the world will know You sent me and will understand You love them as much as You love me. Father, I want them with me-those You have given me- so they can see Your glory. You gave me the glory because You loved me before the world began." said Jesus Christ

336   U

UNLESS   LUKE 13;2-3

"Do you think there are worse sinners than the men from Galilee? "he asked "Is that why they suffered? Not at all! And don't you realize you will perish unless you leave you evil ways and turn to God?" said Jesus Christ

JOHN 3;3

Jesus replied, "With all the earnestness I possess I tell you this: Unless you are born again, you can never go into the Kingdom of God."said JesusChrist

JOHN 4;48

Jesus asked, "Won't any of you believe in me unless I do more and more miracles?"

JOHN 12;23-24

Jesus replied that the time had come for him to return to his glory in Heaven, and that, "I must fall like a kernel of wheat that falls into the furrows of the earth. Unless I die I will be alone-a single seed. But my death will produce many new wheat kernels- a plentiful harvest of new lives. If you love your life down here-you will lose it. If you despise your life down here-you will exchange it for eternal glory." said Jesus Christ

UNRIGHTEOUS   MATTHEW 5;43-48

"There is a saying, 'Love your friends and hate your enemies.!' But I say: Love your enemies! Pray for those who persecute you! In that way you will be acting as true sons of your Father in Heaven. For He

UNRIGHTEOUS   MATTHEW 5;43-48 cont'd
gives His sunlight to the righteous and **unrighteous,**
the just and unjust too. If you love only those who
love you what good is that? Even scoundrels do that
much. If you are friendly to only those who are
friendly to you how are you different from anyone
else? Even heathen do that. But you are to be
perfect, even as your Father in Heaven is perfect."
said Jesus Christ

UNSEEN   MATTHEW 6;6
   " But when you pray, go away by yourself, all
alone, and shut the door behind you and pray to
your Father who is **unseen,** and your Father who
knows your secrets will reward you." said Jesus
Christ   MATTHEW 6; 16-18
   "And now about fasting. When you fast,
declining your food for spiritual purposes, don't do
it publicly, as the hypocrites do, who try to look
wan and disheveled so you feel sorry for them.
Truly, that is the only reward they will ever get. But
when you fast, put on festive clothing, so that no
one will suspect you are hungry, except your Father
who is **unseen** and who knows every secret will
reward you. " said Jesus Christ

UNWORTHY   LUKE 17;7-10
   "When a servant comes in from plowing or
taking care of sheep, he doesn't just sit down and
eat, but first prepares his master's meal and serves

UNWORTHY   LUKE 17;7-10 cont'd
him supper before he eats his own. And he is not
even thanked , for he is merely doing his job. Just
so, if you merely obey me, you should still consider
yourself **unworthy** of praise, for you have simply
done your duty!" said Jesus Christ

UPROOT   LUKE 17;6
   "If your faith were only as tiny as a mustard
seed," Jesus answered, "it would be large enough to
uproot that mulberry tree over there and send it
hurling into the sea! Your command would bring
immediate results" said Jesus Christ

UTTER   MATTHEW 13;35
   " I will talk in parables: I will **utter** mysteries
hidden since the beginning of time." said Jesus
Christ

V

VAIN   MATTHEW 6;7-8
   "Don't recite the same prayer over and over in
vain repetition as heathen do, who think prayers are
only answered by saying them again and again.
Remember, your Father knows exactly what you
need even before you ask Him.!" said Jesus Christ
     MATTHEW 15;8-9
   "You hypocrites! Well did Isaiah prophecy of
you, ' These people say they honor me, but their

VAIN   MATTHEW 15;8-9cont'd
hearts are far away. Their worship is in vain for the
teach their man-made laws instead of those from
God.'" said Jesus Christ

VINE   JOHN 15;1-9

" I AM THE TRUE VINE, and my Father is the
Gardener. He lops off every branch that doesn't
produce. And He prunes those branches that bear
fruit for even larger crops. He has already tended
you by pruning you back for greater strength and
usefulness by means of commands I gave you. Take
care to live in me, and let me live in you. For a
branch can't produce fruit when severed from the
vine. Nor can you be fruitful apart from me.

"Yes, I am the vine, you are the branches.
Whoever lives in me and I in him shall produce a
large crop of fruit. For apart from me, you can't do a
thing. If anyone separates from me, he is thrown
away like a useless branch, withers and is gathered
into a pile with all the others to be burned. But if
you stay in me and obey my commands, you may
request anything you like and it will be granted! My
true disciples produce bountiful harvests. This
brings great glory to my Father.

"I have loved you even as the Father has loved
me. Live within my love. When you obey me, you
are living in my love, just as I obey the Father and
live within His love. I have told you this so that you

VINE   JOHN 15;1-9 cont'd

will be filled with my joy. Yes, your cup will overflow!" said Jesus Christ

VINEYARD   MATTHEW 21;33

"Now listen to this story: A certain landowner planted a **vineyard** with a hedge around it, and built a platform for the watchman, then leased the **vineyard** to some farmers on a sharecrop basis, and went away to live in another country.

"When the time came to harvest the grapes, he sent three of his employees to the farmers to collect his share. But the farmers attacked his men and killed one of them, beat one, and stoned the last.

"Then he sent more of his men to these farmers to collect, but the results were the same. Finally the owner sent his son, surely they would respect him.

"Instead, when the farmers saw the son coming they said to themselves, ' He is the heir to the estate: come on , we will kill him too and get the land for ourselves!' So they dragged him out to the **vineyard** and killed him.

" When the owner returns, what do you think he will do to those farmers?"

{The Jewish leaders replied, " He will put the evil men to a horrible death and get new farmers who will pay their share.}

Then Jesus asked them, "Don't you read the Scriptures: 'The stone rejected by the builders has

VINEYARD   MATTHEW 21;33 cont'd

been made the honored cornerstone; how
remarkable! What an amazing thin the Lord has
done!

"What I mean is that the Kingdom of God shall
be taken away from you, and given to people that
will give Him His share of the crop. All who
stumble on the Truth shall be broken, but those it
falls on will be scattered like dust." said Jesus
Christ

VIRGINS   MATTHEW 25;1-13

"The Kingdom of Heaven is to be illustrated by
this story of ten bridesmaid **virgins** who took their
lamps and went to meet a bridegroom. But only
five of them were smart enough to to fill their lamps
with oil, while the other five were foolish and
forgot.

"So when the bridegroom was delayed, they lay
down and rest until midnight, then they were roused
by a shout, 'The bridegroom is coming! Come out
and welcome him.'

" All the girls jumped up and trimmed their
lamps. The five who hadn't any oil begged the
others to share for their lamps were going out.

"But the others replied, 'We haven't got enough.
Go to the shops and buy some for yourselves.'

"But while the others were gone, the bridegroom
came, and those that were ready went in with him to

VIRGINS   MATTHEW 25;1-13 cont'd
the wedding feast and the door was locked.

"Later, when the other five returned, they stood outside calling. 'Open the door for us!'

"But he called back, 'Go away, it is too late.'
"So stay awake and be prepared, for you do not know the date or moment of my return." said Jesus Christ

VOICE   JOHN5;25

"And I solemnly declare that the time is coming, in fact it is here, when the dead shall hear my voice-the voice of the Son of God- and those who listen shall live." said Jesus Christ

JOHN 10;3-5, 7-10

"The gatekeeper opens the gate for him; and calls his own sheep by name and leads them out. He walks ahead of them and they follow him, for they recognize his voice. They won't follow a stranger, but will run from him, for they don't recognize his **voice.**"

7-10 "I am the Gate for the sheep," he said "All others who came before me were thieves and robbers. But true sheep did not listen to them. Yes, I am the Gate. Those who come by way of the Gate will be saved and will go in and out and find green pastures. The thief s purpose is to steal, kill and destroy. My purpose is to give life to its fullest." said Jesus Christ

VULTURES   MATTHEW 24; 23-28

" Then if anyone tells you, 'The Messiah has arrived in this place or that place or has appeared here or over there,' don't believe it. For false christs shall arise, and false prophets, and will do wonderful things, miracles, so that if it were possible, God's chosen ones would be deceived. See, I have warned you!

"So if someone tells you I, the Messiah, has returned and is in the desert, don't bother to go look. Or, that he is hiding at this place or that, don't believe it! For as lightning flashes across the sky from east to west, so shall my coming be. When I, the Messiah, return. And wherever the carcass is , the **vultures** will gather." said Jesus Christ

W

WALK (S)   JOHN 8;12

Later, in one of his talks, Jesus said to the people, " I am the light of the world. So if you follow me you won't be stumbling as you **walk** through the darkness, for living light will flood your path." said Jesus Christ   JOHN 11;9

Jesus replied, "There are twelve hours of daylight every day, and during every hour a man can **walk** safely and not stumble. Only at night is there danger of a wrong step in the dark." said Jesus Christ

344   W

WANT (ING)   MATTHEW 20;26-27

"But among you it is quite different. Anyone **wanting** to be a leader among you must be your servant. And if you **want** to be right at the top, you must serve like a slave. " said Jesus Christ

MARK. 8;35

"If you **want** to save your life, you will lose it. Only those who throw away their lives for the my sake and the sake of the Good News will ever know what it means to truly live." said Jesus Christ

MARK 10; 42- 45

"Whoever **wants** to be great among you must be your servant. And whoever **wants** to be greatest of all must be slave to all. For even I, the Messiah am not here to be served, but to help others and give my life as ransom for many." said Jesus Christ

WARN (ED) (ING) (S) in many verses...seek

WARS   MATTHEW 24;4-8

Jesus told them, "Don't let anyone fool you. For many will come claiming to be the Messiah, and lead many astray. When you hear of **wars** and the rumors of **wars,** this does not signal my return; the end must come but not yet. The nations and the kingdoms will rise against each other and there will be famines and earthquakes in many places. But this is only the beginning of horrors to come." said Jesus Christ

W   345

WASH (see **FEET**) LUKE 11;39-40

Then Jesus said to them, " You Pharisees **wash** the outside, but your inside is still dirty- full of greed and wickedness! Fools! Didn't God make the inside as well as the outside? Purity is best demonstrated by generosity." said Jesus Christ

WATCH   MATTHEW 7;15

" **Watch** out for false teachers who come disguised as harmless sheep, but are wolves who have come to tear you apart." said Jesus Christ

MATTHEW 24;42

"Therefore keep a **watch** as you don't know what day your Lord is coming." said Jesus Christ

MATTHEW 26;41

"Keep **watch** and pray. Otherwise temptation will overpower you. For the spirit is willing, but the body is weak!" said Jesus Christ

MARK 13;35-37

"Keep a sharp lookout! For you do not know when I will come, at evening, at midnight, early dawn or late daybreak. Don't let me find you sleeping. *Watch for my return!* This is my message to you and to everyone else." said Jesus Christ

WATER (see also **WINE)**

MARK. 9;41

"If anyone gives you a cup of **water** because you are Christ's- I say this solemnly- he won't lose his reward. " said Jesus Christ

346   W

WATER   JOHN 3;5-8

Jesus replied, "What I am telling you so earnestly is this: Unless one is born of water and the Spirit, he cannot enter the Kingdom of God. Men can only reproduce human life, but thre Holy Spirit gives new life from Heaven; so don't be surprised at my statement you must be born again!" said Jesus Christ

JOHN 4;10

Jesus replied, "If you only knew what a wonderful gift God has for you, and who I am, you would ask me for some living water!" said Jesus Christ   JOHN 7;38

"For the Scriptures declare that a river of living water shall flow from the inmost being of anyone who believes in me. "said Jesus Christ

MARK. 6;50

(when walking on the water)... But he spoke to them all at once. "It is all right," he said. "It is I! Don't be afraid.!" said Jesus Christ

WAY   MATTHEW 5;11-12

" When you are reviled and persecuted and lied about because you are mine- wonderful! Be happy about it! Be very glad! For a tremendous reward waits for you in Heaven. And remember, the ancient prophets were persecuted that way too." said Jesus Christ

WAY   LUKE 7;25-28

"Did you find him dressed in expensive clothes? No! Men who live in luxury are found in palaces, not out in the wilderness. But did you find a prophet? Yes! And more than a prophet. He is the one who Scriptures refer to when they say, 'Look, **I** am sending a messenger to prepare the way before you.' In all humanity there is no one greater than John. And yet the least citizen of Kingdom of God is greater than he." said Jesus Christ

JOHN 14;6

Jesus told them, " I am the Way-yes, and the Truth and the Life. No one can get to the Father except through me." said Jesus Christ

WEAK   MATTHEW 26;41

"Keep watch and pray. Otherwise temptation will overpower you. For the spirit is indeed willing but the body is weak." said Jesus Christ

WEALTH   (see RICH) MATTHEW   13; 22

" The ground covered with thistles represents the heart of a man who hears the message, but the cares of his life, his longing for money, the deceitfulness of wealth choke out God's Word, and he does less and less for God." said Jesus Christ

MARK 12;43-44

Jesus said to his disciples, "That poor widow has given more than all those rich men put together! For they gave little of their extra wealth while she gave

348   W

WEALTH (see **RICH**)

MARK 12;43-44 cont'd
her last penny." said Jesus Christ

THE PRODIGAL SON
LUKE 15; 11-32

To further illustrate this point, he told this story; "A man had two sons. When the younger told his father, ' I want my share of your estate now, instead of waiting until you die!' His father agreed to divide his **wealth** between his sons.

"A few days later this younger son packed all his belongings and took a trip to a distant land, and there wasted all his money on parties and prostitutes. About the time his money was gone a great famine swept the land and he began to starve. He persuaded a local farmer to give him a job feeding pigs. The boy became so hungry that even the pods he was feeding the pigs looked good. And no one gave him anything.

"When he finally came to his senses, he said to himself, 'At home, even the hired help have food enough to spare and here I am starving to death! I will go home to my father and say, ' Father, I have sinned against both Heaven and you, and I am no longer worthy to be called your son, please take me on as a hired hand.

"So he returned to his father. And while he was a

WEALTH   THE PRODIGAL SON
LUKE 15; 11-32 cont'd

long distance away, his father saw him coming, and was filled with loving pity and ran and embraced him and kissed him.

"His son said to him, ' Father, I have sinned against Heaven and you and am not worthy to be called your son-'

"But his father said to his employees, ' Quick! Bring the finest robe from the house and put it on him! And the jeweled ring for his finger and shoes! And kill the calf we have in the fattening pen. We must celebrate with a feast, for this son of mine was dead and has returned to life. He was lost and now is found. So the party began.

"Meanwhile the older son was in the fields working; when he returned home, he heard music and dancing coming from the house, and he asked one of the servants what was going on.

"' Your brother is back!' he was told, ' And your father has killed the calf we were fattening and has prepared a great feast to celebrate his coming home again unharmed.'

"The older brother was angry and wouldn't go in. His father came out and begged him, but he replied, 'All these years I've worked hard for you and never once refused to do a single thing you told me to; and in that time you never gave me even a

WEALTH THE PRODIGAL SON
LUKE 15; 11-32 cont'd

goat for a feast with my friends. Yet when this son of yours comes back after spending your wealth, his money on prostitutes, you celebrate by killing the finest calf we have on the place.

" 'Look, dear son,' his father said to him, ' you and I are very close, and everything I have is yours. But it is right to celebrate. For he is your brother; and he was dead and has come back to life! He was lost and now he is found!" said Jesus Christ

LUKE 16;11

"And if you are untrustworthy about worldly wealth, who will trust you with the true riches of heaven? And if you are not faithful with other people's money, why should you be entrusted with money of your own?" said Jesus Christ

WEARY MATTHEW 11;28-30

" Come to me and I will give you rest- all of you weary from hard work beneath the burden of a heavy yoke. Wear my yoke- for it fits perfectly-let me teach you; for I am gentle and humble, and you shall find rest for your souls; for I give only light burdens. " said Jesus Christ

WEEDS MATTHEW 13;24-30

Here is another illustration Jesus used: " The Kingdom of Heaven is like a farmer sowing good seed in his field; but one night as he slept, his

WEEDS MATTHEW 13;24-30 cont'd
enemy came along and sowed thistles among the
wheat. When the crop began to grow the weeds
grew too.

"The farmer's men came and told him, 'Sir, the
field where you planted the choice seed is full of
thistles!'

"'An enemy has done it.' he exclaimed.

"'Shall we pull out the thistle weeds?' they
asked.

"'No,' he replied. 'You will hurt the wheat if you
do. Let both grow together until the harvest, and I
will tell the reapers to sort out the weeds and burn
them and put the wheat in the barn.'" said Jesus
Christ

MATTHEW 13; 37-43

"All right, "he said, "If I am the farmer who
sows the choice seed. The field is the world, and the
seed represents the people of the Kingdom: the
weeds, the thistles are the people belonging to
Satan. The enemy who sowed the thistles among the
wheat is the devil; the harvest is the end of the
world and the reapers are the angels.

"Just as the story of the weeds, the thistles are
separated and burned, so shall it be at the end of the
world. I will send my angels and they will separate
out of the Kingdom every temptation and all who
are evil, and throw them into a furnace and burn

WEEDS   MATTHEW 13; 37-43 cont'd
them. There shall be weeping and gnashing of teeth.
The godly shall shine as the sun in their Father's
eyes. Let those with ears listen!" said Jesus Christ

WEEP (ING)   MATTHEW 8;12

"And I tell you this, that many Gentiles ,like this
Roman officer, shall come from all over the world
and sit down in the Kingdom of Heaven with
Abraham, Isaac, and Jacob. And many an Israelite -
those for whom the Kingdom was prepared - shall
be cast into the outer darkness, into the place of
weeping and gnashing of teeth.
     MATTHEW 13;42

" I will send my angels and they will separate out
of the Kingdom every temptation and all who are
evil, and throw them into a :furnace and burn them.
There will be weeping and gnashing of teeth." said
Jesus Christ   MATTHEW 22;13-14

"Then the king said to his aides, 'Bind him hand
and foot and throw him into the outer darkness
where there is weeping and gnashing of teeth. For
many are called, but few are chosen." said Jesus
Christ   MATTHEW 24;48-51

"But if you are evil and say to yourself, ' My
Lord won't be coming for a while, and begin
oppressing your fellow servants, partying and
getting drunk. Your Lord will arrive unannounced
and unexpected, and severely whip you and send you

WEEP(ING)   MATTHEW 24;48-51 cont'd
off to the judgment of the hypocrites; there will
be **weeping** and gnashing of the teeth." said Jesus
Christh   MATTHEW 25;29-30

"For the man who uses well what he is given
shall more be given. But for the man who is
unfaithful, even what little responsibility he has will
be taken away. This useless servant will be thrown
into the outer darkness where there is **weeping** and
gnashing of teeth." said Jesus Christ

LUKE 6;21

" What happiness there is for you who are now
hungry, for you are going to be satisfied. What
happiness is there for those who **weep** now, for the
time will come when you laugh with joy!" said
Jesus Christ   LUKE 23;28 -31

But Jesus turned to them and said, " Daughters of
Jerusalem, don't **weep** for me, but yourselves and
for your children. For the days are coming when the
women who have no children will be considered
fortunate indeed. Mankind will beg the mountains
to fall on them and crush them, and the hills to bury
them. For if such things are done to me, the Living
Tree, what will they do to you?" said Jesus Christ

WEIGHED   LUKE 21;34

"Watch out! Don't let my sudden coming catch
you unaware; don't let me find you living in
careless ease, carousing and drinking, and your

WEIGHED   LUKE 21;34 cont'd

hearts **weighed** down with problems of this life, like all the rest of the world. Keep a constant watch. And pray that if possible you may arrive in my presence without having to experience the horrors" said Jesus Christ

WELCOME   MATTHEW 10;14-15

"Any city or home that does not **welcome** you, shake off the dust of that place from your feet as you leave. Truly, the wicked cities of Sodom and Gomorrah will be better off at Judgment Day than they." said Jesus Christ

                 MATTHEW 18;5

"And if any of you who **welcomes** a little child like this because you are mine, is **welcoming** me and caring for me." said Jesus Christ

                 MARK. 9;37

Then he placed the little child among them; and taking the child into his arms he said to them, "Anyone who **welcomes** a little child like this in my name is **welcoming** me, and anyone who **welcomes** me is **welcoming** the Father who sent me!" said Jesus Christ

WHATEVER   MATTHEW 16;19

"And I will give you the keys to the Kingdom of Heaven; whatever doors you lock on earth will be locked in Heaven; and **whatever** doors you open will be opened in Heaven!" said Jesus Christ

W   355

WHATEVER   MATTHEW 18;18

"And I tell you this- **whatever** you bind on earth is bound in Heaven, and **whatever** you free on earth will be freed in Heaven," said Jesus Christ

MARK 11;23-24

..."All that is required is that you really believe without a doubt! Listen to me! You can have **whatever** you want , and if you believe, have it , it is yours. But when you are praying, first forgive anyone you have a grudge against, so that your Father in Heaven will forgive you too!" said Jesus Christ   JOHN 14;13

" In solemn truth I tell you, anyone believing in me shall do the same miracles I have done, even greater ones, because I am going to be with the Father. You can ask for anything using my name, and I will do it, for this will bring praise to my Father, because of what I, the Son will do for you. Yes, ask **whatever** you want using my name and I will do it." said Jesus Christ

JOHN 15;16

" You didn't choose me! I chose you! I appointed you to go out and produce lovely fruit always, so that **whatever** you ask from the Father using my name, He will give it to you." said Jesus Christ

JOHN 16;23-24

"At that time you won't need to ask me for anything, for you can go directly to the Father and

WHATEVER   JOHN 16; 23-24 cont'd
ask Him, and he will give you **whatever** you ask for using my name. You haven't tried this before, but begin now. Ask using my name and you will receive and your cup will overflow with joy!"said Jesus Christ

WHEREVER   MARK 14;9

"She has done what she could and has anointed my body ahead of time for burial. And I tell you this solemn truth, that **wherever** the Good News is preached throughout the world, this woman's deed will be remembered and praised." said Jesus Christ

WHITE/ WHITEWASHED

MATTHEW 5;33-37

"But I say: Don't make any vows! And even if you say 'By Heavens!' is a sacred vow to God, for the heavens are God's throne and if you say, 'By the earth!', it is a sacred vow for the earth is God's footstool. And don't swear 'By Jerusalem!' for Jerusalem is the capital of the great King. Don't even swear 'By my head!' for you can't turn one hair black or **white.** Say, just a simple 'Yes, I will.' or 'No, I won't.' your word is enough. To strengthen your promise with a vow shows something is wrong." said Jesus Christ

MATTHEW 23;27-28

"Woe to you Pharisees and you religious leaders! You are like beautiful **whitewashed** tombs-full of

WHITE/ WHITEWASHED

MATTHEW 23;27-28 cont'd
dead men's bones and of foulness and corruption. You try to look like saintly men, but underneath those pious robes of yours, your hearts are besmirched with every type of hypocrisy and sin." said Jesus Christ

WHOLE   MATTHEW 16;25-26

"For anyone who keeps his life for himself shall lose it; and anyone who gives his life up for me shall find it again. What point is there if you gain the **whole** world- and lose eternal life? What can be compared to eternal life? "said Jesus Christ

WICKED (NESS)   LUKE 6;35

"Love your enemies! Do good to them! Lend to them! And don't be concerned about the fact they won't repay you. Then your reward in Heaven will be very great, and you will acting like true children of God; for He is kind to the unthankful and those who are **wicked.**" said Jesus Christ

LUKE 11;39-40
Then Jesus said to them , "You Pharisees wash the outside, but inside you are dirty- full of greed and **wickedness!** Fools! Didn't God make the inside as well as the outside? Purity is best demonstrated by generosity. "said Jesus Christ

WIDE   MATTHEW 7;13

"Heaven can entered only through a narrow gate! The highway to hell is broad and its gate is **wide** enough for the multitudes to choose its easy way. But the Gateway to life is small, and the road narrow, only a few will ever find it." said Jesus Christ

WILL(ING)   MATTHEW 26;41

"Keep watch and pray. Otherwise temptation will overpower you. For the spirit is **willing** and the body is weak.!" said Jesus Christ

LUKE 22;42

"Father, if you're **willing,** take this cup of horror away from me. But I want Your **will** not mine." said Jesus Christ

WINE (also see COMMUNION)

MATTHEW 9;17

"And who would use old wineskins to store new wine? For old skins would burst spilling the **wine** and the skins ruined. Only new wineskins to preserve new **wine.** That way they are both preserved. " said Jesus Christ

WINGS   LUKE 13;34

O Jerusalem, Jerusalem! The city that murders prophets. The city that stones those sent to help her. How often I have wanted to gather your children together even as a hen protects her brood under her

WINGS   LUKE 13;34 cont'd

wings, but you wouldn't let me. And now-now your house is desolate. And you will never again see me until you say. 'Welcome is he who comes in the name of the Lord.'" said Jesus Christ

WINTER   MARK 17;20

" Woe to pregnant women in those days, and mothers nursing. Pray that your flight will not be in **winter.** For those will be the days of such horror as have never been seen since the beginning of God's creation and will never be seen again. And unless God shortens that time of calamity, not a soul on earth will survive. But for the sake of His chosen ones, He will limit those days." said Jesus Christ

WISE (DOM)   MATTHEW 7;24-27

" All who listen to my instructions and follow them are **wise,** like a man who builds his house on solid rock. Though the rain comes in torrents, and floods rise and storm winds beat against his house, it won't collapse, for it is built on rock." said Jesus Christ   MATTHEW 11; 25-26

And Jesus prayed this prayer: " O Father, Lord of Heaven and earth, thank you for hiding the truth from those who think themselves to be so **wise,** and revealing it to the little children. Yes, Father for it pleased You to do it this way." said Jesus Christ

WISE(DOM)   LUKE 12;42-44

And the Lord replied, "I'm talking to any faithful wise man whose master gives him the responsibility of feeding other servants. If the master returns and finds that the job he had done was good, there will be reward-his master will put him in charge of everything he owns." said Jesus Christ

WITHIN   MATTHEW 6;23

" If your light is pure, there will be sunshine in your soul. But if the clouds **within** are evil thoughts and desires, you are in deep spiritual darkness. Oh how deep that darkness can be!" said Jesus Christ

MARK 7;20-23

And then he added, "It is the thought life that pollutes. For from **within,** out of men's hearts come evil thoughts of lust theft murder, adultery, wanting what belongs to others, wickedness, deceit, lewdness envy, slander and pride and all other folly. All these things come from within and make you unfit for God. " said Jesus Christ

LUKE 17;20-21

Jesus replied, "The Kingdom of God isn't ushered in by visible signs. You won't be able to say, 'It began here in this place or there in that part of the country.' for the Kingdom of God is **within** you," said Jesus Christ

WITHOUT   JOHN 8;7

"If anyone of you is **without** sin, you be the first to throw a stone at her." said Jesus Christ

WITNESS   MATTHEW 18;16

"If a brother sins against you, go to him privately and confront him with his fault. If he listens and confesses, you have won back a brother. But, if not, take one or two others with you and go back to him, proving everything you say by these witnesses. If he still refuses to listen, take it to the church, and if the church verdict favors you and he still won't accept it, excommunicate him." said Jesus Christ

        (the term 'witness' to Christ came after the Resurrection and was used by the disciples throughout the rest of the New Testament.)

WOLF (VES)   MATTHEW 7;15-16

"Beware of false teachers who come disguised as harmless sheep, but are wolves and will tear you apart. You can detect them by the way they act, just as you can identify a tree by its fruit." said Jesus Christ   MATTHEW 10;16

"I run sending you our as sheep among wolves. Be as wary as serpents and harmless as doves." said Jesus Christ   JOHN 10;11-16

"I run the Good Shepherd. The Good Shepherd lays down his life for his sheep. A hired man will run when he sees the **wolf** coming and will leave the sheep because they aren't his and he is not their

WOLF (VES)　　　JOHN 10;11-16 cont'd

shepherd. And so the **wolf** leaps on them and scatters the flock. The hired man runs because he has no real concern for the sheep.

"I am the Good Shepherd and know my own sheep and they know me, just as my Father knows me and I know the Father; and I lay down my life for my sheep. I have other sheep in another fold. I must bring them also, and they will heed my voice; and there will be one flock with one Shepherd.." said Jesus Christ

WORD(S)　　　MATTHEW 4;4

"But Jesus told them, "No! For the Scriptures tell us that bread alone won't feed men's souls: obedience to every **Word** of God is what we need. " said Jesus Christ　　MATTHEW 7; 24

"Everyone who hears these **words** and follows them are wise like a man who builds his house on solid rock." said Jesus Christ

　　　　　　　MATTHEW 12;36-37

"And I tell you this, you will be held accountable on Judgment Day for every idle **word** you speak . Your **words** now reflect your fate then: either you will be justified by them or condemned." said Jesus Christ　　MATTHEW 25;35-36

"Heaven and earth will disappear, but my **words** remain forever. But no one knows when the date or the hour that the end will come- not even the angels.

WORD (S)   MATTHEW 25;35-36 cont'd

Not even God's Son, only the Father knows. "said Jesus Christ   MARK 4;14

"The farmer I talked about is anyone who brings God's **Word** to others, trying to plant good seeds in their lives." said Jesus Christ

LUKE 6;47

"But all those who come and listen to my **words** and obey them are like a man who build his house on a strong foundation of rock." said Jesus Christ

JOHN 8;37-38

"...And yet some of you are trying to kill me because my **words** do not find a home within your hearts. I am telling you what I saw when I was with my Father, and you are following the advice of *your* father." said Jesus Christ

JOHN 15;7

"But if you stay in me and obey my **words,** you may ask any request you like and it will be granted! My true disciples produce bountiful harvests." said Jesus Christ   JOHN 17;17

"Father, Make them pure and Holy through teaching them Your **Words** of Truth. As You sent me into the world, I am sending them into the world, and I consecrate myself to meet their need for growth in Truth and Holiness." said Jesus Christ

WORK (ED) (ING) MATTHEW 9;37

{JOHN 9;36 and what pity he felt for the crowds that came, because their problems were great and they didn't know what to do or where to go for help. They were like sheep without a shepherd.}

9;37 "The harvest is so great, and the **workers** are so few," he told the disciples. "So pray to you Father, the one in charge of harvesting, and ask him to recruit more **workers** to harvest his fields. "said Jesus Christ   LUKE 10;2

These were his instructions to them , "Plead with the Lord of harvest to send more **workers** to help you, for the harvest is plentiful and the **workers** so few. Go, now, and remember I am sending you out as lambs among wolves." said Jesus Christ

LUKE 10;7

"When you enter a village, don't shift around from home to home, but stay in one place, eating and drinking without question whatever is set before you. And don't hesitate to accept hospitality, for the **worker** is worth his wages. "said Jesus Christ

JOHN 4;37

"For it is true that one sows and someone else reaps. I sent you to reap where you didn't sow; others did the **work,** and you received the harvest. " said Jesus Christ   JOHN 5;17

"My Father is always at His **work,** doing good and I am following His example." said Jesus Christ

WORK (ED) (ING)   JOHN 6-27-29

'Do not **work** for food that spoils. Spend your energy seeking an eternal life that I, the Messiah, can give you. God the Father has sent me for this purpose." said Jesus Christ   JOHN 9;4

"All of us must quickly carry out the tasks assigned to us by the One who sent me, for there is little time left before night falls and all **work** comes to an end. But while I am still here, I will give light to the world.' said Jesus Christ

JOHN 17; 4-5

"I brought glory to You by doing all the **work** You told me to do. And now Father, reveal my glory as I stand in Your presence, the glory we shared before the world began." said Jesus Christ

WORLD (LY)   MATTHEW 5;14

"You are the light of the **world**- a city on a hill glowing in the night for all to see." said Jesus Christ

MATTHEW 16;26

" What profit is there if you gain the whole **world** - and lose eternal life?" said Jesus Christ

LUKE 16;11

"And if you are untrustworthy with **worldly** wealth, who will trust you with the true riches of heaven?" said Jesus Christ   JOHN 3;16

"For God so loved the **world** that He gave His only Son so that anyone who believes in him shall not perish, but have eternal life." said Jesus Christ

366   W

WORLD
   LY

JOHN 3; 17

" God did not send His son into the **world** to condemn it, but to save it." said Jesus Christ

JOHN 8;12

" I am the Light of the **world.** So if you follow me you won't be stumbling through the darkness, for a living light will flood your path." said Jesus Christ

JOHN 9;5

"But while I am still here, I am the Light of the **world** and I will give it my light." said Jesus Christ

JOHN 15;19

" The **world** would love you if you belonged to it; but, you don't- for I chose you to come out of the **world,** and so it hates you." said Jesus Christ

JOHN 16;33

" I have told you this so you will peace of heart and mind. In this **world** you will have many trials and sorrows; but cheer up, I have overcome the **world."** said Jesus Christ

JOHN 17;8

"Now they know that everything I gave them is a gift from You, for I passed on the commands You gave me; and they accepted them and know of certainty that I came to this **world** from You and they believe you sent me." said Jesus Christ

JOHN 18;36

" I am not an earthly king. If I were, my followers would have fought when I was arrested by Jewish

WORLD (LY)   JOHN 18;36 cont'd
leaders. My kingdom is not of this **world.**" said
Jesus Christ

WORRY (IED) (IES) MATTHEW 6;25-27

" So my counsel is: don't **worry** about things-
food, drink and clothes. For you already have life
and a body- and they are far more important than
what you eat and wear. Look at the birds! They
don't **worry** about what to eat-they don't need to
sow or reap or store up food- for your Heavenly
Father feeds them. And you are far more valuable to
Him than they are. Will all those **worries** add one
single hour to your life?" said Jesus Christ

MATTHEW 6; 34

" Don't **worry** about tomorrow. God will take
care of your tomorrow too. Live one day at a time."
said Jesus Christ   MATTHEW 10;19

" When you are arrested, don't **worry** about what
you say at your trial for you will given the right
words at the right time. For it won't be you doing
the talking- it will be the Spirit of your Heavenly
Father." said Jesus Christ

LUKE 8;14

" The seed among the thorns represents those
who listen and believe God's words but whose faith
afterwards is choked out by the **worry** and riches
and the responsibilities and pleasures of everyday

WORRY (IED) (IES) LUKE 8;14 cont'd
life. And so they are never able to help anyone else
to believe in the Good News." said Jesus Christ

WORSE   JOHN 5;14
..."Now you are well; don't sin as you did before,
or something even **worse** might happen to you."
said Jesus Christ

WORSHIP   LUKE 4;8
"Jesus replied, " We must **worship** God, and
Him alone. So it is written in the Scriptures." said
Jesus Christ   JOHN 4;21-24, 26
" The time is coming ma'am, when we will no
longer be concerned about whether to **worship** the
Father here or in Jerusalem. For it is not where we
worship that counts, but how we **worship-is** our
worship spiritual and real? Do we have the Holy
Spirit's help? For God is Spirit, we must have help
to **worship** as we should. The Father wants this
kind of **worship** from us. But you Samaritans know
so little about Him, **worshiping** blindly, while we
Jews know all about Him for salvation comes to the
world through the Jews."...26.."I am the Messiah."
said Jesus Christ

WORTHY   MATTHEW 19;34-37
"Don't imagine I came to bring peace on earth!
No, rather a sword. I have come to set man against
his father and daughter against her mother and a

WORTHY   MATTHEW 19;34-37cont'd
daughter-in -law against her mother-in -law -a
man's worst enemies will be right in his own home!
If you love your father and mother more than you
love me, you are not **worthy** of being mine; or if
you love your son or your daughter more than you
love me, you are not **worthy** of being mine. If you
refuse to take up your cross and follow me, you are
not **worthy** of being mine." said Jesus Christ

WRITTEN   MATTHEW 26;23-4
He replied, " The Son of man will die as it is
written, but woe to the man by whom I am
betrayed. Far better for that one if he had never been
born." said Jesus Christ

LUKE 10;20
"However, the important thing is not that
demons obey you, but that your names are **written**
down as citizens of heaven. " said Jesus Christ

LUKE 24;44 [45]
The he said, when I was with you before, don't
you remember me telling you that everything
written about me by Moses and the prophets in the
Psalms must all come true?" said Jesus Christ

{45 Then he opened their minds to understand
at last the many Scriptures!}

YEAST   MATTHEW 13;33

" The Kingdom of Heaven can be compared to a woman making bread. She takes a measure of flour and mixes in the yeast until it permeates every part of the dough." said Jesus Christ

MATTHEW 16;6-11

"Watch out!", Jesus warned them; "beware of the yeast of the Pharisees and Sadducees."

Jesus knew what they were thinking and told them, "O, men of little faith! Why are you so worried about having food? Won't you ever understand? Don't you remember all the 5,000 I fed with 5 loaves and basketfuls leftover? Don't you remember the 4,000 I fed, and all that was left? How could you even think I was talking about food? But again I say, 'Beware of the yeast of the Pharisees and Sadducees."said Jesus Christ

YOKE   MATTHEW 11;28-30

" Come to me and I will give you rest-all of you work so hard beneath a heavy yoke. Wear my yoke- for it fits perfectly- let me teach you; for I am gentle and humble, and you shall find rest for your souls; I give you only light burdens." said Jesus Christ

371

The last verses of the Gospels
YOUNG   **JOHN 21;18-25**

Jesus said, "Then feed my little sheep. When you were **young,** you were able to do as you liked and go wherever you wanted to; but when you are old, you will stretch out your hands and others will direct you and take you where you don't want to go. [Jesus said this to let him know what kind of death he would die to glorify God.] Then Jesus told him, " Follow me".

{Peter turned around and saw the disciple Jesus loved following, the one who had leaned around supper that time to ask Jesus, 'Master, which one of us will betray you? Peter asked Jesus," what about him, Lord? What sort of death will he die?"}

JESUS REPLIED, "If l want him to live until I return, what is that to you? *You* follow me."

[So the rumor spread among the brotherhood that that disciple wouldn't die! But that isn't what Jesus said, ' If l want him to live until I come, what is it to you?]

{ I am that disciple! I saw these events and recorded them here. And we all know that my account of these things is accurate.}

[And I suppose that if all the other events in Jesus' life were written, the whole world could hardly contain the books!]

372 Z

ZION MATTHEW 21;5

"Say to the Daughter of Zion, Jerusalem, her King is coming to her riding humbly on a donkey's colt!" said Jesus Christ

Definition;

Zion- God's spiritual Kingdom, the church of God, the people of God, Yahweh, and His Son Jesus Christ and the Holy Spirit

MATTHEW ...written by Matthew ...one of the 12 Disciples

MARK....written by John Mark from stories told to him by Peter who is ...one of the 12 Disciples

LUKE...written by Luke, a physician who traveled with Paul...one of the 12 Disciples

JOHN...written by John...one of the 12 Disciples

After the crucifixion, there were only 11 Disciples as Judas betrayed Jesus and then committed suicide by hanging himself. These eleven men carried the Word of God, the Good News far and wide. They were imprisoned, tortured and killed for their mission. Many books of the New Testament were written while in jail. The message that God is Love and there is something better than what we have going on here was not well received by many. It is not welcomed by very many today.

read on.....next page

373

Experience the
ARGUMENTS

.... what mankind believes to be true and real vs.
God's Truth. Provocative, Angering or
Exhilarating.... it's up to you.
The **BOOK** with 666 decoded in
Hebrew/Greek...English...French ...German...Italian
Russian...Spanish...Swahili
9 languages   ....5 alphabets...all the same...
What are the odds?
Is this the right answer?   Or is it just one answer?
Does it matter?
We are all responsible and
accountable for everything we think, say and
do. This is true at any point in time. It is no
accident. As we are each created as unique miracles
of God and meant to be we are alive now.
The purpose of life is to give each one of us
freedom to determine the meaning of our own life.
How is it going?   Oh yea....   The book?

SOME CHRISTIAN STUFF
FOR YOUR BRIEF STAY
ON PLANET EARTH...

by C.C. Forche

THE END

OR

THE

BEGINNING

YOU

CHOOSE

www.ingramcontent.com/pod-product-compliance
Lightning Source LLC
Chambersburg PA
CBHW052028090426
42739CB00010B/1823